GENUINE
FRIENDSHIP

GENUINE FRIENDSHIP

The Foundation for all Personal Relationships, including Marriage and the Relationship with God

Philip D. Halfacre

To Bishop George Rassas, with humble reverence and respect,

Midwest Theological Forum
Woodridge, Illinois

MTF

Genuine Friendship is published by:

Midwest Theological Forum
1420 Davey Road
Woodridge, IL 60517 USA
Phone: (630) 739–9750
Fax: (630) 739–9758
mail@mwtf.org
www.theologicalforum.org

The editor of this book has attempted to give proper credit to all sources used in the text and illustrations. Any miscredit or lack of credit is unintended and will be corrected in the next edition.

Midwest Theological Forum   ISBN 978–1–890177–78–2

Table of Contents

Foreword by Benedict Groeschel, CFR   ix

Chapter One: We Were Made for Love   1
Some Initial Thoughts   1
The God Who Is Love Made Us in His Image   5
How Are People United?   8
The Different Ways We Use the Word "Love"   10
Emotional Love vs. Intentional Love   12
What Is behind Emotional Love   13
    "Need Love"   14
    "Appreciative Love"   15
    "Gift Love"   16
What Is behind Intentional Love   17
Intentional Love Arising from a Sense of Duty   18
Intentional Love Arising from the Desire to *Be* and *Become* More   21
Love as "Acceptance"   22
Why People Stay Together   23
Fulfilling the Duties of a Relationship   24
Fulfilling People's Hope   26
Questions for Philosophical Consideration and Personal Growth   29

Chapter Two: A First Look at Friendship   31
Some Things that Look Like Friendship but Are Not   31
The People Who "Happen to Be in Our Lives"   33
Companionship   34
From Antiquity to Modern Times—Six Authors' Thoughts on Friendship   37
    Aristotle—The Importance of Virtue   38
    Cicero—Loyalty Sprung from Virtue and Mutual Agreement   40
    St. Augustine—God's Love Perfects and Transforms Our Friendships   41
    St. Aelred of Rievaulx—Distinguishing Real from False Friendships   43
    Michel de Montaigne—The Experience of Union   45
    C.S. Lewis—Friends Are Joined by a Common Interest   46
    Recurring Themes   48
Questions for Philosophical Consideration and Personal Growth   51

Chapter Three: The Love That Is Friendship   53
A Popular Topic   53
What Genuine Friends Pursue When Pursuing Friendship   54

Communicating Our Intimate Love for God 194
    Through Things That Are Said 194
    By the Way We Look at Each Other 194
    Through Touching 195
    Through Sharing Meals Together 195
    Through the Making and Keeping of Promises and Commitments 195
    Through Giving Gifts and Loving Deeds 196
    Through Spending Quality Time with Each Other 196
    Through Doing Things Together 196
Modeling Our Life on the Paschal Mystery 197
The Effect God's Friendship Has on Our Life 201
    Father Walter J. Ciszek: Abandonment to the Will of God—in the Gulag 202
Experiencing Intimacy with God 205
    Mount Tabor and the Transfiguration 206
    Bl. Teresa of Calcutta (Mother Teresa):
    Her Experience of the "Dark Night of the Soul" 207
    Pressing the Issue and Drawing Some Conclusions 209
Questions for Philosophical Consideration and Personal Growth 212

Chapter Eight: Putting It All Together 215
The Loves "Learn" from Each Other 215
What Hinders Us from Loving Heroically? 216
    The "Divorce Mentality" 218
Tools for Generous (and Even Heroic) Loving 219
    Virtuous Living in General 219
    Forgiveness 221
    Loving Well Requires Effort on Our Part 224
One Last Look 225
    Making and Keeping Friends 225
    Happy Marriage 227
    Developing a Friendship with God 228
Intimacy in the Kingdom of Heaven 230
Questions for Philosophical Consideration and Personal Growth 234

Endnotes 235

Index 239

Foreword

by Father Benedict J. Groeschel, C.F.R.

The human person is a fascinating creature. Our capacities both for good and evil seem endless. The pages of human history are filled with stories of many figures who stand out for their greatness—or for the opposite. We have all witnessed the life and death of Pope John Paul II and have seen reactions from people all over the world to the greatness of this man. Their words, tears, and presence in Rome during his final illness and in the days following his death were a powerful testimony. He had a remarkable ability to give. We also have examples of people whose memory is an everlasting shame and disgrace—people like Adolf Hitler and Joseph Stalin. Of course, the vast majority of us are not like either extreme. We are neither great saints nor dreadful sinners. A lot of us more or less schlep through life, doing the best we can with the circumstances we face.

We see a similar pattern in people's relational lives. I am fortunate to know some people who are capable of being a good friend or a good spouse. Many of them also have a remarkable love for God. They are rather simple souls whom the world hardly notices, although those who really know them value their friendship. It is a joy for me to be with such people because they seem to have an easy time communicating their love and fulfilling their commitments to the people in their lives. They are the great lovers of the world, and they make it look easy because they do it so well.

Some people, however, do not make good friends, nor are they good spouses. The worst among them have a way of consuming people, using them for their own purposes. Others, without any malicious intent, neglect their responsibilities to the people in their lives. And some are so emotionally disorganized and have such underdeveloped relational lives that they truly do not know how to relate better than they currently do, though they often wish that they could. For many people—men and women, young and old, rich and poor—that area of life never really came together. They may be tremendously successful in other areas, but their personal relationships are not what they would like them to be.

It is important to remember that we can improve the quality of our personal interaction with others. We can love better. This is what the Gospel is about. My experience as a priest and as a psychologist tells me that people often want to improve the way they relate, but they simply do not know how. They feel like they are stuck in a rut. Perhaps you would describe yourself that way. Maybe that is why you have picked up this book. If so, you are in luck because the purpose of this book is to explain the basic framework of interpersonal relating, while giving practical suggestions for relating better. The author has done his work in a very competent and imaginative way. I have been studying relationships all my life, and I learned a number of things from this book.

This book is based on the fascinating idea that in all of our personal relationships, including marriage and our relationship with God, there is a basic underlying friendship that unites the persons involved. The quality of these relationships is determined by the way in which that underlying friendship is lived out. This is the genuine friendship that this book is about.

We refer to the experience of genuine friendship as intimacy. Many people seem to have an impoverished idea of intimacy and equate it simply with sexual interaction of some kind. Fundamentally, intimacy is a matter of people uniting with one another at a deeply personal level. That is why we can speak of intimate friendship and intimacy with God. Many saints have spoken of their intimacy with God, which touched them deeply within their soul and allowed them to experience his presence. Whether it is with one's spouse, with God, or with a friend in the ordinary sense, these genuine friendships come about when we make a sincere gift of ourselves.

Conversation and shared activities are important in establishing intimate friendships. Conversation need not be intense to be intimate, but it needs to be conversation about something, even if it is only about the events of the day. Years ago I visited a Carthusian monastery, where the monks live an austere life. I vividly recall a conversation with one of them about our respective spiritual lives. We spoke for a couple of hours, and it created a bond between us. Shortly afterward, I sat next to a well-meaning woman on a train who talked for two hours about absolutely nothing. Her prattling revealed a life of superficiality that made me wonder whether she was even capable of meaningful conversation. Paradoxically, meaningful conversation—the variety that genuinely unites people—is the fruit of solitude, silence, and reflection. C. S. Lewis was right when he said, "Those who have nothing can share nothing; those who are going nowhere can have no fellow travelers." We need not be particularly intelligent, creative, or articulate to establish genuine friendships. We simply have to be willing to share a part of our private lives. And it has to be done in a way that involves some sort of give-and-take. If you listen to the way people talk, however, you will notice that some people never really converse. They comment: on the weather, their favorite sports team, or their collection of ginger ale bottle tops. Or worse still, they perpetually complain. Certainly not every conversation between friends is a serious one, and friends do comment to one another about the events of their day. However, intimate relationships are founded on and sustained by conversations that involve mutual sharing and vulnerability. Developing the ability to relate this way and sharing what is deep within us is one of the fundamental tasks of early adulthood.

Relationships are a matter of communion—a union together—and linking people to one another. People can be linked in a variety of ways, but it usually includes some sort of psychological coming together, where we experience each other's presence. It is the opposite of being alone and isolated. Members of a family or a real religious community can be said to experience this communion with one another. In his writings Pope Benedict XVI has often taken the idea of community and used it to interpret our spiritual relationship with Christ and his Church. Obviously this is to use the word communion in a comparative way. Using it in the most intimate way, we might say that mothers experience communion with their children even before they are born. Spouses, in particular, experience a union through deep emotional and psychological bonds.

I have found it interesting to observe spousal relationships from a psychological and relational point of view. Though united in a variety of ways, not all married couples would describe themselves as friends. I saw this many times among immigrant couples in the neighborhood where I grew up in Jersey City. I recall an old cobbler and his wife who lived near us. Every Sunday afternoon he would put on a business suit and his gray homburg. With gloves to cover his work-stained hands, and carrying his walking cane, he and his wife would take their weekly walk, but she was always nine or ten paces behind him. If she wanted to say anything to him, she had to shout. I find these relationships interesting. For the old cobbler and his wife, and for many of that generation, marriage was about simply fulfilling the expected roles of the husband/father and the wife/mother—little more than a legal, contractual agreement. Perhaps that was the only way those immigrant people could survive. They often fulfilled their roles with extraordinary generosity and care, with dedication and appropriate self-forgetfulness, and in many ways they could serve as an example to today's generation. Yet marriages often bore little resemblance to what people today think of as friendship. It does not have to be one or the other—either a marriage of commitment and duty, or an emotionally satisfying marriage of intimate friendship. It can be both, though at times it may be experienced more like the one than the other. That is simply the nature of personal relationships. I am convinced that spouses who relate to each other like the best and dearest of friends are happier because of it. The idea of a husband and wife having a genuine friendship is a prominent theme of this book.

Something like this friendship is possible in our relationship with God. Jesus called his Apostles "friends," and he wants us to relate to him in that way. Friends, especially close friends, open up their hearts to one another. They share their joys and their sorrows with each other. If we see God in this way, our prayer will be both hopeful and honest, resembling two dear friends conversing with one another. It is as though God is holding out his hand to us, inviting us to walk and talk with him.

Some people are not capable of this type of relating because they lack the virtue necessary to fulfill the commitments that are an essential part of these relationships. Virtue is a forgotten word today. Even those who use the word do not agree on what it means. Since there seems to be little agreement on what people recognize as good, we water down goodness and equate it with being nice. Real virtue, though, is much more. It is the inner strength we need to overcome our narcissistic and self-indulgent tendencies. We naturally have expectations of the people we love, especially our family and closest friends. When we enter a person's life, we begin to assume responsibility to some degree for the person. If I lack the inner strength— the virtue—to fulfill my responsibilities to the people in my life, I lack the capacity to be a friend. The particularly virtuous man or woman is the one who is able to continue giving, in spite of the temptation to focus one's energies on oneself. It is not easy to do, and it is especially difficult to do consistently. Think, for example, of the young parents who greatly struggle to meet the seemingly endless needs of their children. It takes courage and patience—and many other virtues as well—to continue giving of oneself, creating an atmosphere of acceptance, peace, and joy. When they do, they create a culture of love.

If you are interested in the inner workings of friendship, marriage, and the relationship with God and the ways in which you might strengthen those relationships, this book is for you. Healthy relating is not a matter of luck. As the book says, it is both an art and a science. The underlying message of the book is that we can indeed grow in the ability to relate well and communicate love. It is full of stories and examples that will inspire you to do just that.

Acknowledgments

Books do not simply drop from heaven, nor are they the work of the author alone. Many people have contributed to the production of the book you have in front of you, and I wish to acknowledge some of those who have helped me along the way.

I wish to begin by thanking my mother, father, and brother. They have supported me in this project from its inception.

There are three bishops I wish to acknowledge and thank: His Excellency Daniel R. Jenky, C.S.C., the Bishop of Peoria and my bishop; His Grace John J. Myers, the Archbishop of Newark and the former Bishop of Peoria who ordained me to the priesthood; His Excellency Carl F. Mengeling, the Bishop of Lansing and my mentor and former pastor. It is difficult to overestimate the fatherly role of a bishop in the life of a priest.

I thank Fr. Benedict J. Groeschel, C.F.R., for his continued support of the project and for having written the Foreword.

Several of my friends have provided hands-on assistance with this work, foremost of whom is Robert Prescott, Ph.D. As the associate chair of the Department of English at Bradley University, his assistance was inestimable. I am also deeply grateful to my friends who served as readers: Msgr. Steven P. Rohlfs, Msgr. Stuart W. Swetland, Rev. Edward Maristany, Mrs. Nancy J. Conness, Mr. Michael J. Hall II, Mr. Robert Thompson, Mrs. Tanya Thompson, Mrs. Carrie Harrison, and Miss Antoinette Calhan.

Finally, I wish to thank Rev. James Socias, Mr. Jeffrey Cole, Mr. Stephen J. Chojnicki, Mr. Jerry Dempsey, and all the staff at Midwest Theological Forum who published this book.

To my family and friends—
many of whom are in Heaven.

You have taught me nearly
everything I know about love.

Chapter One

We Were Made for Love

> "A person is an entity of a sort
> to which the only proper and adequate way
> to relate is love."
>
> From *Love and Responsibility*
> Pope John Paul II

Some Initial Thoughts

This book is about relating. It is about the art of friendship considered broadly, including the friendship between a husband and wife and the friendship between God and his people. Most people value their close personal relationships more than anything else in life. In the Scriptures we read, "A faithful friend is a sturdy shelter: he that has found one has found a treasure. There is nothing so precious as a faithful friend, and no scales can measure his excellence."[1] It is interesting to note that the "faithful friend" is described as a "treasure." We usually use that word to describe something that is not only very good but also somewhat *rare*. Since antiquity the true, faithful friend has been viewed as something rather uncommon. Aristotle, who saw genuine friendship as a virtue, said that this type of friendship is rare because this type of *man* is rare. How many *really* virtuous men or women are there? C.S. Lewis made the same point: "few value it because few experience it."[2]

Even those who are not blessed with many friends or with particularly good friends recognize that friendship is an important part of life. When asked what he or she values most in life, most will answer something like, "The people I love." Our greatest joys in life are our associations and relationships with people. Whether it is our spouse, our children, our best friend, or God, our lives are centered around other people. We need them. The *things* in our life simply will not do. And the reason for that is simple—*things* cannot love us. We want to love and to be loved. It is the way we were made. We were made for *interpersonal union*—made to give ourselves to others and to receive the gift of others. And this sharing in the life of others is an integral aspect of our fulfillment. The human person "finds himself only by the sincere gift of himself."[3] While some seem to live this way with the greatest ease and naturalness, there are many for whom this is the greatest struggle of their lives.

In my life as a priest, I encounter people both young and old who express a desire to have deeper and more satisfying relationships. Many feel *disconnected* from others. High speed internet access, instant messaging, e-mail, and cell phones have become a permanent part of our culture. Yet, ironically, people today seem to be *less* connected in the deeper, substantial, and more personally satisfying ways. It is as though technology is rebounding back on us. People claim they have no time. Think of the last time you wrote a letter—or even a note. Written—not typed. There is something about a handwritten note that is different from one that is typed—much less an e-mail. It is a *personal* communication in a richer sort of way. One might ask, "Who has time for a handwritten note today?" That is our problem. We do not have time today. Is it that we do not *have* time or that we do not *make* time? There has been a cultural shift in the way we communicate, and that, in turn, has had an effect on our relating. We have traded substance and depth for speed and convenience.

If this topic of friendship and deeper relating interests you, then, this book is for you. It will not answer all your questions or solve all your problems. You cannot *read* yourself into good relationships. But you might pick up an insight or two. If that insight gives rise to better relating, then the time spent reading this work will be time well-spent.

Looking at the way people relate, you can see people at every point along a continuum. Some seemingly relate with ease and freedom, while others appear to be perpetually awkward in social settings. Some relate only superficially while others connect very deeply with others. How do we account for this? A number of factors influence the way we relate to others. Our natural dispositions—our personality and temperament—have a lot to do with it. Personality flaws and temperamental quirks are relational handicaps that make interpersonal relating challenging, both for the one with handicaps and for those who befriend him or her—or who try to. It is hard to get close to those who are, say, perpetually crabby and critical.

Sometimes these characteristics are seen as early as infancy. Some babies are blessed with sweet and agreeable dispositions, while others seem to cry no matter what you do to them or for them. It is their natural disposition.

To some extent, the "rule of reciprocity" helps to explain why people relate the way they do. As a general rule, people tend to relate to others according to the way they perceive others to be relating to them. If I think somebody likes me and enjoys being around me, I relate differently than I do with the person who generally dislikes me and does not enjoy having me around. To an extent, there is a natural reciprocity in our interaction with others. This is illustrated in the story of two cowboys. One day a cowboy rides into town and stops at the saloon. He sits down at the bar and says to the bartender, "I have just arrived here. What are the people like?" The bartender asks, "What were the people like in the last town you were in?" The cowboy answers, "They were kind people, gently disposed, agreeable and generally pleasant to be with." The bartender replies, "I suspect you will find the people here to be the same way."

A little while later another cowboy rides into town and stops at the saloon. He sits down at the bar and says to the bartender, "I have just arrived here. What are the people like?" And the bartender asks, "What were the people like in the last town you were in?" Then the cowboy answers, "They were sour, difficult, disagreeable folk." To which the bartender says, "I suspect you will find the people here to be the same way." In other words, we tend to relate to others in the manner we perceive them relating to us.

One's confidence plays a role in the way one relates. When people go into a social setting confident that they have something to offer, that they are lovable and wanted, this very confidence affects the way they relate. It is not arrogance but a healthy belief in oneself that carries with it a natural cheerfulness.

Finally, healthy relating—the kind found in healthy friendships and happy marriages—is a matter of *virtue*. *Great* friends, *great* spouses, begin as great *men* and great *women*. It is hard to be a really good friend *all the time*. That is why we seldom see it. Great lovers love even when their love is not reciprocated. That is hard to do, especially over the long haul. And loving people well means loving them virtuously, which means that all love must be based on and rooted in *truth*. Not everything that looks like love is in fact love. Indeed, there are many things that look like love, that feel like love, that are said to be love, but are really little more than sentimentality, sensuality, and self-centeredness. Many hearts have been broken, spouses abandoned, and friends rejected by things that were done "in the name of love." Infidelity has many faces, and none is more treacherous than the one that passes itself off as love.

Looking at the state of affairs in the world today, we might easily conclude that there is a crisis in interpersonal relating—in both friendship and in marriage. Is "crisis" too strong a word? I will let readers decide that for themselves, but one should take careful note of the findings that were reported in the June 2006 issue of the *American Sociological Review. ASR* is the flagship journal of the American Sociological Association. Though primarily a journal for professionals in the field of sociology, *ASR* also publishes articles of general interest. The June 2006 issue featured an article that was widely covered by the national news media. A sociological study was conducted by researchers at the University of Arizona and Duke University that replicated a study done twenty years earlier. The participants were asked to give the first name or initials of all the people, including family members, with whom they discuss "important matters." When this question was asked in 1985, the respondents, on average, said they had three such people. When this same question was asked in 2004, the average had dropped to two. What I find particularly alarming is that one fourth of the participants indicated, even after further probing by the researcher, that they had *no one* with whom they could discuss important matters. Twenty-five percent of the population has no one to talk to about the things that really matter to them—not even a spouse or some other family member.

The experience people have of feeling disconnected affects more than friendships. Relational difficulties affect family life as well. There are many people who want to end the relationship with the person with whom they were once madly in love! Perhaps the real problem lies in their misunderstanding of genuine intimacy, and their lack of experience thereof. People today seem confused about what real intimacy is, and too often simply equate it with sex. Intimacy is a matter of really *connecting* with another—two persons deeply sharing their inner selves. It happens between two close friends, and it should happen between a husband and wife. But it often does not happen. The crisis in genuine friendship is particularly visible in the casual sexual relationships and casual marriages that are part of today's culture. It is not uncommon to hear of marriages ending after one or two months. How can this be? Certainly, relationships vary in intensity and vary in depth. But if one's deepest friendship and one's greatest intimacy is with one's spouse, how can that relationship end after only a few months? It is incomprehensible. Where is the friendship? And when there is a lack of genuine intimacy in marriage, people can begin to look to satisfy their need for intimacy in other ways, perhaps repeating over and over their superficial or unhealthy or dysfunctional patterns of relating that only deepen their isolation and increase their loneliness.

The good news is that it does not have to be that way. We are capable of making improvements. Successful interpersonal relating—including the relating that is an integral part of marriage—is both an art and a science. God has endowed each person with gifts and talents, as well as with a temperament. That is the "science" part. But there are also *skills* of interpersonal relating that need to be acquired and, to some degree, perfected. That is the *art* side of it. I am convinced that the *art* of friendship, including the friendship of marriage, and friendship with God, offers each of us opportunities for growth. All of that, in a nutshell, is what this book is about.

The God Who Is Love Made Us in His Image

St. John writes in his first letter, "God is love."[4] But God is mysterious. So if God is love then love must be mysterious as well. Perhaps this is why definitions we propose for love always seem to come up short. Every definition captures an aspect of love but not love in its entirety. The attention a mother gives to her child is called love. It is commonly called *affection.* The devotion of a lifelong friend is the love of *friendship.* There is the passionate desire of *erotic* love. Jesus said there is no greater love than to lay down one's life.[5] That is the love of *charity.* My philosophical question is whether there is some one thing that unites the four. We want to be able to point to something and say, "*That is what love is.*" We want it to be something that all of the various types of loves have in common. Is this possible? Can we say this is the true *essence* of love?

I do think it is possible, and I think we should take our cue from St. John who told us "God is love." Though all authentic love has its origin in God, not everything our society calls "love" is divine, and not everything done in the name of love has God's approval. That being said, I do think that there is something that all the loves have in common. They are all, in one way or another, about *union of persons*. The union that is implied is one that is real, though not always felt; moreover, when it *is* felt, it can be experienced in different ways. It can be experienced as affection, as sentimental attachment, as erotic passion, or as confidence in another's continued presence in one's life. But interpersonal union itself is not a feeling—it transcends our feelings. Sometimes there are no feelings attached to it—as, for example, when things are done out of charity. But the unity between the persons involved is nevertheless real. In all of these examples, we see the reality of one person willingly being united with another.

God is love. In God's deepest and most profound existence, God is *not a solitary*—but a *family*, a trinity of persons. God is three persons in the one triune God. From all eternity God existed as Father, Son, and Holy Spirit—not merely three names or ways of looking at the divine, but three distinct persons. And we, according to the book of Genesis, were made in God's image—*imago Dei*.[6] What does it mean to be made in God's image? It means several things. It means we have an inner life; we are not merely objects, we are subjects. We have an intellect that enables us to reason. Hence we can know. We can know what is good and we can know the origin of that good. This inner life that is ours is also marked by a certain *striving* or *aspiring*. We *desire* the good; we desire to be and to possess goodness to the fullest. We want to be fulfilled. We *choose* to pursue that which we perceive to be good, and we do so freely. This is free will. All of this is what makes us *persons*.

There is a likeness, a similarity between God and us, and that similarity is found in our *personhood*. We have personhood in common with God; and persons, because they are persons, seek interpersonal union. The personalist philosophy of Pope John Paul II provides fresh insights into the way we look at God and into the way we look at ourselves. It is part of the personalist philosophy that we acquire insights about ourselves by reflecting on the personhood of God and that we acquire insights about God by reflecting on human persons.

Because we were made in God's image, we desire at our deepest level to live in union with other persons. The human person grasps long before the age of reason that possessing the good to the fullest cannot be done in solitude. As we grow and mature, our understanding of the role that people have in our lives develops more fully. This is more than saying that we humans are social beings. We desire to live in union with others not simply because it helps us meet biological needs, but as the bishops at the Second Vatican Council said, "man, who is the only creature on earth which God willed for itself, cannot find himself except through a sincere gift of himself."[7]

A principal theme of this book is that love is the gift of one's self, a gift that brings about interpersonal union. This is how the Father, Son, and Holy Spirit love each other. It is a love that unites. And, though not always felt, it is real. We must not make the mistake of reducing all love merely to the experience of feeling love.

Love is the gift of self, and we can give a small gift or a large gift. When I was a boy, there was a retired gentleman who lived several houses down the street. I was about seven-years-old, and he was in his seventies. In the summertime, I would often go down to his house and sit outside with him. I even had my own little pint-sized chair. We would sit and visit. Though we did not think of it in these terms, we each made a gift of self to the other. It was a small gift—but a gift nonetheless. The experience of the gift of self and the interpersonal union that is created thereby is what I call *intimacy*.

Imagine two friends who have known each other for many years. They have reached the point where they have no fear of revealing their deepest secrets. Besides feeling free to speak about very private things, they are genuinely concerned about the welfare of the other and are willing to make personal sacrifices for the other's well-being. Here we see a greater gift of self than in the previous example. The union is deeper, and so is the intimacy. Intimacy must not be thought of in an exclusively sexual or romantic way. There is certainly intimacy in sexual love—but non-sexual relationships can be intimate as well. The experience of intimacy is the feeling of being *connected* with another. It is the sense that somehow my life is a part of your life, and *vice versa*.

What happens when one experiences intimacy with no one? Then one has the experience, the feeling, of aloneness. Going back to Genesis, after God created the Garden of Eden complete with all the plants and all the animals, he, at last, created the very highest point of creation up until that point—*Adam*. It is a name that in Hebrew simply means "man." He gave Adam work to do—the naming of the animals—and in so doing he showed his dominion over them. But for all of the Garden's beauty and all its harmony, there was something missing. There was nothing in the Garden to which Adam could give the gift of himself. He was in the most profound and existential sense *alone*. "For the man there was not found a helper fit for him."[8] So the Lord God created Eve. One can only imagine the look with which Adam first gazed upon Eve. Here at last was one to whom Adam could give the gift of himself. Here at last was someone Adam could love, and who in turn could love him. Adam was no longer alone. Some*one* had entered his life; someone he could live his life *with* and live his life *for*.

God made us in such a way that we are completed, we are fulfilled, by living in communion with others. This living in union with others and sharing our lives with them is what I mean by friendship. "Friendship" as I use it here has a richer connotation than the way the word is commonly used. By *friendship* I intend to include the relationship between a husband and wife, but I intend to exclude the casual relationships that, in ordinary language, are sometimes called friendship. I will make this distinction more clear later on. In the end, friendship is about interpersonal union; it is about people—including husbands and wives—sharing their lives.

How Are People United?

In our living and interpersonal relating, there are a variety of ways that we can be united with others. Going to a major-league ballpark one senses the feeling of unity the fans have for the home team. The players themselves have their own sense of unity—a sense of *esprit de corps*. People feel in some way connected with the members of their profession, their co-workers, classmates, and neighbors. In a particular way we feel united with our family and our friends. Looking more closely, we see that there are various ways that we can be united.

One way people are united is in their *feelings* for each other. Whether the feelings are affectionate or erotic, the people who share the feelings between them have an experience of unity. In this case the unity between the two is *felt*. There are other types of unity. It is an important insight to realize that people can be united—truly united—without particularly *feeling* united, or at least without feeling united all the time. The absence of emotion does not, by that fact, make the unity less real.

Susan and Mary, for example, are united in their ideas. They both think the governor's policy on gambling is wrongheaded, and their common way of thinking unites them in a way far different from emotional unity. There is the unity that arises when two people *will* the same thing—volitional unity or unity of purpose. If Susan and Mary not only *think* the governor's policy is wrongheaded but work together to bring about a change, then the two of them are united in a unity of purpose. They *will* the same thing.

There is also the unity that exists between two people who seek the same ultimate end. This is spiritual unity. It is seen, for example, among people who share the same religion. Many who have had the experience of being present at a Papal Mass or audience with the Pope say that it was an experience of unity not only with the Holy Father but also with the thousands of people who were also present. Those who have attended World Youth Day have had this same experience. Spiritual unity is the awareness that, in the final analysis, our lives are about knowing, loving, and serving the Lord.

Husbands and wives have a unity that is present on a number of levels. Besides the emotions that husbands and wives have for each other, they also share each other's bodies and experience what the Church refers to as "one flesh" unity. It is more than an erotic feeling. It is the experience of the two of them coming together in sexual union and realizing that by their coming together they may love a child into existence. Those who have children have the further experience of being united by the very fact that they are the parents of these children.

An exhaustive list would also have included the unity all of us have in virtue of sharing a common human nature; the unity that family members have because they have common ancestors; the unity of fellow citizens, etc. But the five I have listed are sufficient to make the point—there are various ways that people are united.

All five types of unity—emotional, intellectual, volitional, spiritual, and bodily—are real, but each is *experienced* differently. Emotional and bodily unity are types of unity one can feel, while intellectual, spiritual, and volitional unity, in themselves, are not felt—though there may be a concurrent emotional unity that is also present. But even when unity is not felt, or not felt particularly strongly, it is nonetheless real unity. For example, I am a priest living in the northeast corner of my diocese. Say I attend a meeting at the chancery where there is a priest from the southwest corner of the diocese, a priest whom I do not know very well and whom I rarely see. Nevertheless, the two of us are firmly committed to the well-being of the diocese, and we spend our lives to bring that about. Because of that fact, the two of us are truly united even though there really is little that we feel between us. We are intellectually united (we see things the same way), we are spiritually united (we are both priests committed to the same spiritual ends) and we are volitionally united (we are choosing to work toward the same purpose and goal).

But for all that, though there may be unity on a number of levels between two persons, there is still something more that is needed. Something is needed to *keep* them united. We need to have things in common with the people we love, but we need more than that. Sometimes we will feel the unity and sometimes not. Real unity—real love—is something more complex, something richer than what we experience from day to day. Rather, something about the person attracts us, something that we may or may not be able to articulate. There is something we find to be *good*. As the philosopher Josef Pieper puts it in his book *Faith, Hope, Love*, something about the person leads us to say, "*It is good that you exist*."[9] We say, basically, that "because of the goodness I perceive in you, I willingly commit myself to you." It is here that real love, a love that is worthy of persons, develops between two people.

The Different Ways We Use the Word "Love"

If you want to have an interesting conversation, ask a group of people what it means to love someone. You will get lots of answers. "Love" is an interesting word because we use it in so many ways: I love my dog; I love that idea; I love summertime; I love my mother; I love my job; I love my girlfriend; I love ice cream; I love God; I love my school; I love myself; I love the way that sofa looks in here; I love my child. We use the word in so many ways that simply saying to someone "I love you" can mean any of a number of things. Human love has been recognized and written about for a couple of millennia. In the ancient world, Aristotle wrote about this in his *Nicomachean Ethics,* and Cicero's *De Amicitia* explicitly treats the topic of friendship. There have always been authors to write about or comment upon human love.

Though we use the word "love" in many ways, in every case, "love" carries with it this meaning: I am responding to something I perceive to be good. And though our perceptions may be wrong, if we did not perceive something as good, we would not love it. Two things flow from this. First, because I perceive something to be good, I *desire* it in some way. I desire to be enriched by its goodness. Secondly, the goodness I perceive elicits some sort of a *return* from me. Putting these two things together, we see the twofold receiving and giving dynamic of love.

People will sometimes say they *like* rather than say they *love*. What is the relationship between liking and loving? *Liking* is more generic. It is, as it were, broader than *loving*. When we like something, we have an attraction to it because at some level it resonates with us and we take pleasure in it. I like watching football. I like the city of Rome. I like this music. It is the opposite of *disliking*. "I really do not like that painting." In this case I experience a certain disharmony. "It does not sit right with me." "I do not like it. I cannot really tell you why—I just do not. Something about it is not right." These are common expressions for expressing dislike.

We all have things that resonate within us. Perhaps it is more illustrative to begin with things rather than persons. It makes sense, when referring to inanimate objects, to say we *like* rather than *love* them. "I like my new cell phone." But certain other things, such as my Christmas tree, carry deeply important associations with persons and events in my life. The Christmas tree is far, far more than a nice holiday decoration. It would be odd to say, "I love my Christmas tree," and so we usually do not speak that way. But we are moving in that direction.

For some things the word "like" is clearly inadequate. This is so because at a certain point our identification with something is so strong—it so resonates with our being—that we want to cry out, *I love that!* This is particularly true of music. Here our *liking* becomes indistinguishable from our *loving*. Do we not say that we *love* some song or piece of music that, perhaps for reasons unknown, seems to touch our soul? I think we do.

It is understandable, and it is accurate for people to say, "I love teaching"; "I love being a priest"; or "I love being a mother." But I could also understand someone saying, "I *like* being a cashier at the store."

I like playing golf; my friend loves it. I enjoy it if the weather is suitable and I am with friends. He will golf alone—in the rain. It does something for him. He loves it.

It certainly seems inadequate for the devout Catholic to say he *likes* the Church. It is a part of who he is. He loves the Church. What about liking persons? There are many people we like—even like a lot—but we would not say we love them. Why? Loving implies more than liking. And it is even possible to love someone we do not much like. Loving is more complex than liking. Love has a stability about it that can be missing in our feelings and emotions. For love to be genuine, there must be some sort of commitment, and commitment can be present with strong positive feelings, with no feelings, or with negative feelings. It is hard to love someone for whom you (presently) have negative feelings, but it can be done. So loving and liking are not the same. Nor is loving simply a matter of liking someone a lot.

To sum up then, *liking* implies taking pleasure in something or finding it to be in some way enjoyable. *Loving* may include all of that, but it might not. Real love—love that is worthy of human persons—always includes an act of the will. We call this *intentional* or *volitional love*.

Emotional Love vs. Intentional Love

Sorting through the various ways we use the word *love*, it seems that the first and most basic distinction is between emotional and intentional love. Emotional love is the love we *feel* for another. Our positive feelings for another can be strong or slight, steady or intermittent, affectionate or erotic. We will have a lot more to explore on this subject.

Intentional (or volitional) love is a very different way of loving, and it comes about not because of an emotion, but because of a choice. It is a willingness to do something for another simply because one chooses to do it. There may be no *emotional content* associated with it, or one may even have an emotional aversion to doing it. In the end, I am doing it because I *choose* to. Suppose Catherine particularly dislikes giving blood; it always makes her feel sick to her stomach, and she comes very close to fainting. She considers the blood test to be the worst part of her annual physical exam. Now Catherine has a neighbor who is disagreeable. Not only is she not "neighborly," but she often scolds Catherine's children if she thinks they are playing too loudly. Suffice it to say that Catherine does not "like" this neighbor. One day the neighbor is involved in a bad accident and needs blood. It just so happens that both Catherine and the neighbor have the same rare blood type. Even though Catherine hates giving blood and generally dislikes the neighbor, she willingly gives blood to help the woman. This is intentional love. It is an act of love that arises not from an emotional response to a person, but simply from an act of the free will. She does it because it is the right thing to do. We *can* love someone we do not like.

Loving someone often requires "going against the grain" and doing things we would just as soon not do. Whether it is accompanying your boyfriend to the grand opening of the hardware store, sitting in the rain to watch your child's ball game, or visiting your uncle in the nursing home, there are things we do—not because we feel like doing them, but because it is good to do them. They are indeed acts of love.

What Is behind Emotional Love

Emotional love—the love that we *feel* for someone—can either be erotic (which we will call *eros*) or non-erotic. Non-erotic emotional love can be present in varying degrees of intensity. It begins as generally *liking* someone, such as a familiar cashier at the supermarket. Beyond that, we speak of having a *fondness* for someone. It is more than simply liking another, and it presumes a greater familiarity than is associated with "liking." Teachers will sometimes say they are fond of their students. Finally, *affection* is the word I use to describe the strongest non-erotic feelings and emotions we can have for another.

These three—generally liking, being fond of, and having affection for—differ from each other, as the philosophers say, *in degree*, not *in kind*. The difference between erotic love and non-erotic love is a *difference in kind*. They are different kinds of things, like apples and oranges. But the difference between *liking* and *fondness* and *affection* is a matter of greater or lesser intensity. Some authors, such as C.S. Lewis, have categorized all non-erotic feelings as affection. I reserve the term *affection* for the stronger, more intense emotions than those commonly associated with *liking* and *fondness*.

But what lies behind these emotions? Why do I like this thing, this event? Why am I fond of this person? What accounts for the affection I have for my friend? Up to a point we can identify why we are drawn emotionally to some people. I say "up to a point" because many of our own attractions remain mysterious even to ourselves. There is a certain subjectivity to it. It is like our attraction to foods. Why do I really like some foods? I do not know—I just do. Why do I have such affection for that one friend of mine? I do not know—I just do. There are, as it were, ingredients that go into our emotional loves. They generate a certain liking or attraction. These ingredients are *"need love," "appreciative love,"* and *"gift love."* C.S. Lewis commented on these three in great detail in *The Four Loves.*

"Need Love"

Consider the following. It is a hot day. You have just finished mowing the lawn, and you are really thirsty. You pour yourself a glass of water, and it tastes great. This is *need love.* Your attraction to the water is determined by your need: you are really thirsty. If you were not so thirsty, the water would not hold the same attraction. Once the need has been met, the attraction drops off quickly. The smell of food cooking in the kitchen produces a different reaction in us after dinner than it did before. Our love for many things is this kind of love. The smoker's attraction to cigarettes—like any addiction—is *need love.* We love them when we need them. When we do not need them they go back on the shelf. With *need love* the source of the attraction is within *me*—it is *my need*, and the things that I love are the things that satisfy my need.

I am intentionally not making the distinction between needing and wanting. In distinguishing between needing and wanting one could say one *wants* a new set of golf clubs, but does not *need* them. That is a helpful distinction for ethical considerations, but it is not helpful here. The emotions as such cannot distinguish between needing and wanting. So when I refer to *need love*, I am simply referring to one's *inner experience* of needing. One's needs can be legitimate—such as the need for food, warmth, emotional security, and intimacy. Or they can be illegitimate, like the need to act out sexual desire outside of marriage or the insecure employer's need to dominate the people in the office. Either way, whether the need is legitimate or not, it is experienced as a "need," and for that reason we call the attraction to those things *need love*.

While people can and do have *need love* for persons it is only love in a qualified sense. It is certainly not a mature love. People have needs that others can meet, and having those needs met creates a certain bond. But my love for you, if it is only *need love*, is self-centered. It is really based on me, on what you can do for me. This is the essence of *need love*—it is about my need, it is not about you. Think, for example, of the relationship between a professional and his or her client. The professional helps the client meet a particular need. There is nothing wrong with this, but it is a professional, not a personal, relationship.

Some relationships that pose as personal relationships are nothing more than the mutual satisfaction of each other's needs. Underdeveloped romantic relationships may be based on little more than *need love*. Each enjoys the company of the other, and they satisfy each other's emotional needs. The relationship could be described as, "I love what you do for me." Each of them experiences strong feelings when with the other person. However, the relationship is defective—or at the very least, it lacks the qualities of a mature, loving relationship—because it is not a *person* that each of them loves. What they love is the *feeling*, the subjective experience, each of them has when they are with one another. And the relationship is characterized by a mutual accommodation of each other's emotional needs. This kind of relationship rarely lasts. When it does last it is because their love is transformed into something more than *need love*.

We all have needs, and it is understandable that we do things to have those needs met. Those who love us and are committed to us willingly reach out to us when they see that we have a need that they might reasonably meet. But there is more to love than meeting another's needs, and as long as a relationship is primarily *need love* it is vulnerable. By definition, it only lasts as long as the need remains.

"Appreciative Love"

Unlike *need love*, which is based on a certain lack—or need—in the lover, *appreciative love* is based on the perceived goodness of the beloved. There is something in the beloved object that we value, something we judge to be *good*, to be desirable. I have an appreciation for the goodness I perceive, and its goodness and desirability draw me to itself.

Consider this example. It is your girlfriend's birthday. You walk through the front door of the flower shop and you smell the fresh flowers. You think to yourself, "Those flowers smell great." This is *appreciative love.* You were not craving flower scent. No need of yours was being met. You encountered the fragrance, and you found yourself attracted to it. We are drawn to that which we perceive to be good. Unlike *need love,* it is not based on "me" but on some perceived good quality *in the object.* Something about this thing or this person attracts me—I perceive something that I value. There is a fulsome presence of *appreciative love* in our mature interpersonal relationships.

We would like to think that it is *appreciative love* that moves the people in our lives to love us. We hope that there is much about us that draws people to us and makes them "love us for who we are." We do not like to think that people stay with us simply because it enables them to have their needs met. And we certainly would not want to think that the people in our lives are with us simply out of pity or duty. But in truth, there are a variety of reasons and motives why we do the things we do. Why do I go to see that old friend of mine who lives a couple of hours away? Perhaps I have something I really *need* to discuss with him. Perhaps we have not seen each other in a while and that effervescent personality of his, as it were, draws me to himself. Or maybe he has asked me to come for a visit, and though I am busy at present, I spend an afternoon with him because I see it as a duty of friendship. Are not all of these ways of responding to another person different modes of loving? Indeed they are. Again, we would all like to think that we are being loved with *appreciative love* all the time. In reality, there are a variety of motives prompting the people in our lives to love us.

"Gift Love"

The third in the set of the three ingredients of love is *gift love,* the desire to give of one's self to another. We give ourselves in lots of ways. We hold the door for the mother pushing a stroller, we shovel the elderly neighbor's snow, we wash and iron our son's shirt, we see a little something at the store that we know our friend would like and so we buy it. These are all *gifts* we give to another that in some way symbolize and are a token of the gift of *ourselves.* Have you ever noticed that it can be very difficult to buy a birthday or Christmas gift for someone you really love? It is hard to find just the right thing. That is because the gift itself is a token of, is a material representation of, the gift of one person's life to another. That makes it difficult to find just the right gift for the special people in our lives. The gift seems somehow inadequate, unable to *say* what I want it to say.

We can desire to give a lot of ourselves or a little. The desire to give is an aspect of the union for which we all long, the entering into the lives of others, and the giving of ourselves to them. Parents, especially mothers, have *gift love* for their children. It gets them not only to *do* but even to sacrifice for their children, and to do so in a way that others seldom would. It is *gift love* that motivates a man to cook dinner for his friend or moves the girl to buy her co-worker her favorite kind of candy.

So then, these three ingredients combine in various proportions to make up emotional love: *need love, appreciative love,* and *gift love.* Emotional love is a love one *feels* for another. But there is another way of loving—intentional love.

What Is behind Intentional Love

Intentional (or volitional) loving arises from the free will. I do this for you *because I choose to.* Suppose you have an annoying co-worker who asks you to go to lunch; you would rather eat alone than spend your lunch hour with him. But you cheerfully and graciously accept his invitation. Why? You do it because at some level of your thinking and evaluating you judged that *it would be good to do so.* You saw that somehow, in a way that cannot be clearly articulated, doing this rather minor good thing says something about *you* and in a particular way also says something about *him* and his importance as a person. This is why intentional love is a profoundly important part of the life of every person. This kind of loving, the loving that is a particular exercise of one's freedom, makes us to be the persons we are.

Sub-humans (dogs, cats, chimps, etc.) are not capable of intentional love for the simple reason that they do not have a will that is *free.* Animals do what they do because of their instincts, or simply to meet some biological need. Human persons do a lot of that too—but we do not *have* to. We can *choose* to act in a way that is contrary to our instincts and does not meet a biological need. A man I know once saw a gasoline tanker truck crash into a stalled car on I-80 near Ottawa, Illinois. The car caught fire and could have exploded the tanker, yet this onlooker ran to the car to help the driver escape. Doing so was completely *contrary* to his instincts. His instincts told him to run away, to run to safety. No biological need of his was being met—indeed, he was putting himself in great danger. He ran to the car because he *chose* to.

Why do we do these things? What is *behind* intentional love? (Note I do not ask what *causes* intentional love. Intentional love arises because of a *free* choice. If something *caused* it, then it would not be free. Nevertheless, we are motivated to choose one way rather than another, to choose *this* good rather than that one. It is these motivating forces that we are exploring when we ask what is *behind* intentional love.) I think there are two ways that one is moved, prompted, or motivated to choose the way one does. They are not neat categories that are mutually exclusive; there is a lot of overlapping. A sense of duty can prompt us to choose the way we do, as can the desire to *be more*, to *become more*, to *love more*. These latter are not duties in the strict sense, but rather the desire to become the man I could be, the man I desire to be, the man that I desire to be for you.

Intentional Love Arising from a Sense of Duty

Intentional love is at times experienced as something, so to speak, pushing us on, prompting us to do what we ought to do. This is the intentional love that arises from one's sense of duty. In every relationship there are duties, though we rarely spell them out.

Some duties arise from having made prior commitments. We count on people to do what they say they will do. When we make a commitment, we have the duty to fulfill it. Consider the following. Jerry, an avid golfer, asks Tom to play golf on Monday. Monday comes around, and it is a crummy day for golf. Tom does not particularly feel like golfing, but because of his commitment he goes anyway. Tom understands that part of friendship includes doing the things one has committed to doing—like fulfilling the commitment to play golf. In this example, does Tom want to play golf? The answer is both yes and no. On the one hand, Tom does not particularly want to golf in foul weather. That is the *no* part. On the other hand, Tom understands that being friends with someone means making commitments and keeping them—even when doing so is inconvenient. Tom really does value Jerry's friendship, and as such he *wants* to keep the commitment he made. That is the *yes* part. Again, loving someone means making commitments and keeping them. Are there any limits here? Certainly. Circumstances can change that would make it gravely inconvenient or even wrong for one to keep one's commitment. We are not going to play golf if it is pouring rain, if I get the flu, or if your wife is taken to the hospital. But the keeping of our commitments has to be based on more than simply whether I happen to *feel* like it at the time.

To a large degree, the process of maturation involves one's growing in the ability to make and keep commitments. This is one of life's great insights. We can commit ourselves on a number of levels. In general, we make personal commitments and professional commitments—with each of these having numerous sub-categories. One's religious commitments, for example, are a part of one's personal commitments. The people that are in your life personally or professionally know how well you keep your commitments. Again, loving people means making commitments to them and keeping them. Keeping one's commitments means more than, "I will do it if something better does not come along" or, "I will do it if I feel like doing it at the time." Watch the way high school kids interact. They are notorious for keeping their options open when it concerns social events. When Matt asks Tim if he wants to do something on Friday night after the game, Tim responds by saying, "I will have to see what is going on." This way of interacting is pervasive among this age group. For many of them a sense of loneliness sets in when they realize that no one seems to be particularly committed to them. Some find the commitment they desire in a boyfriend-girlfriend relationship, though those who cannot or will not fulfill commitments in a friendship, likely will not consistently fulfill commitments to their boyfriend or girlfriend either. They will, however, fulfill such commitments as long as doing so fits in with the larger picture of a relationship that helps to meet their own emotional needs.

Some obligations arise from specific vocational commitments. Vocational commitments are open-ended in the sense that one does not know specifically what one will be asked to do when one commits to being a spouse, a priest, a doctor, a school teacher, etc. We do not know the details in advance because we *cannot* know them in advance. When Katie commits herself to being Dr. Anderson's nurse, she does not know precisely what she is getting herself into. Yet she can, in a very real way, commit herself in an open-ended way to living the life of a nurse and embracing the obligations that such a vocation entails. These are the obligations that we did not specifically commit to but which arise specifically because of our vocation. A priest, for example, is having dinner with some friends when the hospital calls with an emergency. The priest simply has to go to the hospital—it is part of his vocational commitment. The father of a family wants to watch the game on Sunday afternoon, but his wife has planned a party for her mother. He has to go to the party, and if he is smart he will do so cheerfully and without complaining. It is part of his vocation of being a husband. The custodian is scheduled to get off work at 4:00 but at 3:55 the toilet overflows. This man's vocation, among other things, includes being a custodian. He must stay and clean up this mess, though he clearly does not *feel* like doing so.

Some commitments follow from our commitment to God. Catholics, for example, have the obligation to attend Mass every Sunday and holy day of obligation. Occasionally someone will say, "You should go to Mass because you want to, not because you have to." I understand this sentiment, but imagine if we all had as a principle of living, "I only do what I feel like doing at the moment." Imagine if parents and spouses lived that way. The clothes would never get washed, the house would never get cleaned, and the kids would spend all their day at home because neither mom nor dad felt like taking them anywhere. It is a simple fact of life, and a fact of every relationship, that from time to time we have to do things that we would just as soon not do. Our relationship with God is no different. Anyone who has a substantial prayer life will attest that there are many days when they go to prayer—not because they feel on fire with the love of God—but because loving the person of our Lord, as with loving any person, means "spending quality time with Him." This is what spiritual writers mean when they speak of the "battle of prayer." Praying is not always easy, but those who love God pray anyway because conversation with God is one of the duties of our friendship with Him.

Finally, some things in life we feel duty-bound to do simply because they seem like the right thing to do at the moment. So, although you are running late to your son's ball game, and though it is a hot, humid summer evening, you stop to help an elderly man who is struggling to change a flat tire. There is no personal commitment nor specific vocational commitment that gives rise to a duty; nevertheless, you have a general sense that you *must do this.* You feel, in a way, obligated to do this. And after you have changed the tire, you will have a sense of satisfaction—tempered by the fact that you know that *you hardly could have done otherwise.*

These are all examples of intentional love—love that follows not from a feeling but from an act of the will—and which we do because of some sense of duty. The duty may follow from a personal commitment I have made; it may follow from my vocation, from my relationship with God, or simply from a general sense of doing the right thing. In all of these cases, my will is prompted to choose to fulfill a duty.

Intentional Love Arising from the Desire to **Be** *and* **Become** *More*

If you are like most, at some point in your life you looked at someone you deeply admire, someone who possesses a certain quality of greatness, and you said to yourself, "I would like to be like that." What is it about these people that makes them great? They seem to stand head and shoulders above everyone else. What makes them that way? I think one finds in these people a certain quality of living and loving and acting that enables them to live consistently *for others* in a way that goes beyond what duty would require. Fulfilling one's duties entails doing what one could reasonably expect in a relationship. There are things we can reasonably expect from our spouse, from our parents, from our friends, etc. Some people go beyond that. They do more than what is reasonably expected, and we say of such people that they are *generous.* But God has blessed the world with some men and women whom the word "generous" seems inadequate to describe. They are more than simply generous because they are generous *all the time.* They are *heroic.*

Consider Bl. Teresa of Calcutta (Mother Teresa). In the Western world it is unimaginable that one would find people lying in the street—dying of disease and hunger. But in Bl. Teresa's world it was sadly commonplace. Looking at the life of this holy woman we see someone who went to these people—not simply the poor, but the *poorest* of the poor—and brought them back to her residence. Their bodies were covered with sores that filled the air with a nearly unbearable stench. Bl. Teresa did far more than bathe and feed them—

she *convinced* them that she was genuinely interested in them. By what she said, by what she did, and by the way she said and did these things she convinced them that she loved them. For some of them, their last days on earth were the first time they experienced being loved. And they died in peace. She once said, "I picked up one person—maybe if I did not pick up that one person I would not have picked up the others."[10] This is heroic selflessness and generosity. We look at her life and we say, "I could never do that." Perhaps not. But perhaps we could move a few steps in that direction, trying to forget about ourselves and our wants and desires—living instead in the presence of others and trying to live our lives for them. Living for others, rather than for ourselves, is the foundation of authentic human greatness.

In the end it comes down to the kind of person *we want to be*. Not every spouse is a good spouse. Few are great. Not every friend is a generous one. But we can be—or at least we can be *better*. It does not happen overnight, but making the conscious decision is the first step. All of us have hurts and wounds from our past, and not a few are hampered in their relating by their own emotional needs. But to the extent that it is in our power we must try to move on. As Jesus said, "Rise, let us be going."[11] I need to begin thinking less about myself and my own little world. I need to enter more deeply into the lives of others, and make their well-being the desire of my soul.

Love as "Acceptance"

Surveying the literature on the topic of love, one finds that it is described either as an emotional response to another, or as an act of the free will whereby one willingly gives oneself to another. I think there is another mode of loving—love as acceptance. It is more akin to intentional love than to emotional love, but it includes elements of both. It is not intentional love in the sense of *doing* something for the other, but of choosing to accept the other. The statement, "I want to be loved," expresses the idea that we want to be known by another—known deeply, as I know myself—and accepted in spite of my deficiencies.

This aspect of love—the love whereby I am an important part of your life, and I have the experience of being deeply accepted by you—is not something that happens quickly. Emotional responses can develop rapidly as we suddenly discover we like somebody, and intentional responses of our free will can take place in an instant. I can decide in "the blink of an eye" that I will do something for you—but love as acceptance takes time to develop. It grows over the years as my inner life is revealed to you. Over the years, you have discovered patterns in my behavior; you know what I am like at my best, and at my worst. You do not accept my shortcomings, but you accept *me* in spite of them. Having seen me in countless circumstances through the years, you still say, "It is good that you exist."[12] This is love as acceptance. When we experience it, we are made to feel important, made to feel in some way wanted. It is a kind of love that makes us humble—humble because we are aware of our own imperfections.

Why People Stay Together

As we have seen, people can be united on a number of levels. But the fact that two people are united now does not mean they will be united later. What keeps people together? Why do some friends *stay* friends? When a couple gets married they pledge their love for life—yet many, many marriages end in divorce. What is there about lifetime friends and spouses that keeps them united? What is the cement that bonds them together?

To begin with, while lifetime friends and spouses almost always have strong emotions and feelings that bind them, what keeps them together is *more* than an emotional bond. Emotions and feelings by themselves are far too unreliable and fickle to cement a lifetime friendship or marriage. We simply cannot depend on our emotions to carry the day every day. Emotions are sufficient to hold together a casual relationship, but not one that has any depth, one where real issues are discussed and difficulties are faced. Some expect the intensity of emotion often associated with a new relationship to carry them through the years. They are often disillusioned when they come to the discovery that the real love that is present in lifetime friendships and marriages is something that requires real effort and is not always experienced as something sweet. Real? Yes. Beautiful? Yes. But not always sweet.

Long-term friendships and lifelong marriages are characterized by *breadth*, *depth*, and *commitment*. People are united by the things they have in common. If the only thing Jason and Danny really have in common is their love for baseball, their friendship will, for that reason, be limited. Their friendship needs more breadth. This is important for people who are considering marriage. A man and woman who are in love take great delight in each other, rejoicing in their mutual love. Still, they should look at how much they really have in common. It is helpful—though often difficult—for people to put their emotions aside for a moment and soberly evaluate how much they have in common with the person they think would be a good spouse.

People struggle to keep a relationship alive when there is not a lot of overlapping in their interests. When a man and a woman fall in love, their primary interest and focus is on *each other*—as one would expect. But romantic and erotic attraction is not enough. They need common interests to sustain the relationship—activities they enjoy doing together and topics they enjoy discussing. This will be particularly important for the couple when life begins to be experienced as routine and with a degree of monotony. Experience tells us that the excitement of a new job, a new school, or a new gadget eventually wears off. It happens in relationships too. In happy marriages, the husband and wife have a number of areas of common interest that unite them.

Depending on what they are, these common interests can unite us *deeply*. Children deeply unite parents. We all have things that really matter to us. Unity in these aspects of life give a relationship depth.

Fulfilling the Duties of a Relationship

Every personal relationship, whether casual or deep, entails some sort of commitment. Once people are committed to each other, they can no longer relate as strangers, and to do so would be odd. Indeed, the degree to which we are willing to commit ourselves determines the nature of the relationship and its depth.

What is it the commitment we make? At one level, we commit ourselves to a person by committing ourselves to fulfilling the *duties* that are inherent in the relationship. Every relationship has duties. Many of the duties are more or less vague and duties are rarely spelled out. Yet we have an intuitive sense when a certain something is due to someone in our lives because of the nature of our relationship.

Katie and Ann live next door to each other. As two people who happen to live next door, they could relate more or less as strangers—as some neighbors do. Or, not wanting to remain strangers, they could begin to relate as neighbors and continue relating that way through the years. Katie and Ann indeed interact as neighbors— greeting each other and looking out for each other. Katie is going to be gone for several days, and she asks Ann to keep an eye on her place and pick up her mail each evening. That is a reasonable expectation of neighbors. One could say Ann has the duty to do this. There are some neighbors who do more—or even *far more*—than one could reasonably expect of a neighbor. They are more than neighbors, they are *good* or even *great* neighbors.

Every relationship has these duties. There are duties associated with friendship and the closer the friends, the greater the duties. There are fewer duties in a casual friendship than in a deep one. With a friend who is like your *other self*, there are a lot of duties. Take a simple example: A father just arrived at his daughter's wedding rehearsal when he notices the battery in his camera has died. He says to his dear friend who is also at the rehearsal, "My camera battery just died. Would you run to the drugstore and get me a new one?" Does the friend have the *duty* to do this? Given the context (it is his friend's daughter's wedding rehearsal) and the friendship between them, I would argue that he does have a duty to do this. It is part of the nature of friendship. Friends not only share each other's joys and sorrows, they are committed to each other and desire each other's *good*, their *well-being*. We want our friends to flourish and to be happy, and we are willing to do what we can to bring that about. These are the duties of friendship. Closer friends have more duties than casual friends; still, some friends (close or casual) do more or even far more than their friendship would require. They are *good* friends, *great* friends, or even *heroic* friends.

The same can be said of marriage. In the Rite of Marriage, just before the couple exchanges vows, the priest says, "[The Lord Jesus] has already consecrated you in Baptism and now seals and strengthens your love with a special sacrament so that you may *assume the duties of marriage* in mutual and lasting fidelity." What are these *duties of marriage*? There are the obvious things like sexual fidelity, but certainly it includes more than that. One would be hard pressed, however, to come up with a list that spells them out. One is *obliged* to fulfill one's duties, and in so doing one is simply *doing one's duty*. One can also do *more* than one's duty, and in so doing one's love is greater because he or she willingly goes *beyond* the fulfillment of his or her obligations. Suppose Jessica develops a sinus infection and feels miserable. Does her husband, Tim, have a *duty* to go to the pharmacy to pick up Jessica's prescription? I would argue that he does. But Jessica also likes to have an attractive garden. Does Tim (who cares little for flowers) have a *duty* to spend every Saturday in May planning, buying, arranging, and planting the garden? I would argue he does not. He may nevertheless choose to do so, and if he does so choose he is doing more than his duty. Every relationship is this way: we have things that we have a duty to do, and if we do more we move into the realm of generosity. Jesus said to his disciples, "When you have done all that is commanded you, say, 'We are unworthy servants; we have only done what was our duty.'"[13] When we enter into a relationship with someone—whether it is a professional relationship, a friendship, a marriage, or parenthood—we willingly assume duties. We must not think of ourselves as generous because we do that which we are obliged to do.

Fulfilling People's Hope

Faith and hope are two aspects of interpersonal relating without which it is impossible to have satisfying human interaction. Without faith in each other and without hope in each other, we live in a state of existential aloneness.

The first people to enter our lives are our parents. Siblings and playmates follow. Life experiences train us to evaluate the believability of those with whom we come into contact. Some are highly believable—hopefully mom and dad are in that category—while others give one cause to doubt. The degree to which I believe you determines the way we will interact. Having faith in people means believing them and believing *in* them—believing them to be genuine, of upright intention, and sincere in what they say and do. One's faith in another can be minimal, moderate, or strong. It could be rated on a scale of one to ten. Perhaps we believe someone in our life to be generally honest, but what if in a particular instance that person would stand to gain a lot if he were slightly dishonest? Am I confident that he would still be completely honest? We make these judgments about people—about their trustworthiness—and it is reasonable that we do so. Having judged someone to be worthy of trust, we say we have *faith* in him or her. That, in turn, then enables us to place our hope in the person.

Hope is different than faith. Hope, which seems to be a forgotten virtue, is not simply wishful thinking—but the confident expectation that others will do what they say they will do. We place our hope in people because of our faith in them. Hope enables us to go out on a limb in the expectation that others will fulfill their commitments. Many of the worthwhile things we do in life depend on people working together, keeping their promises, and fulfilling their commitments. Consider something as simple as a football team. I commit myself to attending practice and working hard, and I have the expectation that my teammates will do the same. But suppose I thought my teammates were undependable, lazy, and lacking in genuine commitment. Suppose it had happened more than once that game-day came, and there were not even enough players to field a team. My own commitment to the team would be diminished. "I cannot do this alone. They do not seem to be interested. I will do something else instead."

We depend on others to keep their commitments. Say a friend who lives 100 miles away agrees to meet for dinner in a town that is halfway between us. When he arrives at the designated place, he has the reasonable expectation—the hope—that I will be there. Our hope is generalized in that we want our friends to *do* and *be* what friends are supposed to do and be. We see this very clearly in marriage. As a man and woman fall in love, their faith in each other grows. Each believes the other to be genuine, sincere, and honest. They want to spend the rest of their lives with each other and raise a family together—believing that the other is capable and willing to assume the responsibilities of a spouse and parent. They have hope in each other. In keeping their mutual commitments, they fulfill each other's hope as they strengthen their marriage and raise their children.

We might reflect on the fact that Our Lord has placed us in other people's lives. How well do we fulfill our commitments to them? Being the friend, the co-worker, the spouse that we *ought* to be brings out the best in others. It raises their own confidence and gives them a share of the good we accomplish by our mutual cooperation. Seeing that others care about me, and are committed to me, gives me a healthy self-confidence that motivates me to be a good friend in return.

There are many things I cannot do by myself; you have promised to do this with me. I have hope—the expectation—that you will fulfill what you have promised to do. We count on our spouse to fulfill his or her role, just as children depend and count on parents to fulfill their parental commitments. My friend promises to pick me up at the airport—I expect him to be there. The football players expect their coach to *be* their coach, doing the things that coaches do. By working together and fulfilling our commitments to each other we build up the Kingdom of God on earth. It begins now, in seed form. Recall how Jesus, in one of his parables, compared the Kingdom of God with a mustard seed. It starts off small, but when full-grown and flowering in eternity it is the largest of shrubs.[14]

Understanding and experiencing the fulfillment of our hope here and now enables us to grasp what is meant by hope in God—the theological virtue of hope. The believer has faith in God. And one who fully embraces the Christian Faith believes not merely that God exists, but also believes that God has communicated his love for us and his plan for us. Because many of the good things God has promised us will be received in eternity, it is often difficult to live as we should *now*. This is why we need hope. The theological virtue of hope is the confident expectation that God will make good on his promises. Just as the hope we have in our friends gets us to "go out on a limb" in the expectation that they will do as they promised, so too the theological virtue of hope—hope in God—motivates us and pushes us to live the life proposed in the Gospel in the expectation that God will fulfill his promises in heaven. In both cases, whether it is fulfilling the demands of our relationships with each other, or fulfilling the demands of our relationship with God, it involves far more than simply *being a swell guy*. We were made for far more. "Unless a grain of wheat falls into the earth and dies, it remains alone; but if it dies, it bears much fruit."[15] We were made to give ourselves away. It is the stuff of which heroes are made, and it is hope that enables us to do it.

Questions for Philosophical Consideration and Personal Growth

1. Why is a handwritten note a richer form of communication than, say, an e-mail?

2. Suppose someone met you for the first time (maybe somebody new at work) and spent five minutes with you. What would be his or her first impressions of you? Would this person think you seemed:
   - Preoccupied?
   - Friendly?
   - "Full of yourself"?
   - Eager to impress?
   - Interested in me?
   - Like a jerk?

   Why would he or she think this?

3. Write down the first names or initials of the people with whom you would discuss "important matters."

4. Explain what it means to be deeply connected with someone. What is the relationship between *being connected* and *feeling connected*? Is the measure of the one always an accurate measure of the other? In other words, can I *feel* deeply connected with someone while not actually *being* deeply connected? And can I *be* connected with someone but not particularly *feel* it—at least not feel it all the time? Explain this. What insight does this provide about the nature of real interpersonal connectedness?

5. Do you think people's concept of loving someone changes over time? Explain.

6. Loving someone for the long haul requires, at least from time to time, going against the grain. Does that detract from our love, or in some way ennoble it? Would the "perfect relationship" be one where every aspect of it was "sweetness and light"?

7. The text states, "Underdeveloped romantic relationships may be based on little more than *need love*." What does this mean, and what would it mean for the relationship to be further developed?

8. Suppose you and I are friends. I ask you to go see a new science fiction movie with me. You do not really like science fiction and you are tired from working all day. But you go anyway. How do these feelings (your dislike of science fiction and your feeling tired) affect the quality of your "gift" of accompanying me to the movie? What insights can be discerned from this?

9. If we can be moved to do something by a desire to *be more* and to *become more*, what does that tell us about the nature of true human greatness? What then is the relationship between greatness and love?

10. We all have emotional needs and it is natural for us to want these needs to be fulfilled. Can you envision a relationship that is little more than a mutual accommodation of each other's needs? Can a person's emotional needs be so great that they hinder normal relating? Can one's emotional needs be so *little* that they hinder normal relating? Ideally, what role would our emotional needs play in our relationships?

11. The degree to which we give of ourselves is a measure of our greatness. What are some of the things that keep one from giving more of themselves? What keeps you from giving more of yourself? Perhaps you are already doing a lot. Perhaps it does not occur to you how you might do more. Suppose you began to see how you might do more in your personal relationships, would you be inclined to do so? Are you cheerful about your giving of yourself? How would an objective observer rate your generosity regarding the giving of your time and your attention?

12. Some people seem unwilling to ask anybody to do anything—not even close friends. Is this helpful to the relationship? Explain.

13. How well do you fulfill the implicit and explicit commitments to the people in your life? In what instances do you do particularly well? In what instances (at what times, or with which people) could you do better?

14. Suppose you were giving a talk on this chapter to a group of people in their early twenties. What three points would you want them to be sure to remember?

Fill in the blank: If you forget everything else I say today, remember this:

Chapter Two

A First Look at Friendship

"To the Ancients, Friendship seemed
the happiest and most fully human of all loves;
the crown of life and the school of virtue.
The modern world, in comparison, ignores it."

From The Four Loves
C.S. Lewis

Some Things that Look Like Friendship but Are Not

As we begin our consideration of friendship, I think it will be helpful to exclude from our conversation things that might look like friendship but in fact are something else. The word "friend" is like the word "love" in that it is often used loosely. To begin with, being *friendly* is not the same as being friends. Perhaps there is someone who works in the same building with you and the two of you often happen to be going into or out of the building at the same time. You each smile and say, "Good morning," or, "Have a good evening." You are friendly—you are not friends. Nevertheless, friendliness, or the virtue of affability, is a positive trait that we would do well to cultivate. My high school students sometimes say that being friendly toward someone you do not particularly like is being hypocritical or fake. I do not think that is true. Pretending to be *friends* with someone with whom one is clearly at odds would be hypocritical. But the simple gestures of friendliness, which are often merely a matter of civility, should not in themselves be taken for friendship. If we cannot be friendly toward others—including those who oppose us—we will begin to live like barbarians.

We have all heard it said that a *dog* is man's best friend. I am a dog-owner and a dog-lover myself. And while dogs can be fiercely loyal and display tremendous affection, for all that, they are not capable of human friendship. Only *persons* are capable of making the gift of themselves and entering into the lives of others.

Neither are children capable of adult human friendship. Young children have *playmates*. These playmates play an important role in their lives and are integral to a child's development. Further, children are indeed capable of having genuine concern for others and can act selflessly and generously. But a child's lack of reflectivity and undeveloped communication skills hinder the establishment of friendship as it is experienced in adulthood. With the passing of years, the ever-growing ability to outgrow the self-centeredness of childhood makes friendship progressively more possible and increasingly desirable.

Professional relationships are not friendships. I might like my barber, my student, or my teacher, and perhaps I see them often. That, in itself, does not make us friends. It is a professional relationship, not a personal one. We could become friends, which would mean that in addition to our professional relationship we are also friends.

Also, familial relationships, in themselves, are not necessarily friendships. But family members can, and often do, relate as friends. As the expression goes, "You pick your friends—you do not pick your family." Familial relating is a type of relating unto itself, in both the immediate and the extended family. Within the various familial relationships, individuals can relate as friends as well. Siblings are not siblings by choice, and being siblings does not make them friends—but they could begin to relate as friends. If they do, their friendship does not replace the sibling relationship, it enhances it by connecting them on levels that neither relationship alone could do.

The point I am trying to make is that while one may be surrounded by people—in relationships that bear a certain resemblance to friendship—one can nevertheless feel very much alone. Many struggle with loneliness, with the feeling of not being *connected* very deeply with others. Some are embarrassed by it, thinking their loneliness is because of some personal defect on their part. Perhaps they wonder why they feel alone even though they are surrounded by people all the time. They feel lonely because the experience of intimacy has eluded them. The goal for them is not to increase the *number* of people in their lives, but to deepen their relationships. As relationships deepen, the experience of intimacy diminishes loneliness.

In the next section, we will look at the people who "happen to be in our lives." These people are not yet our friends. But people who eventually become our friends nearly always begin in this group.

The People Who "Happen to Be in Our Lives"

In the last section, we excluded some concepts that are sometimes loosely connected with friendship. Most can see how mature, adult friendship is something other—something deeper—than any of those. But there is another type of relationship, and a very important relationship at that, which is often taken for friendship—but is not friendship. It is the relationship with the people who "happen to be in our lives."

Imagine if, by some feat of technological wizardry, you could get a computer printout of *every person* you encountered in the past twelve months. Along with their names would be their photos and a listing of every time you saw each other. Remember, it includes *every person*. You would not even recognize most of them. With some of these people, encountering them was a one-time-occurrence, such as your interaction with a waiter at a restaurant. Others, we see regularly but we do not interact with them. If you regularly shop at the same grocery store, you may come to recognize those who stock the shelves. You have nothing but the most brief and superficial interaction as you ask, perhaps, where to find something. Then there are those you speak with a bit more, with varying degrees of interaction. Depending on what we do for a living, or otherwise spend our days, we could have many people who regularly enter into our lives. They are the people who *happen* to be in our lives because circumstances have placed us in the same place at the same time. They are our classmates, teammates, co-workers, and neighbors. We belong to the same clubs and organizations, the same churches and synagogues. It is not uncommon that with some of these people we have more frequent contact than with anyone else, except perhaps our spouses. We see these people often, even daily. The receptionist, the secretary, and the bookkeeper all work in the same office. Fifteen people are on my softball team, and naturally I talk to some more than others. I know all of my classmates by name; I have a little interaction with many of them, and more significant interaction with a few of them.

Which of these people are my friends? Are they all my friends? Are none of them? We see each other everyday, work side by side, and know basic details of each other's lives—does that make you my friend? Clearly, we interact with people in widely varying degrees. At what point do we draw a line and say, "Friendship begins here"? The way that question is answered is determined by the way we define "friendship." And that issue is a primary focus of this book. But before we continue looking further into the nature of friendship, I want to discuss more fully the relating that falls just short of friendship.

Although we sometimes use the word "friend" to describe the various people in our lives, many of these relationships, though good in themselves, have not yet reached the level of what we will later define as friendship. So what do we call these people, if they are not friends? C.S. Lewis understood this issue very clearly and he chose to call these people *companions*. The word "companion," like the words "friend" and "love," encompasses a variety of meanings—which complicates our task. The real difficulty lies in the fact that there is no single English word that corresponds to the relationship we are trying to describe, without also having other meanings that we intend to exclude. But other words that come close include, *buddy, comrade, cohort,* or *associate*. So if I say, "He is a buddy from work," one would assume that this is someone I know and interact with at some level—but the relationship falls short of friendship. C.S. Lewis chose to use *companionship* to describe this relationship, and I am doing the same—not because I am beholden to Lewis, but because I, too, find the other words even less satisfactory.

The word "companion" originally referred to a person with whom one ate bread (*cum panis*). Today the word sometimes connotes an *accompanying person*, such as in "traveling companion." The word can even refer to one's spouse, as in "my companion for life." But as I use the term, I intend neither of these meanings. And throughout the book, I use the word in the same sense as Lewis used it.

Companionship

When the word "friendship" is used loosely, it is often applied to what should properly be called *companionship*. We have lots of companions, and it is good that we do. We need them. They are the people that *happen* to be in our lives. But they are not our friends, and those who *have* real, genuine friends easily see the distinction.

I recall hearing a talk on charity given years ago. The speaker told the assembled crowd that he had over 100,000 friends. The question for me at the time was, "How many are *true* friends?" When we understand the distinction between *friendship* and *companionship* we can begin to see how someone can have many companions while at the same time being painfully lonely. The reason for this is obvious enough. We are not *personally committed* to our companions, and they are not personally committed to us. Co-workers are *professionally* committed to each other, and teammates and classmates share a certain *esprit de corps*, but there may be no personal commitment beyond that. This is why they are simply companions. Companionship, by definition, lacks the personal commitment that one finds in friendship. Companions may have strong professional bonds—just as teammates experience a certain sense of unity—but in their *personal* lives they are not united in the way that friends are. Though we work with companions and interact with them, we are not committed to them in the way we are committed to our friends, and we do not reveal private matters to them.

With this in mind, companions are more than acquaintances. The fact that they are companions and not friends, though, does not mean that they are not important to us. Our companions are *very* important to us. *We spend most of our day with them.* In the last century it was called a "clubbable" relationship. Some are fortunate enough to have a friend at the workplace or at school, but most of those who surround us each day are our companions. Some authors, like Lewis, have said companions are like silver—friends are like gold. No one ever says, "That is cheap—it is only silver." Silver is a precious metal, but it is not gold.

As we have seen, one of the difficulties we face in trying to discuss these matters lies with the language itself. We have already seen how the words *love, companion,* and *friend* have a wide variety of meanings. As I see it, there is a continuum, or a range of relating, that has the total stranger at one end, and the "friend who is like my other self" at the other. Along that continuum, every difference is one of degree. Using the example of color, sky blue and navy blue differ in degree. In other words, every difference along that range is a matter of having more of something or less of something. Companions become casual friends, and casual friends become friends by "adding more" of the qualities that make up friendship. On the other hand, the difference between friends and lovers—non-erotic and erotic love—is a difference *in kind*. They are different kinds of things. Just as sky blue does not become red by having a little more or a little less of something, friends do not become lovers by having a little *more* of something. Friendship and erotic love are different *kinds* of things.

With this continuum in mind, we mark off certain sections along the range and give it a name. Our acquaintances—people whom we have met—are midway between the stranger and the companion. Casual friends are midway between the companion and the friend. We can begin to see some elements of friendship in casual friends. They have more of a commitment to each other than companions do; but it is not the heartier, fulsome sort of commitment that one sees in genuine friendship.

It is sometimes difficult to distinguish two things along a range that lie next to each other. Getting back to our color example, one can easily distinguish sky blue from navy blue. But it is not so easy to distinguish navy blue from midnight blue, or midnight blue from black. I once purchased a pair of pants that I thought were black. When I brought them home, and saw them next to my black coat, I realized the pants were midnight blue. One easily distinguishes acquaintances from friends because they are far enough apart along the range. But in between acquaintances and friends, where I have situated companions and casual friends, distinguishing one from another can be difficult to do in practice. Suppose there is someone you have worked with for several years. You enjoy pleasant conversation. You talk about work-related matters, and you know a few basic details about each other—like his or her spouse's name and favorite sports teams, but you have never had what one might call a private or personal conversation. If you have not discussed personal matters, it would be a stretch to call the relationship a friendship. My companion knows my face—my friend knows my heart.

College freshmen who go away to school learn the distinction between friendship and companionship on their visits home. It is not possible to see everybody when I am home, since I only have a few days. But there are a few people that I will *make sure* I see. These are my friends. We hope the people we really want to see also want to see us.

Companions are an important part of our life inasmuch as the bulk of our day is usually spent with them, and because we spend so much time with our companions we would do well to learn healthy ways of interacting with them. Friendliness, dependability, other-serving, thoughtfulness, and professionalism are just a few virtues we would like to find in those that are around us all the time.

From time to time, one of our companions stands out from the rest. We see in this person more than a few qualities, values, and virtues that we ourselves admire. We have interests in common. We find it easy to identify with this person since we tend to see things in a similar way, and we begin to desire to get to know this person better. Again, the distinction between a companion and a casual friend is difficult to make in practice, but as people begin to be friends, they begin to have an interest in each other beyond the circumstances that initially brought them together. When co-workers begin to share their personal lives, they begin to be friends. If two co-workers are merely companions their relationship ends when they cease being co-workers. If they have become friends they will remain friends even though they no longer work together. The same is true of classmates. Companions come and go. We let them pass into and out of our lives. Friendship is more stable. People do not become friends overnight, and the bond between friends keeps them together even when the original circumstances cease that brought them together in the first place.

From Antiquity to Modern Times— Six Authors' Thoughts on Friendship

Now that we have distinguished companionship from friendship, let us begin our look at friendship itself. Everyone has a general sense of what friendship is. Friendship is part of the somewhat mysterious interaction between people who love each other. But if pressed to explain more clearly what they mean, different people explain friendship differently. At the very least, there is a difference in emphasis as regards the essential elements.

We learn a great deal from reflection and enlightened conversation with, and about, people who have both experienced friendship and thought a lot about it. I want to proceed by introducing several authors who have made a worthy contribution to the discussion of the nature of friendship. We will look at Aristotle, Cicero, St. Augustine, St. Aelred, Montaigne, and C.S. Lewis.

Aristotle—The Importance of Virtue

It hardly seems that Aristotle needs an introduction. He was chronologically the third of the three great Ancient Greek philosophers, Socrates, Plato, and Aristotle. From his eighteenth to his thirty-seventh year, Aristotle lived in Athens as a student of Plato in the Academy. He wrote many philosophical works and is, so to speak, one of the founders of Western thought.

Aristotle wrote what some say is the most well thought-out and comprehensive treatise ever written on friendship. It is found in Books VIII and IX of his *Nicomachean Ethics*. He discusses friendship in the context of a treatment of ethics because, as he says, friendship "is a kind of virtue, or at least accompanies virtue." It is a subject of moral philosophy inasmuch as friendship is necessary for human persons to live well, flourish, and be happy. "No one, even though he had all other goods, would choose to live without friends." But a difficulty arises from the fact that Aristotle wrote on the topic of *philia*, which is a particular way of loving. It includes the love of friendship, but it includes other things as well, such as the love of parents for their children.

Philia is a kind of love, distinct from *eros* and *agape*. *Eros*, of course, is erotic love; and *agape* is a selfless love that is akin to charity. *Philia* is a loving, affectionate bond that one has with another, and it is applicable to the relationship one has with friends, relatives, or fellow citizens in general. We speak the same way in English when we speak of the "loving ties" one has with one's children, friends, fellow countrymen, etc. So one type of *philia*, or loving relationship, is that which exists between friends, or *philoi*.

Aristotle says that we can have a loving tie, *philia*, with someone for one of three reasons. They are the three reasons we have for finding something lovable, namely: it is pleasant, it is useful, or it is good in itself.

Some people are simply enjoyable to be around. They are pleasant, or in some way or another they give us pleasure. Aristotle says young people often establish friendships on this basis. But while we can, and often do, establish affectionate bonds with them, these relationships are not friendships properly speaking. While they bear a resemblance to friendship, some essential qualities of friendship are missing, such as altruism, reciprocity, and the mutual recognition of each other's goodwill.

Other people are not so much pleasant as they are useful. And I can establish a loving bond with the people who, in one way or another, make my life easier by the things that they do. For instance, the horse trainer has a good working relationship with the black-smith, whose services he needs. If the loving, affectionate bond ex-ists merely because his abilities suit my needs, then this is a useful relationship—but not friendship.

If these two relationships—those based on someone being plea-surable or useful—are not genuine friendship, why does Aristotle mention them at all? Aristotle wants to point out that we can, and often do, have loving affection for these people. But so as not to confuse simply having or experiencing these loving, affectionate ties—*philia*—with genuine friendship, he acknowledges their exis-tence and then excludes them from consideration.

Genuine friendship, the *philia* that exists between *philoi* (friends), is rooted in goodness or virtue. I am drawn to my friend by a good-ness I perceive in him or her. This is a tremendous insight that Ar-istotle gives us as to the nature of interpersonal relating and pro-vides an answer as to why we find ourselves attracted to certain people. Even in Aristotle's day, different opinions were offered as to why people become friends. Is it because, "Birds of a feather flock together," or "Opposites attract"? Aristotle commented that it is nei-ther *because* people are similar, nor *because* they are dissimilar, that they are drawn to each other. Rather, what draws them to each other is their *goodness*.

Friendships that are rooted in goodness or virtue have several essential characteristics. First of all, friends of this sort want what is good for each other. And they are *aware* of each other's good inten-tions. It is part of our friendship that I know you desire what is in my genuine best interest. Secondly, you not only *desire* what is good for me—you willingly *help* to bring it about. When two people mutually love each other in this way, they are friends in the truest sense of the word. Aristotle says, "Friendship between such men remains as long as they are virtuous; and virtue is a permanent habit." He says these are the most intense and most noble of friendships; and they take a long time to establish. But, he adds, "Very likely friendships of this kind are rare, since virtuous men are scarce."

Cicero—Loyalty Sprung from Virtue and Mutual Agreement

Cicero does not really add anything new to the conversation, but he provides sort of a synthesis of ancient thought on the subject of friendship. In Roman tradition, friendship was a virtue by which a man was perfected. It was an altruistic relationship which paradoxically made one's own life worth living.

Marcus Tullius Cicero, the noteworthy Roman statesman of the first century BC, was particularly admired for his skill as an orator, and his thoughts on friendship reflect the environment in which he lived. Living as a statesman during the decline of the Roman Republic, he witnessed the rise and fall of Julius Caesar. It was an exciting and dangerous time as political alliances were regularly formed and betrayed. Politics and political life in ancient Rome were not determined by political parties and ideologies, but by means of loosely or firmly held personal commitments and friendships. At the end of the day, who can I trust to stand with me? Who can I trust to be at my side—not simply as a political ally—but as a man? This environment clearly affected Cicero's thoughts on the nature of friendship.

Cicero would agree with everything Aristotle said about friendship, but his emphasis would be different. While Aristotle saw the ideal friendship as an affectionate attachment (*philia*) that arises because of a person's inner goodness (virtue), the Romans, for their part, placed a particular emphasis on trust and loyalty. This is not surprising since the Romans were eminently practical people by comparison with their philosophy-minded counterparts in the ancient Greek world. And Cicero, who was eventually murdered, understood that having loyal people around you was of great practical importance.

He defines friendship in his work *De Amicitia* (On Friendship), and his definition has been the benchmark in nearly every conversation on the topic since that time. Because education formerly included reading classical authors, Cicero's works were widely known by those who came after him, and it is not surprising then that we see his definition of friendship appearing again and again.

Cicero believes that while all of us, by our nature, are meant to have some sort of friendship with others, true and perfect friendship (*vera et perfecta amicitia*) is only enjoyed by a few. He writes, "Friendship is so concentrated and restricted a thing that all the true affection in the world is shared by no more than a handful of individuals."[16] The reason for this is evident from the way he defines friendship. First (and he agrees with Aristotle here), genuine friendship is only possible among people who are good. He states, "I want to say first of all that friendship can exist only between good men."[17] Secondly, friends are in harmony on all matters of importance. Cicero writes, "Now friendship is just this and nothing else: complete *consentio* (agreement, consent, harmony, accord) in all matters, divine and human, plus goodwill and affection."[18] As Cicero sees it, if two people do not agree—having this harmony and accord between them—they cannot be true friends. It is these two things—goodness and *consentio*—that motivate one to be loyal and make people friends.

Immediately after defining friendship, Cicero adds that he is inclined to think that—except for wisdom—there is not a greater gift that the immortal gods have given to men than friendship.

It is interesting to note Cicero's insistence that virtue is essential to friendship. One might wonder whether, say, a band of thieves could be friends? According to the Ciceronian notion of friendship, they could not—at least not the true and perfect friendship of which he writes. He says, "Wrongdoing, then, is not excused if it is committed for the sake of a friend; after all, the thing that brings friends together is their conviction of each other's virtue."[19]

Finally, Cicero saw that because people's ideas, interests, and values change over the years, "There was nothing harder than to maintain a friendship all the way to the last day of life."[20] But loyalty—the crown of friendship—is proven over time. It is made possible by one's virtue and is motivated by harmony and agreement between friends.

St. Augustine—God's Love Perfects and Transforms Our Friendships

St. Aurelius Augustinus was a fifth-century bishop of the North African city of Hippo. He hardly needs an introduction. His autobiography, *Confessions*, is still widely known and read. In it one reads of the circuitous path that he followed on his emotional, relational, intellectual, and spiritual journey.

Three elements are blended and woven together in the thinking and the rich personality of this great man: he was educated in classical literature, including Cicero; his thinking was steeped in Sacred Scripture; and his own personal life gave him vast experience in the school of human love.

It has been said that St. Augustine, in a sense, "baptized Cicero," by essentially leaving his classic definition intact and using Ciceronian language in some of his own letters on the topic of friendship. But, while concepts and phraseology were borrowed from Cicero, St. Augustine's conception of friendship is thoroughly Christian.

A central theme in St. Augustine's writing—and in his life—is the "restless heart." The human heart is ever in search for something that will permanently satisfy. But St. Augustine's experience taught him that nothing seems to satisfy it for long. The human heart, he eventually came to understand, was made to be fulfilled by God. So in the very first paragraph of his autobiography one finds his famous line, "You have made us for yourself, O Lord, and our hearts are restless until they rest in you." St. Augustine's position, formed by his own experience, is that only divine love—never human love alone—will bring peace and rest to our heart. So the struggle for each person is found in letting God's love reign supreme in his or her heart, and to subordinate all other loves to that love. As such, everything—including our friendships—comes under the umbrella of charity. Loving God as we ought, through faith and obedience, we can then—by grace—love each other as we ought. Reflecting on human love, St. Augustine wrote, "The good that you love is from him, and insofar as it is also for him, it is both good and pleasant. But it will rightly be turned to bitterness if whatever comes from him is not rightly loved, and if he is deserted for the love of the creature."[21]

As St. Augustine sees it, one's love for God—with its power to energize, filter, and transform—has an effect on all human relating. From his own experience, he understood very well that in our fallen state all human emotion—not just sexual love—needs something to govern or regulate it. Why does it need to be regulated? On the one hand, we can be lazy, leaving difficult or tedious things undone. On the other hand, one must also be on guard against what one might call "an idolatry of friendship"—or any other human love. Why? Because though we can be tempted to settle for less, our restless hearts were made for God, and anything less will not satisfy. But human friendship can be *transformed* when our friends are loved with charity. It changes the motivation for our love and at times even affects the very loving itself.

How, one might ask, do we love with charity? Loving everyone with charity does not mean that we love everyone in the same way. Because God's love dwells in us, we are able to love strangers, and even our enemies—but we do not stand by them in adversity, share our lives with them, or reveal to them the secrets of our heart. Naturally, that particular way of loving is reserved for those whom we hold dear. But whether we love strangers, enemies, friends, or lovers—we love them with the love of Christ that dwells within us. As a result, the love we have for the various people in our lives becomes a way that we ourselves love God. We grow in our love for God by the love we have for each other.

In a letter to Martianus, St. Augustine uses Ciceronian phraseology when he describes friendship. But he insists that the agreement between divine and human things, along with goodwill and affection *takes place in Christ.*[22] He writes,

> 'Thou shalt love the Lord thy God with thy whole heart and soul and with thy whole mind' and 'thou shalt love thy neighbor as thyself.' . . . In the first of these, there is agreement on divine things; in the second, on human things, joined with good will and love. If one is with his friend in holding firmly to these two commandments, his friendship will be true and everlasting, and it will unite him not only to his friend, but to the Lord Himself.[23]

God, in his providence, places people in our life—including our friends. It is our duty to God, and to them, that we love them. These friendships, because they are in Christ, last forever. Reflecting on the death of a friend, Augustine wrote, "Blessed is he who loves Thee, and who loves his friend in Thee, and his enemy also, for Thy sake; for he alone loses none dear to him, if all are dear in him who cannot be lost. And who is this but our God?[24]

St. Aelred of Rievaulx—Distinguishing Real from False Friendships

This twelfth century Cistercian abbot wrote a book entitled *Spiritual Friendship*, and it is widely regarded as a classic. St. Aelred's point to his monks is this: How wonderful it would be if everyone in the monastic community loved each other in the way that two dear friends love each other. It would be a foretaste of heaven.

St. Aelred sees friendship not simply as a social grace, nor as an aid for making one's way through the difficulties of life. Friendship, for St. Aelred, is a means to Christian perfection and part of the life of sanctity. But he was keenly aware that not everything that presents itself as "friendship" is genuine friendship.

St. Aelred begins by asking what we should choose for our enjoyment. He notes we cannot create our own happiness. It is a universal human experience that our lives need to be *about* something, something that will occupy our minds, hold our attention, overcome boredom, and give us a sense of fulfillment and satisfaction. This is reminiscent of St. Augustine's idea of the restless heart. Since we cannot fulfill ourselves, we reach to things to fulfill us. Some of them, St. Aelred observes, drag us down and bring us misery; other things raise us up, and bring us happiness. Good friendships raise us up.

St. Aelred, like Aristotle, delineated three kinds of friendships. In his account, only spiritual friendships are genuine friendships, while the other two—carnal friendship and worldly friendship—lack some essential element. *Carnal friendships* are formed by mutual affection, and as such these relationships have the appearance of friendship. They are called "carnal" because the only thing uniting these "friends" is their mutual affection for one another and their feeling of mutual harmony. But the relationship is lacking in goodwill—and therein lies its defect. The affection between them may well be a mutual harmony in vice.

Worldly friendships are formed for the sake of some mutual advantage. It is a self-seeking relationship lacking in charity and mutual goodwill. Some benefit, other than the friendship itself, keeps these so-called friends together. In both carnal and worldly friendships, cupidity (desire) is the operating principle. In the case of carnal friendship, the desire is for the experience of affection; in worldly friendship, it is desire for mutual advantage. Both are lacking in charity.

Spiritual friendships, on the other hand, are genuine friendships. Motivated not by cupidity but by charity, they seek no benefit other than the friendship itself and the good of one's friend. Through the power of God's love (charity) that is working within them, spiritual friends willingly sacrifice for one another as they seek to bring about what is genuinely good for their friends. While carnal and worldly friendships seek mutual harmony and mutual advantage, a spiritual friend willingly sacrifices both of these if doing so will benefit his or her friend. It genuinely seeks the good of the other. St. Aelred writes, "And so spiritual friendship among the just is born of a similarity in life, morals, and pursuits, that is, it a mutual conformity in matters human and divine, united with benevolence and charity."[25] The definition clearly has a Ciceronian ring to it.

God commands that all be loved with charity, but not that all be loved as friends. Hence St. Aelred writes, "But only those do we call 'friends' to whom we can fearlessly entrust our heart and all its secrets."[26] In the Kingdom of Heaven, the love we have for our friends will be extended to all. In that Kingdom, when anxiety, fear, adversity, and death have been dispelled, "We shall rejoice in the eternal possession of Supreme Goodness; and this friendship, to which here we admit but few, will be outpoured upon all, and by all outpoured upon God, and God shall be all in all."[27]

Michel de Montaigne—The Experience of Union

Michel de Montaigne was an influential French Renaissance writer. This sixteenth century humanist, skeptic, and author is considered by many to be the first to employ the personal essay as a form of writing. One of his essays is on the topic of friendship.

Montaigne was born in Perigord, France, on the family estate Chateau de Montaigne, in a town now called Saint-Michel-de-Montaigne, not far from Bordeaux. His family was very wealthy, and his father provided him with a very thorough education. He eventually served at the Bordeaux Parliament, and it was at this time that he became very close friends with the humanist writer, Etienne de la Boetie, whose untimely death deeply influenced Montaigne. When he composed his essay, *Of Friendship*, he had his departed friend in mind.

What stands out in Montaigne's view of friendship is his emphasis on the *experience of union* one has with one's friend. It is both a union of affection and a union of wills where the two friends are so taken with each other, so well acquainted with each other, and bound to each other, that nothing is as close to either of them as their friend.

When he writes of friendship, he distinguishes the common variety from this friendship of complete union. He writes:

For the rest, what we ordinarily call friends and friendships, are nothing but acquaintanceships and familiarities formed by some chance or convenience, by means of which our souls are bound to each other. In the friendship I speak of, our souls mingle and blend with each other so completely that they efface the seam that joined them, and cannot find it again. If you press me to tell why I loved him, I feel that this cannot be expressed, except by answering: Because it was he, because it was I.[28]

Though Montaigne eventually married and had five children, it is clear from his writing that he considered friendship superior to erotic love. He sees the latter as "more active, more scorching, and more intense." He continues, "But it is an impetuous and fickle flame, undulating and variable, a fever flame, subject to fits and lulls, that holds us only by one corner."

By comparison, the love of perfect friendship is a more settled, calm, and secure love. Montaigne writes, "In friendship it is a general and universal warmth, moderate and even, besides, a constant and settled warmth, all gentleness and smoothness, with nothing bitter and stinging about it."

Montaigne, in comparison to the way he sees friendship, has a tragic-comical view of marriage, about which he states "only the entrance is free." Its continuance is constrained and forced. He does think that if one could marry a friend with whom one has this love of perfect friendship, "It is certain that the resulting friendship would be fuller and more complete." He sees the many duties and activities of daily married life as something that strains the relationship, "Whereas in friendship there are not dealings or business except with itself."

Because of the nature of these perfect friendships, it is only possible to have such a friendship with one other person. Otherwise, our obligations would conflict. Finally, such perfect friendships—which Montaigne admits are rare—come to us as a gift from Heaven.

C.S. Lewis—Friends Are Joined by a Common Interest

Clive Staples "Jack" Lewis is probably best known for his writings in defense of the Christian Faith—most especially, *Mere Christianity*—and his retelling of the Christian mystery in the children's books, *The Chronicles of Narnia*. Born in 1898 in Belfast, he attended prep schools in England before serving in World War I. After the war, he finished his education and in 1925 was elected Fellow of Magdalen College, beginning his professorship at Oxford University. For the next twenty-five years or so, he lived the life of a "confirmed bachelor." In a peculiar series of circumstances, Lewis—by then in his fifties—met and eventually married Joy Gresham. In 1960, four months before Joy died of cancer, *The Four Loves* was published. Lewis would live another four years. He died November 22, 1963, the same day as Aldous Huxley and John F. Kennedy.

In *The Four Loves*, Lewis discusses affection, friendship, *eros*, and charity. Though he does not say so explicitly, Lewis seems to believe that the Greek *philia* is too broad, and that further distinctions need to be made. In modern Greek, *philia* means "friendship." But in the way it was used by Aristotle, it meant a "loving relationship" that one could have for family, friends, or fellow-countrymen. Lewis looks at the relationship one has with friends and says there are two loves occurring simultaneously: affection and friendship. We nearly always have fine feelings for our friends. But, Lewis believes, those affectionate feelings are something distinct from friendship itself. All of the fine feelings one has for a friend, Lewis puts into the category of affection. But friendship itself, as Lewis sees it, has no emotional content. Though he would quickly point out that affection nearly always accompanies friendship, and—in the case of a friendship between a man and a woman—*eros* can accompany the friendship as well. His view of friendship is very different from the one presented by Montaigne. Indeed, Lewis himself says, "If a man believes (as I do) that the old estimate of friendship was the correct one, he can hardly write a chapter on it except as a rehabilitation." He thinks the sentimentalists of the Renaissance got it wrong.

Lewis begins his discussion of friendship by distinguishing friends from companions. I happen to think his conception of a companion—as distinct from a friend—is a helpful one, and my discussion of companionship toward the beginning of this chapter is distinctly "Lewisian." Our companions are the people who "happen to be in our life." They are our co-workers, classmates, and teammates. We do not choose them to be our companions; the circumstances of our life have brought us together. By inserting the notion of the companion, Lewis is attempting to move his readers away from the tendency to see the people in our life in two categories: *acquaintances*, whom we have met, but do not really know; and *friends*, with whom we have varying degrees of closeness. Instead, Lewis locates the category of companion in between acquaintance and friend, substantially reducing the field of the latter.

Having all but evacuated friendship of its emotional content, and having eliminated from consideration those who are merely companions, Lewis then spells out his concept of friendship. A friend is someone who sees something that I see, and we see it in a way that separates us from those who do not see it. Friendship typically begins when one says to another: "What? You too? I thought I was the only one!" It makes no difference what the subject is that unites them. It need not be a *cause* they are committed to, though it might be. But they could just as well be united by seeing, for example, that desk lamps—besides being useful—are also beautiful; that the gods are not only powerful, but holy; that cooking can be a form of art. All that is necessary is for the two—or more, perhaps many more—to have this common interest, this common way of looking at things. In *The Four Loves* Lewis writes, "The man who agrees with us that some question, little regarded by others, is of great importance, can be our friend. He need not agree with us about the answer." While previous commentators believed that people who lack goodness are incapable of genuine friendship, Lewis, on the contrary, thinks friendship—the uniting of two or more people in a common interest—can make good people better and bad ones worse, as determined by whether their common interest is good or bad.

This common way of looking at something is, for Lewis, the essence of friendship. As for the other things that are going on in my life, such as my health, my job, my children, or my happiness, Lewis responds, "What have all these 'unconcerning things, matters of fact' to do with the real question, *Do you see the same truth*?" These, for Lewis, are a distraction from what the friendship is really about. You eventually come to know these things about your friend, but only casually, bit by bit, as they furnish an illustration or an analogy. They are never discussed for their own sake. This is why Lewis says that friends meet, "Like sovereign princes of independent states." Their lives never really come together, except in that particular area of their common interest.

Recurring Themes

If we compare these various descriptions of friendship, what do we see? Clearly, the various authors emphasize different things. For instance, the role of goodness, virtue, and moral quality is present in Cicero, St. Augustine, St. Aelred, and it is strongest in Aristotle. But it is entirely absent in both Montaigne's and Lewis' treatment.

All but Lewis think there is an emotional component to friendship, though the experience of union that Montaigne writes of is different than Aristotle's description of *philia*. Aristotle sees friendship as a loving attachment one has to another which, in genuine friendships, is based on the friend's goodness. The way Montaigne describes the union of perfect friendship may lead some readers to conclude that this relationship is a sort of erotic love in disguise, though Montaigne would deny it. Lewis, on the other hand, thinks the loving attachment of *philia* is no part of friendship. Lewis grants that friends nearly always happen to have affection for each other. But on his account, friendship properly speaking is completely nonemotional.

All six of them agree that friends, at some level, have things in common. But for Lewis, it is the defining element of friendship.

Every author we have looked at since Cicero has maintained that God (or the gods) is somehow involved. Cicero and Montaigne see friendship as a divine gift. St. Augustine, St. Aelred, and Lewis see God as intimately involved in all of our relationships and especially in friendships.

All six of them see friendship existing in different levels and degrees. And they all agree that true and genuine friendship is something that is rare. As Lewis put it, "Few value it because few experience it."[29]

As we move toward a synthesis, we can see a number of themes emerging. Some of them are simply grasped intuitively. But an adequate theory of friendship must in some way account for and in some way include the following.

- Friendship as a personal relationship
- Mutually and freely entered into
- Exists in varying degrees
- Goodwill toward one's friend and a willingness to help bring it about
- Moral quality or virtue
- The sense of harmony and solidarity
- Feelings of affection and sympathy
- Mutual trust and loyalty
- Having things in common that they share

- Shared intimacy
- God's role in the friendship

In the following chapters, we shall see these various elements woven together as I offer my own view of friendship. If we can see farther than those who came before us, it is because we are standing on their shoulders.

Questions for Philosophical Consideration and Personal Growth

1. How does it happen that someone has many people with whom he or she interacts every day, and yet he or she remains deeply lonely?

2. Let us look philosophically at friendship. What is friendship? What makes two people friends? Friends nearly always share between them a bond of warmth and familiarity. The Greeks called this *philia*. But we also have people in our lives for whom we have these feelings of warmth and familiarity but whom we do not call our friends. What then makes someone our friend?

   Suppose we add trust. If two people have a loving attachment of warmth along with trust—does that make them friends? Or is friendship something more than that? If it is more—what is it?

3. What role, as you see it, does virtue play in friendship? Is it helpful to a friendship? Is it necessary for friendship? What is it that friends want for each other? Do I want you to get and achieve what you want? Or do I want you to get and achieve what is truly good—even if you do not want it?

   Suppose you are my friend, and I tell you that I am considering a new business undertaking. But this new adventure is highly unethical by nearly anyone's standards. If you are my friend, what do *you* want for me? Do you want me to achieve what I want? (The way you answer this question reveals your philosophy of friendship.)

4. Cicero believed that harmony or agreement (on all things divine and human) was essential to friendship. He believed that this is what motivates one to be loyal. You must, according to Cicero, agree with me in order to be my friend. Do you agree with Cicero on that point? Do you think friends need to agree on everything? Must they agree on *some* things? What role, if any, does agreement/harmony/accord play in a friendship?

5. Do you believe that human love—the giving and receiving of love between human persons—can satisfy all the desires of one's heart? Why do you think that is the case?

6. What role, if any, do you believe that one's love for God (and God's love for us) plays in a friendship? Do you agree with St. Augustine?

7. How is it that good friendships—besides the enjoyment we have in them—also make us better men and women? Can a good friendship ever make someone worse? What does that say about the nature of true friendship?

8. Montaigne places the experience of union at the heart of friendship. What do you make of Montaigne's description of friendship? Do you think two people could be genuine friends without such an experience of union? Do you think a "willingness to do for the other" needs to be part of the definition of friendship? Or, is it enough simply to experience union? As you answer this question, your philosophy of friendship is developing further.

9. For one reason or another, many give a benign interpretation to Lewis' description of friendship. But taken at face value, Lewis says that friends are not really interested *in each other*. The things that are going on in my life—my health, my happiness, my job, etc.—are a distraction to what our friendship is really about, which is our *common interest*. What role do you think these common interests play in a friendship? How important are they? Are they, as you see it, the core of what friendship is all about?

10. Lewis thinks friendship makes good men better, and bad men worse. Aristotle does not think people who are lacking in virtue can be genuine friends because he believes virtue (character strength) is at the heart of friendship. The issue is not whether fraternal camaraderie and *esprit de corps* is possible—of course it is. The issue is whether this is genuine friendship. What do you think?

11. Are you ready to sketch an outline of the definition of friendship that is neither too strict nor too loose? If you try doing this, you will see that writing a definition of friendship is more difficult than it looks. Everybody has an intuitive sense of what friendship is. Yet when we try to articulate it clearly, an adequate definition seems elusive. Try writing a definition for genuine friendship.

Chapter Three

The Love That Is Friendship

"A faithful friend is a sturdy shelter:
he that has found one has found a treasure.
There is nothing so precious as a faithful friend,
and no scales can measure his excellence.
A faithful friend is an elixir of life;
and those who fear the Lord will find him.
Whoever fears the Lord directs his friendship aright,
for as he is, so is his neighbor also."

Sirach 6: 14-17

A Popular Topic

Friendship is an enormously popular topic. And though it has been defined differently through the ages, everyone wants to have friends. Friendship is something humanly fulfilling—and *not* wanting friends must surely be some sort of pathology.

One reason friendship is so appealing is that friends (unlike spouses) choose their level of involvement in each other's lives—which may be a lot or a little. Friends enjoy each other's company, get together on occasion, and share the events of their lives. If they choose, they may have much more involvement in one another's lives. The point is, they mutually decide the degree they will be involved in one another's life. In this sense, friendship is very different from the commitment one makes in marriage, and this in some ways makes friendship more attractive than marriage.

It is the combination of both love and freedom that makes friendship appealing. If a married man takes a new job several states away, his wife moves with him. If a wife becomes very ill, her husband may take a leave of absence from work to care for his ailing spouse. While friends *could* do such things, such a commitment is beyond what one normally associates with friendship, even a very close friendship. Friends choose the degree that their lives will overlap. And though spouses do that too, spending time and working together in varying degrees, spouses clearly do not have the freedom and independence that one associates with friendship.

While there are clearly differences between marriage and friendship, the love and commitment one finds in genuine friendship prepares one for marriage. One who is incapable of genuine friendship is incapable of marriage. As I see it, friendship is the primordial interpersonal relationship—and other intimate interpersonal relationships are a derivation of it. When there is a breakdown in the desire or ability to relate as a friend, the effect is seen in all of one's interpersonal relationships—not just friendship in the traditional sense, but spousal friendship, and friendship with God as well. We could call the inner dynamic of friendship a kind of "relational trigonometry." When we grasp it and live it, it greatly enriches all of our personal relationships—especially marriage and the relationship with God. But when this friendship is missing, marriage is reduced to something far less than it otherwise could be. And when one does not perceive that God invites us into friendship with himself, then in the relationship with God we become merely rule-keepers, motivated by fear or by slavish obedience.

So these three relationships are types of friendship—friendship in the traditional sense, marriage, and the relationship with God. This is why friendship is so important. It is our most basic and fundamental way of relating personally and intimately with the important people in our lives.

What Genuine Friends Pursue When Pursuing Friendship

Though often not aware of it, people enter relationships pursuing different things. On the one hand, people can enter a relationship to pursue an experience. Be it companionship, friendship, or marriage, they enjoy the positive feelings associated with these relationships. But that is different from pursuing something that is worthwhile—independent of how I may experience it. Whether something is good, and the way I happen to experience it, are two separate issues. Acquiring knowledge, for example, is something good and worthwhile, though one may not enjoy the learning experience—as any student can attest. Friendship is a good that fulfills human persons. So is marriage. But at any given time, the experience of it may not be a positive one. So the question is, when one pursues a relationship—what is one pursuing? Or more precisely, what is one *primarily* pursuing? If what I am really after is a positive experience, then our relationship is a fragile one. It is hard to deny that many people unwittingly enter into relationships—including marriage—precisely this way. Perhaps this accounts for why so many marriages fail. They were seeking a positive experience, and they thought they would find it with this particular person—but it did not work out they way they had hoped.

Genuine friendship, and certainly marriage, is not fundamentally a matter of seeking a positive experience, but of committing oneself to a *person* and to the *good* that will come from the relationship. One may ask, "Can we not pursue both at the same time?" Of course we can, and we typically do. I love my friend; I love what is good for him; I love what is good for me; and I love the experience I have of our friendship. And when these things all "come together" at the same time, life is pleasant. But what happens when they do not? What if being your friend, or your spouse, is experienced as something particularly difficult? What then? Here one can see where one's real commitment lies. Imagine a man whose personality changed after having a stroke, or a woman who begins to show signs of mental illness, or is in a nursing home. A lot of people who were "friends" stop coming around. But the genuine friend still visits even though the experience often is not a positive one. Why does the friend still visit? Because the friend knows—even if he or she is unable to articulate it—that friendship, and the deeds of friendship, are good things and are *humanly fulfilling* even when they are not experienced as such. Life is more than the accumulation of our experiences. This is a fundamental relational concept. Real love—the love that unites and fulfills persons—is something that transcends our feelings and experiences. It is the love of God that permeates our human interacting. So throughout the book, when I talk about friendship and especially when I use the term "genuine friendship," I am referring to a relationship where one is:

1. Committed to the individual as such, and his or her well-being;

2. Committed to pursuing the good that is the relationship itself;

3. Committed to pursuing the good that flows from it.

And while this might sound like heavy philosophy, it really is not. It is saying that love is something other than the experience of unity that people have.

What Makes People Friends?

To the extent that two people relate as friends, they relate as equals. People can simultaneously relate on several levels. An army general and a staff sergeant, a professor and a student, an employer and employee, a bishop and his priest, could be genuine friends. Insofar as they are friends, they relate as equals—individual-to-individual, person-to-person. As Cicero said, "What is most remarkable in friendship is that it puts a man on an equality with his inferior." But the equality of their friendship does not erase the inequality of their other relationship. This is clearly the case in the friendship one has with God. God never stops relating to us as God. He is our Creator and our Judge, the source of every blessing and the giver of every good gift. But in addition to being our God, he also wants to be our friend. He wants a personal, one-on-one, person-to-person relationship. Even when we do relate to God as a friend, the other relationship with him does not cease.

The ancients did not believe friendship with God was possible, and it would not be had not God first offered it to us. We could never, on our own, presume to initiate such a relationship with God. But God, as it were, humbled himself. We read in the Book of Exodus, "The Lord used to speak to Moses face-to-face, as a man speaks his friend."[30] He even goes so far as to call Moses his *intimate friend*. Christians, for their part, believe that God the Son—the Eternal Son of the Eternal Father—became one of us and seeks our friendship. He said to his disciples, "No longer do I call you servants, for the servant does not know what his master is doing; but I have called you friends."[31] And why does he call them friends? Because, as Jesus says, "All that I have heard from my Father I have made known to you." Jesus, so to speak, shares the family secrets with his Apostles and invites them to share in his life and mission. Therefore he fittingly calls them "friends." But being our friend does not mean he ceases being who he is—the Son of Man, who at the end of the world, "Will come again in glory to judge the living and the dead."

At first glance, it seems improper to say that we relate to God, so to speak, as an equal. But we are equal *only insofar* as we are friends—not in any other way. And it is only possible because God himself initiated the relationship. On our own we could never presume to do so. It is easier to accept when we see this same God condescending to become one of us in the Incarnation and inviting us to become a member of his family.

So what makes people friends? To begin with, people are friends because they want to be. It is the nature of friendship that it be mutually and freely entered into. Why do they do this? I do not think it is primarily because of mutual or common interests—but because they are *interested in each other*. That, as I see it, is the single most defining element of friendship. Two people are friends because they want to be. We can entice or cajole, but we cannot coerce a friendship. It has to be free, or it is not friendship.

While friendship is a relationship that is freely and mutually entered into, it requires that one be *capable* of friendship—and not everyone is. Both Aristotle and Cicero saw virtue and character strength as essential to friendship, and I think they were right. Genuine friendship entails much more than identifying emotionally with someone with whom one has things in common. Friendship is a way of *habitually* relating, seeking what is good for one's friend and doing what one can to bring it about. Because of the vicissitudes of life, of human emotions, and the reality of Original Sin, we struggle to remain steadfast in our love. If we are not men and women of character (men and women who do the right thing even when it is difficult), genuine friendship will elude us—though we can have lesser relationships that resemble them.

Friendship comes about by mutual interest; character strength makes it possible; and friendships are typically lived out by having *favorite common activities*. Friends need a context in which to interact and favorite things to do together. In this favorite common activity—be it playing soccer or discussing medieval history—their friendship is lived out. Whether it is a friendship in the customary sense, marital friendship, or friendship with God—friends need things they enjoy doing together that provide the occasion for them to communicate and experience each other's love.

Therefore, as I see it, these three things are the absolutely essential elements of friendship:

- Virtue, which gives us the capacity to be and relate as a friend;
- Mutual interest, which provides the desire for friendship;
- Favorite common activity, which is the way our friendship is lived out.

When these three are present, the conditions are ripest for friendship. The people involved have the capacity for friendship, the interest, and a way for the friendship to be experienced and lived.

Friends Let Each Other into Their Personal Lives,
Creating the Experience of Intimacy

Once a friendship begins, the new friends begin doing the things that friends do. The things that initially brought them together—that which made them companions—only set the stage for real friendship. Real friendship includes letting someone into your personal life in some way, though some are afraid to take this next critical step. So they keep all their conversations "safe." They will talk about harmless things, things of no real personal consequence, or their conversation will be composed mostly of complaining about one thing or another.

The first baby steps of a friendship occur when you tell someone part of your personal story. Enough talking about golf, the weather, the president, or the boss—I want to tell you something about my experience of my life. It is not something I tell everyone, but I want to tell you. It always to some extent involves going out on a limb. I am not sure if I can trust you, but I think I can, so here goes. If it goes well, if I am not rejected, and if you keep my secrets, my trust grows. When the two begin mutually interacting this way the friendship is beginning to develop.

When we begin to let others into our lives—sharing our secrets and the story of our life—the result is a shared intimacy. It is a fruit of interpersonal relating, and it grows through the years as our lives become intertwined and we have the experience of connecting with each other—of knowing and of being known, of accepting and of being accepted, of loving and of being loved. It is this experience of genuine intimacy that overcomes loneliness and isolation.

Intimacy, along with friendship itself, is a fundamental concept in this book. Intimacy is about the closeness and unity—the interpersonal union—that comes about by sharing one's life with another. Whether it is intimacy with a "friend" in the traditional sense, the intimacy of marriage, or intimacy with God—it is always a matter of deeply sharing the things of one's heart and mind (and in marriage, sharing one's body) with someone I love.

The Importance of Character Strength and Virtue

Aristotle, and several who came after him, said that friendship has to be based on character strength and virtue. He is right. But why he is right may not be obvious. It has to do with the nature of virtue itself.

Character strength is the measure of a man or woman's good qualities—their inner qualities. Particularly virtuous people have many such qualities. We say of people that they are men or women of *character* when they habitually act in an upright and virtuous manner. Virtues are good things we do *habitually*. Some people *want* to be good, but very often fall short. We say their character is weak. Some habitually make choices that are inconsistent with what we normally think of as upright living. We say of these people that their character is poor or even awful. But we say of those who consistently seem to live good and upright lives that their character is strong, good, or even unquestionably good. Of course, only God can judge what is in a person's heart, but as Jesus said, we can tell a tree from its fruit.

So why is this important to friendship? Genuine friendship—by definition—requires such traits as honesty, trust, loyalty, goodwill, and sacrifice. These are qualities that are consistently found in men and women of good character. It is the presence of these qualities, along with others, that *makes* them good.

So I do not think that "bad men" can be friends. They can have a certain camaraderie or companionship—but they lack the inner qualities essential to genuine friendship. If I help you do something evil, how is that good for you? We would hope that our friends would love us enough that they would never help us commit evil, even if we begged them to. Or if we understand, for instance, how lying damages a person's authenticity and integrity, it is unthinkable that we would permit a friend to lie for us.

To be a friend, one must be *good*—a man or woman of virtue, of character. Aristotle says inner goodness is what makes people appealing. In the final analysis, it is what draws us to another.

The importance of character strength can be illustrated in various ways. First, because friendship is a form of love, I cannot genuinely love you if I do not want what is genuinely good for you. Desiring what is good for you is not always the same as hoping you get what you want, since people do not always want what is good for them.

I may not know what is truly good for you—but whatever that is, whatever form it takes, I *hope* that good comes your way—and that evil never does. The second part of this is that we *help to bring it about*. One can have goodwill in a lazy sort of way and hope that good things come to everybody. But friendship goes further than that. There is a logic to the love of friendship that expresses itself in service, and the extent to which one is willing to do that is a measure of one's love.

In order for two people to relate as friends, they must trust each other. Sometimes we say, "I feel I can trust that person." But trust, properly speaking, is more than a feeling. It is a general disposition we have toward someone that is based on the degree that we believe in someone's virtue. We count on our friends to tell us the truth, to keep our secrets, and to carry out their commitments. Like all the elements of friendship, trust will increase over the years as the friend *rings true* year after year, as we experience his or her honesty and dependability.

People Differ in Their Capacity for Friendship

Individuals differ in their capacity for friendship. That capacity, in turn, is determined by one's maturity and one's virtue. An analogy may clarify this. On the first day of practice for the basketball season, the coach has the players run up and down the stairs and around the gym. As time goes by, they can run farther and faster. Their capacity for running has increased. Similarly, our capacity for self-giving can increase. Playing basketball well includes a lot more than running. One must be able to shoot, dribble, pass, play defense, etc. Many good qualities—virtues—make one a good friend. Several immediately come to mind: honesty, dependability, generosity, and loyalty are just a few. As these qualities expand, our capacity for friendship expands. Sometimes people say, "This is the way I am. You must simply accept me as I am." One senses in that expression a denial that one is capable of inner growth. But we *can* grow. It does not happen overnight, but real progress does occur.

Suppose we worked in a shipping department for a book distributor. Five hundred orders come in for books today. We have the books—but we only have 200 shipping boxes. The number of shipping boxes *limits* how many books we can send. Students of chemistry would say the boxes were the "limiting reagent." The absence of good qualities limits one's ability to enter into meaningful relationships.

Jared and Ray

Jared is a likeable fellow who works in an office. He is cheerful, agreeable, and has a positive outlook on things. When asked if he will stay after hours or come in on Saturday to finish a project, he always agrees. But while he is quick to agree, he only follows through about half the time. The rest of the time he has some "plausible enough" excuse why he cannot do what he agreed to do. His favorite expression is, "Don't worry. Everything will be fine—it's all good." It is frustrating for the others in the office because they never know whether he will in fact do what he said he would do.

Ray, on the other hand, does not say, "yes" so quickly. But if Ray says he will do something—he will do it. He is dependable.

Lacking dependability, or any of the other essential virtues of friendship, such as honesty, generosity, or loyalty, limits the degree to which one can be a friend. Getting back to our illustration, Ray *likes* Jared and there is a friendship between them. But from Ray's point of view, Jared's lack of dependability handicaps their relating and limits their friendship. Ray really would like to do things with Jared—both social and work-related activities. But Jared's lack of dependability makes Ray reluctant to make plans. But if Jared understood this and, over time, became more dependable, his growth in the virtue of dependability would bring increased possibilities for deeper friendships.

* * * * *

The previous illustration focused on dependability. The same could be said for any of the many virtues that are important in friendship. You might place a higher value on loyalty than on generosity. And I might think honesty is more important than dependability. That does not matter. The point is this: people who are *good* are good because they are virtuous. One cannot be a good friend without being a good man or woman. There is more to friendship than liking someone and having some things in common.

Vices, of course, have the opposite effect. They diminish our ability to enter into and sustain meaningful relationships because they are nearly always aspects of self-centeredness. No one is perfect, of course, and in our fallen human state, it is often difficult to be good habitually. But with time, practice, and effort we can improve. Pope John Paul II used the expression, "the school of self-mastery" to describe the process whereby we grow in the ability and the desire to give of ourselves. The good qualities needed for friendship are not like the uncommon talents seen in, say, a professional athlete. We *have* the ability, but some areas of our lives need to be developed further.

Cicero, like others, saw that goodness is an important part of relating and defined friendship as, "Harmony in all things human and divine along with goodwill and affection." But he saw plainly that goodness is not the same as perfection. If we had to be perfect to be friends, nobody would be or would have a friend. Cicero says the goodness that is required is the goodness that is found, even if only rarely, among real people living in the real world—not the kind of goodness that one can only dream of or find among the gods. We do not have to be perfect—but we do have to be good. And to a large extent, one's capacity for goodness is a measure of one's capacity for friendship.

What exactly do we mean by *goodness*, and how does one measure it? It is common for people to say, "This is good," when what they really mean is, "I like this." But the difference between finding something to be good and finding something to be likeable is an important distinction to make. The goodness we are speaking of here is a moral quality, and it is the capacity for disinterested self-giving. "Disinterested" does not mean "not interested." Rather, it is the habitual quality of being able to give of ourselves without having an eye on what we will receive in return. If I am motivated to do something for you because of what it will do for *you*—not because of what it will do for me—then my love for you is disinterested.

Let us look at an example. Suppose you are a brand new teacher, and I have been teaching for many years. It is August and school is going to start in two weeks. You are trying to organize your classes, but it just is not coming together like you had hoped—it is a more difficult task than you had imagined. You are not sure how to divide the material; you do not know whether to give homework or have quizzes, or both. You cannot decide on how many exams to give, etc. So, on a beautiful Saturday afternoon, I come over and help you organize your material for the first semester. I do this not merely out of sympathy for you, but because I can visualize or imagine something good (namely, the organization of your classes, which will be good for your students and give you peace of mind), and I elect to do what I can to help make that a reality. It is a way of loving, and love is my motivation. I am not doing it for me; I am doing it for you. This is disinterested love. It illustrates someone who is desiring something good for a friend and doing what he can to help bring it about.

People who love in this way are, so to speak, naturally attractive. It is as though we cannot help being drawn to them because of their genuine goodness. This way of selflessly relating to another is present in people to a greater or lesser degree. Some only rarely give of themselves; others do so much more frequently. One might do so with a chosen few, others more broadly. For some it is a rare occurrence, others do so habitually. Understood in this way, we can begin to see how one could measure—at least from this one perspective—a person's relative goodness. So one could say, from the standpoint of personal generosity and selflessness: *you are a good man*. There are many different virtues—character strengths—that one can possess. They are habits, not single instances of good behavior, but they all seem, in one way or another, to be encompassed by the general idea of generous, self-giving.

It is this goodness and virtue that gives one the capacity to be loyal. Loyalty is the virtue whereby I stand with my friend even when it is difficult to do so. I keep his secrets, and I offer support and encouragement during the difficult times of life. Loyalty is a virtue that is essential to friendship, and it enables friends to be with each other for the long haul, standing at each other's side. Loyalty does not mean universal agreement with what someone thinks, nor approval of everything a friend does. But it does mean that we keep our commitments, keep each other's secrets, and we do not let our differences affect our friendship. There is something ennobling about loyalty.

Because friends do not always agree, loyalty presumes a certain measure of tolerance. And though we wish this were not the case, friends can hurt each other. Genuine friends have the humility and the courage to ask for, grant, and receive *forgiveness*. And because real loyalty is not *quid pro quo*, one can be loyal to one's friend even when the friend is not loyal in return. Clearly, authentic character strength is needed to accomplish this.

Let us look at another example, one that illustrates loyalty.

Dustin, Molly, and Jennifer

Dustin is a high school teacher who graduated from college five years ago. He is working in the English department at a very large public high school. There is a noticeable *esprit de corps* in the department, and the teachers—especially the unmarried ones—frequently get together socially. Dustin really enjoys working in this school, and over the past five years he has developed some meaningful relationships. We will look at his relationship with two of them: Molly, also an English teacher, and Jennifer, who teaches math.

Dustin and Molly became friends five years ago when they both started teaching. Both teach English to underclassmen. Dustin finds her to be bright, organized, energetic, and full of good ideas for the classroom. From the time they began teaching, they established a friendship that has deepened over the years. Dustin likes her, and he trusts her.

Jennifer, who started teaching the year after Dustin, works in the math department and also coaches volleyball. She and Dustin have gone on a few dates, and now Dustin is very interested in her. They are not officially "dating" yet, but—at least in Dustin's mind—it seems to be moving in that direction. Dustin has high hopes for this relationship, and he really wants things to go well.

Valentine's Day is a couple of weeks away, and Dustin does not know what he should do. He does not want to, as it were, overplay his hand, but he does not want to underplay it either. He is afraid that if he ignores Valentine's Day that Jennifer might take that as a rejection. But at this point, Dustin is not quite ready to tell her how he feels about her. So he decides to ask Molly what to do.

Molly and Dustin have talked about personal and work-related things in the past, and they have kept each other's secrets. Now, Dustin wants to talk about his developing relationship with Jennifer, but it is tremendously important to him that the information remains just between the two of them. So he reveals to her his thoughts and feelings about Jennifer and seeks her "female advice."

Molly is a *loyal* friend. She sees Jennifer at school everyday and interacts with Jennifer's peers and Dustin's peers. But she never says or otherwise communicates—directly or indirectly—the private things Dustin told her.

The friendship between Dustin and Molly has blossomed because they are able to speak freely in an atmosphere of confidentiality and trust. These friendship-deepening conversations both *presuppose* and *deepen* the relationship between them. Their mutual loyalty has made that possible. If, in the beginning, Dustin doubted Molly's loyalty, the friendship between the two of them would not have grown into what it is today because these friendship-deepening conversations never would have taken place.

Had Molly violated Dustin's trust, he would have been deeply hurt and saddened with a two-fold sadness. First, he would be saddened because of the potential damage to his budding romantic relationship with Jennifer. But secondly, and this is sometimes overlooked, he would be saddened because Molly is not the loyal friend that he thought she was. As it is, Dustin's well-placed confidence in Molly's loyalty has enriched his friendship with her and helped his relationship with Jennifer. Molly's loyalty is a virtue. It is part of what makes her a good person and is a factor in her capacity for friendship.

Virtue by Itself Is not Friendship

The point I wish to make regarding virtue is simply this: without certain good qualities, an individual is incapable of genuine friendship. Spiritual development and human growth are really the same reality considered from different points of view. It is the whole person that needs to develop, mature, and strive for perfection. Those who are extraordinarily virtuous can be truly extraordinary friends. Different people excel in different things. Perhaps you are particularly generous, loyal, or humble. Imagine someone being virtuous to an extraordinary degree, someone whose generosity and loyalty far exceed what is typical for "good people." Figures like St. Francis of Assisi come to mind. What an extraordinary privilege it would have been to be one of his close friends. How our lives would be enriched if we could be surrounded by friends like that! But, as Aristotle noted, *friendships* like this are rare—because *people* like this are rare.

I think Aristotle was right when he wrote that the relationship that is rooted in a mutual appreciation for each other's virtue is the most enduring kind of friendship because virtue—by definition—is something lasting. This, according to Aristotle, is the hallmark of genuine friendship. Good people are capable of being good friends. Great friendship can arise among great people. Though these friendships are not rooted in each other's usefulness nor in pleasure, there is in fact nothing more useful and nothing more pleasant than a true friend.

Virtue has a natural appeal to it. When we encounter it in people, we seem to be drawn to the goodness we perceive in them. But virtue, by itself, is not friendship.

Friends have goodwill for each other, and they do good deeds for each other. Having goodwill and doing good things for another is a way of loving, but by itself it is not the love of friendship. Friendship presupposes goodness, but friendship is more than goodness—something must be added for people who are good to also become friends.

You and the guy next door may be very good men—self-giving and of noble intentions. You may even possess heroic virtue. Your lives may overlap if, say, you both have a daughter in the same grade. But for all that, you may not be friends. You can think alike and have a degree of affection for each other. And yet, though you are *friendly* you have not become friends.

So what is missing? To be friends, they must mutually desire each other's friendship. For that to happen they need to like each other and enjoy each other's company. It would certainly be an odd sort of friendship if we did not enjoy being together. If people are to become friends, they must desire the unity that will come about by their friendship. We can recognize someone's goodness and yet not desire friendship with that person. We can imagine saying, "He is a nice guy and a genuinely good man, we have a number of things in common, but I really do not want him as an important part of my life." We are willing to be friendly, but not friends. Of course, friendship is present in degrees. One can be a friend without being a close friend or a dear friend. Close friends have personalities that seem to fit together, they "click" with each other. And how deeply two people connect is one measure of how close they are. It only really happens when we let it happen—two people are friends with each other because they *want* to be.

Friends Are Mutually Interested in Each Other

We saw in the last chapter that C.S. Lewis thought "having a common interest" was the defining element of friendship. I respectfully disagree. I think people are far more likely to become friends because of their mutual interest *in each other*. This, I believe, is what makes people friends. Assuming two people have the capacity for friendship, they are friends with each other *because they want to be*. Though friendship has a mysterious quality about it that eludes even our best attempts to explain, it is partly accounted for by the emotional bonds that connect friends to one another.

Friendship itself is something richer, deeper, and more stable than our feelings and emotions, yet it seems undeniable (though Lewis denies it) that there is an emotional content to our friendships that is integral to the relationship. In varying degrees, we experience friendship through affection, through mutual understanding and sympathy, and through the unity of shared solidarity.

The feelings we have for each other naturally ebb and flow, and at times they are particularly strong, especially with our closest friends. One can observe an interesting phenomenon at a funeral home visitation. Imagine this scene at Mr. Jones' wake. It is a common one. Just past the casket are Mrs. Jones and her adult children. Family and friends come to pay their respects and to offer support. Mrs. Jones and her children are sad, but they manage more or less to contain their emotions as they greet people. But every now and again someone very close to them comes through the line and it makes them cry. It is the special bond we have with our closest friends that brings out these emotions.

If we look at the people who are our friends, what do we see? We see that we nearly always began as companions. We happened to be at the same place at the same time, perhaps as schoolmates, teammates, roommates, neighbors, or co-workers. If you and I become friends, it is because of our mutual interest in each other. We might both be passionately interested in microbiology, and that may have been what occasioned our meeting each other. But, at some point, I became interested in you personally, as a friend. And you felt the same toward me. This is what is meant when it is said that we *choose* our friends. This element of mutuality is essential to friendship. If we are friends, then I am your friend and you are my friend. It is mutual. There does not need to be perfect reciprocity, and that is not always possible. You may have a larger role in my life than I have in yours. Nevertheless, we both consider each other a friend and relate to each other as such. The two of us have *freely* entered into this friendship.

Imagine two college students, Tara and Mae, who were assigned to be lab partners in their biology class. Each week they do their lab work together. Later in the week they review their work before they hand in their lab report. They have a good working-relationship. But Tara wants to be more than lab partners; she wants to pursue a friendship with Mae. Mae, for her part, is not terribly interested. But Tara is relentless. She *insists* they have lunch together after reviewing their lab notes and a couple of times she has prevailed upon Mae to watch a movie with her. In Tara's mind, the two of them are friends because they do the things that friends often do together. In truth, Mae has simply yielded to Tara's subtle tactics of domination and manipulation. Tara has forced this relationship, and it lacks the freedom and mutuality characteristic of friendship.

In the last section, the section on virtue, we saw how genuine friendship entails more than liking someone. Virtues make one capable of genuine friendship, but it is not a person's virtue that we notice right away. The first thing we notice is that we happen to like them. Friendship begins when two people take a mutual interest in each other. By "mutual interest," I mean the kind of interest that friends take in each other.

Let us look at this taking place on a collegiate football team. The football team will serve us well for this illustration because of the various dynamics involved. There are about one hundred guys on the team who are working together in intense activity in pursuit of a common goal. By definition, all the teammates are companions.

The members of the team are engaged in intense physical activity. They workout together, practice together, and play together. Besides their activity on the field, they must attend team meetings and team meals. They travel many hours together on their way to games, and they interact with each other in the locker room before and after the games. All of these things they do as a *team*, building up one another and compensating for each other's weaknesses.

At team meals, the first-year players are beginning the "natural grouping" process. They each tend to hang around some teammates more than others. At this point, since they barely know each other, the natural grouping could be due to any of a number of factors. Perhaps their lockers are next to each other or they are paired together during practice. So, at team meals, they look for familiar faces as they decide where to sit. And over time the conversations broaden. By the fact that they "look for each other" at team meals, we can say that they have begun *voluntary association*. They did not, properly speaking, *choose* to be teammates with each other. They *happen* to be on the same team. But now, they are voluntarily interacting with some of them. As such, they are now more than merely companions. But it would be premature to say they are friends. Since they are somewhere in between companionship and friendship, I call them "casual friends." At this point, their personal expectations of each other remain low, and there has been very little sharing of personal information. The conversations remain "light" and often revolve around the things they have in common, such as football and classes.

As time goes by, they notice that there are some teammates that they simply *like* more than others, and they begin to take an interest in certain people. If pressed to give a reason why they happen to like a particular person, they probably could not do so. They just do. At this point, they are beginning to pursue and initiate friendships. If it is reciprocated, a friendship will begin at that point. If they are not *mutually* interested, nothing more will come of it, at least not now.

* * * * *

While virtue is a necessary characteristic of friendship, the fact that someone is virtuous does not for that reason alone make him my friend. I may notice that another is genuinely good and noble and yet not particularly desire to be his friend. The ingredients can all be present, and yet a friendship does not develop. To borrow an example from cooking, all the ingredients were present, but the sauce never came together like I had hoped. In personal relationships, the personalities need to come together. Something needs to "click." One's personality and temperament play just as large a role in friendship as does one's virtue. Indeed, it is mysterious why we find a person's personality attractive. Earlier we saw that Aristotle observed that there was no agreement on whether persons are attracted to one another because they are similar ("birds of a feather flock together"), or because they are dissimilar ("opposites attract"), which is obviously the case in male-female attraction.

I do not know that we will ever get to the bottom of why two people, two friends, find the personality of the other so attractive. But I think Plato was on to something with the idea that there is something about you—a goodness that I perceive in you—that in some way fulfills me. We begin with the presupposition that the human person was made for union with other persons and ultimately with God. That is the way we are hard wired, so to speak. It seems that we would naturally seek friendship with those whom we find likeable and good and whom we perceive would complete us in some way. I do not think it is enough to say that they fulfill a need we have because I do not think we can (or should) reduce all attraction to a sort of need-love.

In the final analysis we still have not determined precisely why we find someone likeable, and I suspect we never will. But I do not think it is *because* they are similar, or *because* they are dissimilar, that we like them and want to be friends with them. We can be drawn to the personality of another for reasons we are unable to explain. It is part of the mystery of the human person and the mystery of human interaction, especially in our fallen state. Two people who are very different can become very dear friends. If they do become friends, it is because they both desire a friendship, and because they have the virtues necessary for any two people to establish a genuine friendship.

A man who had recently graduated from college was reminiscing about how he missed his roommate. The two of them are very different and never would have chosen to room with one another. But in spite of their many differences, they became very dear friends. "He has all the qualities that are annoying," one said of the other. He continued, "He is completely unorganized and would do just enough to get by. Whenever we would go somewhere, he always had to go to the ATM for money; or he would borrow money but never pay you back. When he told stories, he always exaggerated and made up stuff." The two of them shared the very small, cramped space of a college dorm room, and each had habits the other found annoying. Besides their personal habits, the two of them varied greatly in their religious beliefs and values. Yet, in spite of their many differences, they genuinely cared about each other and looked after each other. Though they were very different, they were both genuinely *good* men. This fact, coupled with their mutual affection for each other, made friendship between them possible.

One virtue in particular enabled this to happen: the virtue of overlooking each other's bothersome quirks and not defining a person in terms of his or her shortcomings. We could add one more thing: neither succumbed to the temptation—either through impatience or irritability—to say hurtful things when they were annoyed by the other. Because they were both virtuous men, and because they both liked each other and took a genuine interest in each other (which is not always the case between people who claim to be friends), they helped each other to grow—though, perhaps, not as much as the other would have liked. Because they were both good men, and because they both mutually desired to be friends—they indeed were friends.

When friends are together, they "hear each other." What does this mean? Suppose I am making a presentation. It could be to a large group, a small group, or to an individual. What are my listeners hearing? From one point of view, you could say they are hearing *words*. As I speak, their attention can be focused on the words I am using and whether I am using them correctly. Secondly, they could be hearing not words as such—but *sounds*—and their attention is drawn to the fact that I am speaking too loudly or too softly. Thirdly, they could be focused on my *arguments*, my reasoning. As I speak, they are processing the information in terms of whether my point is a good one, whether it is reasonable, and whether it agrees or disagrees with their perception of reality. Finally, they could be focused on me as a *person*. In doing so they perceive that there is an individual before them who has a history and a destiny and who—in some way or another, great or small—is trying to make a connection with them.

What I have just briefly outlined is what philosophers call the four "orders" of reality. As it is applied here, we would say someone "hears" one of four things: words, sounds, arguments, or persons. They are not reducible to each other. Friends, as such, focus on each other *as persons*. When I listen to you speak I hear *you*. I hear *you* more loudly and more clearly than I hear your words, your sounds, or your arguments. This helps explain why we are united. And it also explains why often we are not. This is more than what is meant by active listening; it is a way of, as it were, receiving another. And it only happens when we want it to. For some reason I am drawn to you, to your personality, your personhood. Something about your personality attracts me.

Friends find each other's personality attractive, and they take a mutual interest in each other. But the degree and the way in which they take such an interest is part of the drama of interpersonal relating. You, for example, may take more of an interest in your friend than your friend takes in you. Maybe you wish he or she took more of an interest in you and that the two of you spent more time together. There is a sense in which we *pursue* a friendship. Even after a friendship is established, it does not always, as it were, flow equally in both directions. Who has not experienced this?

Some people have a friend whose sincere interest can seem intrusive. Readers who are familiar with *The Four Loves* may recall the story of Mrs. Fidget. It is a tale created by Lewis to illustrate unbridled affection, though it is equally applicable to our conversation on friendship. Mrs. Fidget was a wife and mother who had far more interest and involvement in her family's life than they wished. She loved them, and they loved her, but she drove them crazy.

Whether we wish people would, so to speak, take a couple of steps closer, or a couple of steps back, things never seem to come together just the way we would like. It is part of the reality of life in this world. It will be different in Heaven. Here and now, we have many different obligations and commitments, and it can be difficult to balance them all. We wish we had more time to spend with the people we love, not having to arrange schedules and not having to work around other commitments. It will all come together perfectly in Heaven.

Friends Have Things They Enjoy Doing Together

We have established that there are certain virtues that a person must possess in order to be capable of friendship. Further, we have seen that friends mutually desire friendship with each other. People are not "friends in theory." If we are going to be friends, then we must have things we do that bring us together. This happens in the things we like to *do* together and in the things we like to *talk about* together. These shared activities provide the context for us to communicate our mutual interest in one another.

We can draw an analogy from marriage. A man and a woman become married by exchanging marriage vows. But having made the choice and the commitment, they must then *live married life*. They decide where to live and set up their home. They carry out the daily domestic work which includes everything from washing the clothes to mowing the lawn. They are present to each other and available for each other as they experience the ups and downs that are a part of their lives. They raise children together and all that that entails. It is precisely in the living of family life that their relationship is lived out and experienced. This life they live is, as it were, the incarnation of their marriage.

Something similar happens in friendship. Having mutually chosen each other as a friend, their friendship must be lived out. It must take some form—it must be incarnated. This, I believe, is the role that temperament and common interests play in a friendship. And because people differ in these respects, friendship takes a different form with different people.

For example, a company called "The Brickyard" employs about a dozen bricklayers. Jerry, David, Pat, and Phil have been with the company for more than ten years. These men work together, eat their lunch together, and occasionally have a few drinks together after work. It is in these activities that their friendship is lived out. There is not a lot of what one might call "serious conversation" between them. While there is genuine mutual interest and concern for each other, they do not talk about the fact that they are friends. They experience their closeness through the common activity of their work. But they work and recreate together in a way that their lives are exposed to one another. They have created an atmosphere of trust and loyalty in their interacting, and because of this, they are friends.

Jack, Susan, and Traci, all university psychology professors, live out their friendship differently. Aside from being professors, the three of them actually have rather little in common. They differ widely in their political and religious beliefs. Jack and Traci represent complete opposites on the liberal/conservative spectrum. But all three are passionate about *ideas*, and they thoroughly enjoy taking a topic and examining it from an intellectual and experiential point of view. Whether it is a topic for possible publication, or new material for classroom presentation, they regularly get together to discuss ideas. Though they are very different from one another, each recognizes the sincerity, generosity, and goodness of the others. Over the years, their lives have been revealed to each other. Although Jack, Susan, and Traci have rather little in common, they share a real concern for each other, they desire each other's friendship, and they live out their friendship through their frequent exchange of ideas.

Joel and Caleb have been friends since their college days when they lived in the same dorm. Now, several years later, Joel is an attorney, and Caleb teaches high school. Both are in their twenties and neither is married, though Caleb will likely be engaged soon. Their favorite activity together is having dinner, which they do at least once a month. Joel and Caleb are especially close friends, and the friendship between them developed in such a way that they easily reveal to each other the details of their private lives. Their dinners typically start with light conversation, but at some point Joel or Caleb will say something like, "So, how are you doing?" For these two men, they communicate and experience their mutual interest in each other—not by working together, nor by discussing favorite topics—but, as it were, more directly. Each of the four bricklayers and the three college professors could easily infer that the other friends in their group took an interest in his own life. With Caleb and Joel it is more explicit. Perhaps they are closer because of it.

If this is what Lewis meant by friends having a common interest, such as bricklaying, discussing ideas, or having dinner, then I think he is right. I am not sure that this, in fact, is what he meant. Lewis seems to be saying that what *makes people friends* is their common interest. If that is what he means, I respectfully disagree. I think people are friends because of their mutual interest *in each other*. But I think friendship is *lived out* through common activity and common interests. Doing things together does not make two people friends—but those who *are* friends *do* things together. There must be some medium, some context, for their friendship to be lived out and experienced. The things they do together could be professional or recreational. Even if it is only talking on the telephone, they must have something they do together. Without it, their friendship cannot take shape. As Lewis says, "Those who have nothing, can share nothing; those who are going nowhere can have no fellow travelers."[32]

The mutual interest is what makes or breaks a friendship. The bricklayers could lay bricks, and the professors could discuss ideas for twenty years—and never really become friends. It is not the activity itself that makes people friends. Fellow workers may experience solidarity in their common activity. But it is the solidarity of companionship, not friendship.

Looking at the many people in our lives that we honor with the title "friend," we see that some of them could accurately be called "a friend from our past." We are still friends. We just do not see each other very often and they do not presently have an active role in our lives. Sometimes people will describe these friendships as follows: When we get together, which is not very often, it is as though we pick up right where we left off. These friends do more than reminisce about the glory days of the past. They keep each other updated on their lives, albeit infrequently. These "friends from our past" remain an important part of our lives. At one point, they may have been active participants in our daily lives. But the present circumstances of our lives do not permit us to spend time together like we used to. As long as we continue to have a mutual interest in each other and have some way of living out our friendship—even if it is only an annual phone call—we will continue to be friends.

The Commitment of Genuine Friendship Prepares One for Marriage

It seems to me that friendship is most clearly understood when it is seen as standing midway between companionship and marriage. We have seen how friends nearly always start out as people who happen to be in each other's lives, but something happens that enables the companionship to become a friendship. Namely, along with the mutual interest they take in each other, they willing commit themselves to each other in some real way. We speak of this in terms of fulfilling the duties of friendship. When you enter a person's life in a serious way, as friends do, relational obligations naturally follow. Those obligations, or duties, will vary depending on the depth of the friendship, and friends more or less work that out as time goes by. As the relationship is developing and the two people are more than companions but not quite friends, we could say they are "casual friends." Friendship is a way of being a part of someone's life. As we saw earlier, it is more than the emotions we feel, though there is an emotional content to friendship. And it is more than the embracing duties and obligations. Friendship itself is something far richer. As we have seen throughout the book, it is a matter of interpersonal union.

More than the emotions and more than the duties, when we accept another's offer of friendship we let the person into our lives in a way that unites the two of us. And as the friends walk down their respective paths of life, they share with each other their experiences.

We share more deeply with our friends who are closest to us. But no matter how close the friends become, even if they reveal their innermost selves, their paths in life are separate paths. I may love my friends dearly and share many intimate stories about my life, but strictly speaking my life is not *about* my friends. They are not the primary focus of my life or vocation.

Here is where we see the clear distinction between friendship and marriage. In marriage, the man and woman freely choose to make each other—and the family they will create—the primary focus of their lives. The man who proposes marriage is saying to the woman, "I want your life, your well-being and happiness, to become my vocation and the way that I serve God." In marriage, our lives are given over to our spouses and our families in a sacrificial love that is lived day in and day out. In friendship, there is a *part* of my life and a *portion* of my heart that is given over to my friend. There is a sense in which friends live for each other. They can, and sometimes do, make heroic sacrifices for each other. But they are not the primary focus of each other's lives. From this perspective, I think it makes sense to say, as Lewis says, "Friends stand side-by-side, lovers stand face-to-face."

If we follow a couple's path from companionship to marriage, we can discern two distinct changes in their relationship. The first change occurred when they went from being companions to being friends. It may have occurred so naturally that they were unaware that the relational change was taking place. Circumstances of life brought them together, making them companions. But they had to *choose* to be a friend to each other. Their lives were adjusted a little by that choice as they began to include their friend in their lives. As the two of them grew closer as friends, they shared more and more of their inner lives. At a certain point, it occurred to them that it would be desirable to redirect their lives in a dramatic fashion. "The one whom I love as a friend could become the focus of my life—by becoming my spouse." But is it not in the *school of friendship* that one first learns what it means to commit oneself to another in a selfless way? This is what I mean when I say that genuine friendship prepares one for marriage.

What Kind of a Friend or Spouse Am I?

Earlier in the chapter we looked at character strength and virtue. As we grow, becoming more virtuous, our relationships improve. And though the measuring is imprecise, one can measure the quality of one's relating by the degree to which one fulfils one's duties—and goes beyond them—in a sacrificial gift of oneself. Earlier we saw that virtue and character strengths make one capable of genuine friendship. Anyone can have a moment, or a day, when he or she is particularly good or uncharacteristically bad. But taking one's general pattern of relating—looked at as a whole—what does one see? This is why virtue matters.

In a friendship, a marriage, or the relationship with God, one's general pattern of relating may be "adequate." Or one might be consistently good—or bad. Let us look at a couple of examples from the Gospels. In the familiar story of the Good Samaritan, a man (presumably a Jew) is coming down from Jerusalem to Jericho when he is attacked by robbers who strip him, beat him, and leave him half-dead. A priest and a Levite pass by without doing anything. But a Samaritan goes out of his way to assist the distressed victim. Recall that Samaritans and Jews shared a mutual disdain for one another. Now, seeing the generosity of this Samaritan toward a Jewish stranger, imagine how he likely related to those closest to him. The priest and the Levite, for their parts, missed a huge opportunity to do something worthwhile.

The story of the Visitation of Mary illustrates the humility and the generosity of the Mother of God. The angel Gabriel has just announced to her that by the power of the Holy Spirit she would conceive a child who would be called "Son of the Most High," and who would sit upon David's royal throne. She must have known that the child would be the long-awaited Messiah. In spite of that, she went *in haste* to the home of her cousin, Elizabeth, who had conceived a child in her old age and was now in her sixth month. She did not rest upon her dignity, but went to wait upon her aged cousin. She saw an opportunity for giving and for serving—and she acted upon it.

My point is that some people do far more than the meeting of reasonable expectations. They look for opportunities to give and to serve—not the Mrs. Fidgets of the world who torture people with their "unkind kindnesses," doing things for others that they do not want done—but people who habitually live for others.

Who would not feel insulted if told that they were "adequate" as a friend or as a spouse? We all want to think of ourselves as being generous. But are we really? I think that all of us *have moments* when we are generous. Most are willing to go out of their way for a special occasion. And for that reason, we think of ourselves as generous. (We also have moments when we were particularly miserly with ourselves and our time—but we like to forget about those times when we evaluate our character.) The fact is many have friends or spouses who adequately meet the reasonable expectations of a relationship—but only rarely do more than that. Some consistently do more than that, and we call them *generous*; or they may even do *far* more, so we call them *great*. Occasionally we find someone who is genuinely *heroic*.

On the other side, we can speak of people in a given relationship as being *inadequate, self-centered, wretched,* or *treacherous*. The following chart is an attempt to distinguish between these various categories. The various titles given to each category, and the way they are differentiated, is not what is important. What *is* important is seeing that some can, and indeed *do*, live in a way that exceeds or greatly exceeds what one could reasonably expect. And some fall short, even far short. This chart lays out four fundamental categories of friendship. Our relationships rarely fit neatly into any given category, and we do not always act consistently, but these categories help us expand our understanding of the way we relate.

To say someone is a great friend speaks not so much of the closeness of the relationship, but of the degree to which the friend fulfills the duties of friendship, and the degree to which he or she goes beyond that. This insight enables us to distinguish on the one hand, the degree to which we enter into each other's lives (i.e. how close we are) and on the other hand, the degree to which we live up to and fulfill the expectations of the relationship. The *degree* of the friendship and the *quality* of the friendship are like apples and oranges and should not be confused with one another. So one could imagine, for example, Cheryl and Marcy, who are (merely) casual friends. They are college students who play on the same softball team during summer vacation. Though they have done this for several years, they have not shared much of their lives with each other. Yet Cheryl fulfills the obligations of casual friendship in an exemplary manner. She greets

Heroic	This person lives for another or others at great personal sacrifice, which may include the emotional toll that the relationship presently brings. We see this, for example, when one cheerfully cares for a dying spouse.
Great	A self-forgetfulness characterizes this person's way of relating and interacting. Whether in friendship or in marriage, it seems to give this person joy to live for others in a selfless way.
Generous	The obligations and duties that are part of the relationship are cheerfully and graciously fulfilled. And the generous friend or spouse often goes beyond the fulfillment of reasonable expectations or duties.
Adequate	The expectations of the relationship are adequately fulfilled. The obligations and duties inherent in the relationship are consistently fulfilled in the spirit of "doing one's duty." It may never occur to the individual that he or she could do more.
Inadequate	Either because of inattention or laziness, the obligations and duties inherent in the friendship or the marriage are often unfulfilled. Relational obligations are not *always* left unfulfilled, but it happens often enough to be noticeable. It is a recognizable pattern of behavior.
Self-Centered	Self-seeking motivates this person to seek his or her interests at the expense of another. The habitual pursuit of one's own needs means that responsibilities to others are left unfulfilled. "My own 'needs' rank higher than my obligations to you." The harm that is done is not intentional but is nevertheless real.
Wretched	In the previous example, the self-centered individual was too busy with his own 'needs' to attend to others. Here, whether knowingly or not, the relationship is such that one *uses* the other, in a harmful way, to meet his or her own 'needs.'
Treacherous	Information shared in an intimate relationship is later used against the person. To cite a familiar example, Jesus' enemies were afraid to apprehend him in broad daylight because they feared the crowds. Only those closest to Jesus knew where he spent his nights. Judas was willing to tell Jesus' enemies where he was in exchange for thirty pieces of silver.

Marcy when she sees her; she always tries to be cheerful; and she makes positive, encouraging comments when appropriate. When Marcy's grandmother died Cheryl sent her a note. In these things she fulfills the duties of casual friendship. Cheryl is a *good*, though not particularly *close* friend.

On the other hand, Tony and Terry are close friends who have shared much of their personal lives with each other over the years. Yet Tony does not consistently fulfill the obligations of friendship and often allows his own selfishness determine his course of action (or inaction). Tony and Terry long ago decided to have dinner every Wednesday evening. But at least once a month Tony calls at the last minute to cancel. He always comes up with an excuse. In truth, he simply did not feel like going. He is not dependable. Apparently, it matters little to Tony that his friend enjoys their time together and looks forward to it. Tony is a *close*, though not a particularly *good* friend to Terry. He is a *close* friend because they have shared very private, intimate details about their lives. But he is not a *good* friend inasmuch as he fails to live up to the expectations one typically has of a friend. Relationships such as these often bring sadness and discouragement.

This distinction between being a *close* friend and being a *good* friend has obvious applications to marriage. Husbands and wives experience a certain closeness in virtue of the fact that they are married and live as spouses. Yet, for all that, it is plainly evident that many spouses do not live the marital relationship particularly well. A man can be a husband, but not a particularly good husband. He could be an inadequate husband, a self-centered husband, a wretched or even a treacherous husband. But the opposite is also possible. Some spouses are not merely adequate, they are generous spouses, great spouses, and a few are even heroic.

On this scale, with heroic loving on the one end and treacherous relating on the other, what determines where any given individual will end up? Why are some people great while others are wretched? In the end, each man and woman decides the sort of person he or she wants to be. This is the drama of each person's life. What kind of person shall I—by my own free choice—become? What kind of friend, what kind of spouse do I want to be? A portion of it is "the hand we were dealt." But most of it—the most important part of it—is "what we choose to do with it." We are who we are—we are the kind of friend or spouse we are—because that is the kind of person we choose to be. Having heroes and positive role models is enormously helpful. If I have people that I admire for their generosity, it is easier for me to aspire to that way of living and relating. We want the ones we admire to be proud of us. In homes where family members generously give of themselves, children are more likely to grow up doing the same. But when a child grows up in an environment where everyone—including parents—simply looks after himself or herself, it is far less likely that he or she will have the motivation (or the practical knowledge) to relate differently.

Relationships Take Time to Develop

So we have this image of two people, of either the same or the opposite sex, who are somehow drawn to each other: they like each other, and perhaps they have a number of things in common. They are beginning to take a personal interest in each other. But they are not yet friends, though a friendship is budding. It takes a long time to establish a genuine friendship. According to an ancient proverb, two people are not yet friends until they have eaten a peck (one-quarter of a bushel) of salt together. This can be painfully obvious to people who have recently moved and are now living far away from their friends. They are open to meeting new people, and they may have established some new relationships. But they are not like their "friends from back home."

The reason true friendship takes time is obvious enough—one must prove one's goodness, perseverance, and loyalty. Being friendly, warm, and agreeable is not the same as being friends. Because friendship involves the revealing of our personal lives, we must know—with increasing certitude—of a person's trustworthiness before we will be willing to reveal the secrets of our hearts. Discretion—the ability to keep secrets and keep matters private—is one of the many virtues needed for genuine friendship. This is where people get hurt. They reveal too much too early. Some people do better than others when it comes to keeping private information private. Everyone can be indiscrete from time to time, and sometimes it happens accidentally. But some people simply cannot be trusted with secrets. They blab. Others may be capable of it, but they have insufficient loyalties (or perhaps they would say "conflicting loyalties"), and information that was to remain between the two of you is made known to others.

Knowing whether someone will keep my secrets is only discovered over time. Revealing too much too fast is a recipe for disaster.

Friendship takes time to ripen, and this can be frustrating for people of all ages. Most people first become capable of real friendship in high school, though some do not bloom relationally until later. A high school student may experience loneliness stemming from the fact that his or her peers lack the maturity necessary for genuine friendship. In the first and maybe second year of college, we see people who have a greater understanding and capacity for friendship but who have not been around each other long enough to know whether they are trustworthy. It can happen to others as well who find themselves in a new setting while their family and friends, whom they count on for support, are far away.

If we look at two people who are the best of friends, and consider how they went from being merely companions to having the friendship they have today, we can discern three phases in the relationship. These three phases are the same whether the friendship is between two men, two women, or between a man and a woman.

The Initiating Phase

In the first phase—when we take steps to initiate a friendship—it has occurred to one or to both of them that they could pursue a relationship that is more than simply companionship. There are many ways one can try to initiate a friendship, but all of them involve some sort of invitation. For instance, one might say to a co-worker, "We should get together after work sometime." Or perhaps, in the context of our work, we begin to reveal a bit of ourselves, and then wait to see how the other responds. In one way or another, we communicate our interest in a deeper relationship. Matt, for instance, may like to pursue a friendship with Dan. And perhaps that unfolds into a lasting friendship. But it might not work out that way. Friendship is based on a mutual interest. In our example, Dan may have no interest beyond a very casual relationship with Matt. Matt may be saddened or frustrated by this—but this is simply part of life. We are never *entitled* to someone's friendship—it is a gift. And we give it to whom we wish.

The Deepening Phase

When the two mutually choose to pursue a friendship, they begin to share their lives with each other in ways they did not when they were simply companions. In this phase they are building their friendship, which can take years, and the line between the phases is a fuzzy one. The deepening begins to occur even toward the end of the initiating phase. But the initiating phase is concluded when both parties would agree that their friendship is an established fact. They are no longer *considering* being friends. In a sense, this is easier in the boyfriend/girlfriend relationship because they mutually *declare* the relationship. They are "going out."

The deepening phase may be a very long road. It is this phase that determines how close the two friends will become and the extent of their interaction. The road along which they travel is the road to intimacy. They are both determining the extent to which they are willing to let the other into the inner recesses of their private lives. It is an essential element of friendship that we share our inner lives; we reveal the things that are hidden from public view.

Why do we keep some things secret? Because of embarrassment or fear—or even because you are humble and, for example, do not want to broadcast the fact that you were the valedictorian of your high school graduating class. We tell our friends the secrets of our inner life, but some things we only share with our closest friends. And we may have deeply personal matters that we share with a very select few or with only one person. It is not true that, given enough time, every friend would get to know us the way our closest friends do. We make the decision on a case-by-case basis as we decide how far we are willing to let someone into our lives. In the deepening phase, we decide how much we are willing to share.

Earlier we saw that there are duties in friendship. As a relationship deepens, the duties increase. The duties we have to our dearest friends are greater than our duties to our more casual friends. You could perceive, for example, that I would like to have a deeper friendship with you, one that would entail more interaction between us. But—as harsh or cold as it sounds—you might have neither the time, nor the interest, in expanding our interaction beyond the friendship we currently have. Furthermore, we should not take on responsibilities that we cannot fulfill.

In the deepening phase, the friends are also determining the way their friendship will be lived out. If we are going to be friends, we must have a way we live out our friendship. The things we do together as friends, and how often we do them, is determined in this middle stage.

The Abiding Phase

In this final phase, the friends are not actively looking for ways to *build* their friendship as they did in the deepening phase. They are happy and comfortable with the way they relate, and they are secure in their friendship. This stage is not just for the closest and dearest friends. Two people can abide in a casual friendship. The fact that it is not a deep friendship does not make it somehow defective.

In the abiding phase, the friendship can continue to deepen. It happens if the people are open to it happening, and if the circumstances permit this to happen. I nevertheless call this the abiding rather than the deepening phase, because the friends are not actively trying to deepen the relationship, and the deepening of the relationship somewhat took them by surprise. We can see this happening in the following example. Laura and Jackie had been very dear friends for many years, and they shared with each other the secrets of their hearts. Laura had an unmarried brother, Robert, who died suddenly. Since Laura's parents were deceased, and since she had no other siblings, the funeral arrangements and the settlement of the estate all fell to Laura. She was completely overwhelmed by it all. Laura's friend, Jackie, was an enormous support. Though it was Laura's responsibility to make decisions, Jackie took an active role in all of this. Jackie took care of a number of the smaller details and helped Laura with the larger ones. Because of this, Laura did not feel as though she were doing this alone. Indeed, she was not alone. All of this deepened the friendship between Laura and Jackie; and it was occasioned by an unexpected event—the death of Robert. Unpredictable and unfortunate events sometimes provide occasions for our relationships to deepen in ways that could not have been imagined.

Laura and Jackie have a friendship that abides. This is due, in part, to the fact that they frequently see each other. Many of us have friends whom we rarely see, yet the friendship between us is something very real. The relationship is continually being fed, not with common activity, but with mutual interest. For example, though I rarely see a certain friend from my college years, she remains an important part of my life. I am still very interested in her well-being, and she in mine.

But it also happens, as the years pass, that we can lose our interest in people. We would like all of our relationships to last forever. But not all friendships abide; some of them pass away. Friends who were once important to us no longer are. Two people, who started as companions and then became friends, could revert to being companions if they lose their mutual interest in each other and in their friendship. This sounds callous. And we would like to think that once someone is a friend, he or she will always be our friend. But, as our experience tells us, it does not always work out that way. This is why the abiding phase of friendship is an important one. If we are going to keep our friends, if our friendships are to abide, they must continue to be fed and sustained by our mutual interest in each other. It seems that some shared activity—even if it is only an annual phone call—is necessary for our mutual interest in each other to be something real. When this is lacking, it seems fitting to say that someone is a "friend from my past."

Finally, some people have what could be called relational-laziness. For one reason or another, they seem unwilling to put forth much effort in sustaining their relationships. It can be evident in their marriages as well as their friendships.

Throughout the chapter, we have looked at the three essential elements for a friendship: virtue, mutual interest, and shared activity. Our relationships—friendships and marriages—will endure over the years to the extent that these three elements remain. When they do remain, they bring with them the peace and security that comes with loving and knowing that we are loved.

Questions for Philosophical Consideration and Personal Growth

1. Think about the people that are closest to you. You experience your interaction with them in different ways. Are you able to see examples of your remaining faithful to a friend in spite of the difficulties that the relationship entails? Can you see how others have remained faithful to you even when doing so was difficult? What insights does this provide regarding genuine love? If genuine love is something other than the positive experience people have of one another, what is it?

2. People who experience difficulty in establishing and maintaining friendships will sometimes focus their attention on doing things that they think will make them more appealing to others—often in merely superficial ways. If you saw this trait in, say, your sibling or child, what advice might you give to him or her?

3. The people who love you, love you because you are *you*. Which of your (hopefully many) good qualities makes you a good friend? Where are your relating skills weakest and most in need of improvement?

4. What is the difference between being "likeable" and being a friend?

5. Think of the people that you are especially close to. What character traits in them do you particularly value?

6. How do you understand loyalty, and what do you consider to be the limits of loyalty? Do I have to agree with you to be loyal to you? Are there some things that are more important than loyalty? What does it mean to have conflicting loyalties? How should one resolve them? As you see it, is there something one might call "loyalty to God" that is like a trump card?

7. Why do you think it is that two people find each other attractive? Do you think that this is an area where one's tastes can be refined? For instance, people who enjoy fine wine nearly always say that their taste in wine has changed and developed over the years. When they first started drinking wine, they did not have an appreciation for the wines they enjoy today. Does the same thing happen in one's appreciation for people? How do you see the change that occurs over the years?

8. What role do you see virtue playing in a friendship? What does it mean to say that virtue and character strength make one *capable* of genuine friendship?

9. What does it mean when we say, "We learn many things about life in the *school of friendship*"? In particular, what does friendship teach us about marriage?

10. Look at the people that are closest to you, including your spouse. Consider them individually. How close would you say you are? Why did you answer the way you did? What kind of a friend (or spouse) is the person? Good? Adequate? Generous? Heroic? Self-centered? Why do you say this?

   Now how about you? How good of a friend (or spouse) are you? Why do you say this? How might things be different?

11. Considering the degree of one's generosity regarding his or her relationships, how important do you think it is that one have "heroes" and mentors? If you have heroes and mentors, who are they? What makes them heroic? How have they influenced your life?

Chapter Four

Friendship Experienced as a Culture of Love

This is what we love in our friends,
and we love it so much that a man's conscience
accuses itself if he does not love one who loves him,
or respond in love to love,
seeking nothing from the other but the evidences of his love.
This is the source of our moaning when one dies—
the gloom of sorrow,
the steeping of the heart in tears,
all sweetness turned to bitterness—
and the feeling of death in the living,
because of the loss of the life of the dying.

Blessed is he who loves Thee,
and who loves his friend in Thee,
and his enemy also, for Thy sake;
for he alone loses none dear to him,
if all are dear in him who cannot be lost.[33]

From *Confessions*
St. Augustine (354–430)

How Friendship Is Experienced:
A Culture Is Created—A Culture of Love

If we had to choose between all the goods of the world and having true friends, we would choose to have friends. The reason is obvious enough—silver and gold cannot love us, but our friends do. We naturally desire friends—people who love us—because we want to love and to be loved. In friendship, especially spousal friendship, we create a culture of love.

The word "culture" is used in many different ways. When I use the word in this book, I have the following notions in mind. A culture is the particular way of *valuing* and *acting* that is characteristic of some specific group. There is, for example, the culture of one's work environment. One could think of nurses on a given floor at a hospital, who as a group have embraced certain values regarding the way they provide health care, and the way they relate to one another. When new nurses come to the department, it would be communicated either formally or informally, "This is the way we do things here."

This idea of culture is seen more clearly in the context of a family. The values embraced by the family members heavily influence the way they live family life. For example, the parents might have the expectation that the children are home for a family dinner on specific nights of the week. Another aspect of the family culture is the way they communicate approval and disapproval. Hopefully, each family member does his or her part to create an atmosphere—a culture— where everyone in the family feels at home in the family home and knows that it is a place where love and acceptance are the operating principles. These things determine the way they live family life. It is the way they do things, and it is based on the values they have collectively embraced as a family.

Friends also create a culture in the way they interact and communicate. In a way that is similar to flourishing families, friends establish a culture of love. It is as though friends say to one another, "I know that I am at home when I am with you." The closer friends are to one another, the more this will be the case.

The creation of a culture of love does not happen automatically. It does not always happen among friends, it does not always happen with people who are dating, and it does not always happen in a family. But it *can* happen and it should. When it does occur, a climate is created where people know (because of their continual experience) that their family/friends are interested in them, that they matter, that they are accepted, and that they have their approval. We communicate to those we love, "It is good that you exist!" This habitual way of relating gives our friends the experience that we are attentive to them. We know what is going on in their lives and we appropriately respond. "I am not in your lives as a spectator—I am a participant."

In creating a culture of love, we form mental and emotional associations. Perhaps you can recall some specific place where you had a very negative experience, causing you much stress. It could have been the ice cream parlor where you broke up with your boyfriend, or the art room of your grade school. Because of the power of association, you can experience stress by returning to those places even years later. "I do not like coming back here. I have bad memories tied to this place." But it works the other way too, with positive associations. We can have a restaurant with powerfully positive associations connected with it. "My best friend and I have had many meals here and shared with each other the stories of our lives." Most importantly, positive associations connect us in a good way with *persons*—the persons who love us most. Just being with them, even when very little is said, is an experience of an established culture of love. This culture of love is precisely what enables people to flourish, and it gives people a healthy confidence in their interpersonal relating.

We were made for love. When we see that we *matter* to the important people in our lives, that they take an interest in us, that we have their acceptance and approval, that they rejoice in our friendship—all of this taken together gives us the experience of solidarity. This is the exact opposite of feeling *alone*. When I know that I am loved, I know that I am never alone—our friends are with us even when they are absent. In spousal friendship, an abiding solidarity can arise from the raising of children, the living of family life, and, of course, in the experience of their marital affection and erotic love. Friendship, affection, and erotic love coming together all at once can create an experience of romance. When marital love is lived well, the spouses know they are never alone. Some have spoken of their marital friendship continuing even after a spouse has died. As one aged widow put it, "Now that he has gone to Jesus, he is with me all the time. I talk to him many times every day. Before long we will be together again in the Kingdom."

Jesus died on the Cross on Good Friday. While he was always united to his Father in Heaven, we do not know how or to what extent he *experienced* that union at any given moment, including the three hours he hung on the Cross. But God the Father, in his mercy, permitted Jesus to have with him the two most important people in his life: his mother and St. John, the "disciple whom Jesus loved."[34] They did not "do things" for him at that moment. It was enough that they were there with him. This is true solidarity. I know that I am not alone because I know—even if you are not physically present—that you are with me, giving me a sense of security and a sense of confidence.

Effectively Communicating Our Love

If we look at the way we relate to the people in our lives, we will likely see patterns. In any given relationship we tend to relate according to a pattern that we have previously established with that person. This explains why, for example, a fifty-year-old college professor, happening upon her sixth-grade teacher years later at the grocery store, will still call her "Mrs. Jones," and give her the marks of respect one typically gives to teachers. They have an established pattern of relating. We do this in our personal relationships too. We have characteristic ways of responding. We can choose to act outside of our established patterns, but we tend not to do that.

Knowing that in each of our relationships we tend to relate according to established patterns, we can garner insights about our own relating by looking at these patterns. We may discover that we relate very well with some people, while certain other relationships bear some marks of dysfunction. Though it is not easy to do, we can change our relating patterns.

A positive pattern of relating can begin with someone being agreeable. It is the opposite of having a contrary or harsh disposition. It is not that we must ignore real differences between us, but some people have a seemingly compulsive need to correct or modify everything that is said. They can never simply nod their head in agreement. They are disagreeable, and Aristotle was right when he wrote that these people have a difficult time making friends.

There are a variety of ways of saying to someone, "You matter to me." Some people struggle with verbal communication, but their actions clearly demonstrate their love. Look at all the things your friends—including your spouse—willingly do for you. These works of love are not really a substitute for the words of love. But when they are motivated by love, they reveal the secrets of the heart. Of course, communicating love is best and clearest when the words and deeds go together. Those who struggle with being verbally affirming could try taking "baby steps." I sometimes encourage people to say things like, "I really enjoy golfing with you," or "I like it when we get together for lunch on Fridays." Later on they can take larger steps, saying things like, "I look forward to the time we spend together," or "I treasure our friendship." People can be anxious about verbally communicating love if they are not sure how the other will respond. If they start small they are often pleasantly surprised by the results.

So the culture of love that we want to establish in our relationships, and most especially in our families, is experienced in three ways:

- In the environment of acceptance and approval that we create by our demeanor and our words;
- In the things we willingly do for each other;
- In the solidarity that, over time, comes from the sharing in each other's lives.

The Different Levels of Friendship

Having made the distinction between friends and companions, we see that even among those whom we rightly call *friends*, there are different levels of friendship. Looking at the life of Jesus, we see that he had twelve Apostles. He was also friends with two sisters and their brother: Martha, Mary, and Lazarus.[35] The Apostles were also Jesus' friends and he identifies them as such.[36] Even among the Apostles, however, there is a distinction in the way Jesus relates to them. Several times in the Gospels Jesus calls aside Peter, James, and John. He has these three with him at some particularly intense moments. Upon the death of the daughter of Jairus, the synagogue official, Jesus entered the girl's room, but "he allowed no one to follow him except Peter and James and John the brother of James."[37] These three are with him on Mt. Tabor when Jesus is transfigured in glory.[38] And they were (rather inattentively) with him in the Garden of Gethsemane when Jesus was agonizing over his impending Passion.[39]

Even among these three Apostles, Sts. Peter, James, and John, we see differences in the way Jesus relates to them. It is to Peter that Jesus entrusts his Church,[40] and after the Resurrection Jesus commands him to "feed my lambs" and "tend my sheep."[41] But St. John will be forever remembered as the "disciple whom Jesus loved."[42]

The other Apostles were also Jesus' friends. He said to them at a certain point: "No longer do I call you servants ... but I have called you friends."[43] Jesus was a better friend to the Apostles than they were to him. He loved them all, and communicated his love. They, in turn, each returned Jesus' friendship in varying degrees. Two of the Apostles, John and Judas, stand out, in particular, for their response to Jesus' love. John was the faithful friend who was with Jesus to the bitter end. Judas Iscariot betrayed him.[44]

We, too, make distinctions among our friends. It is as though they surround us in concentric circles. Some are closer in and some are further out, but they are all our friends. We may have some who are truly friends, but whom we only see or hear from once a year or so—perhaps through a Christmas card. Perhaps we were really close in high school and continue to keep in touch periodically. We share a loyalty and affection between us—we just do not see each other all that often. These friends are kept aware of the major events in our lives, but not the lesser details. Most people have a lot of friends like this, and the older we get the more of them we have. People in their sixties or seventies can have friends from childhood, high school, college, their old neighborhood, their first job, etc.

As these concentric circles get smaller and closer to the center, we find friends with whom we have more frequent contact and of whom we have greater expectations. As such, they are kept abreast not just of the major happenings in our lives but the smaller things as well. We are more likely to seek their input and rely more heavily on their support and encouragement.

Finally, we have the innermost circle or circles. These are the people in our lives that are closest to us. They know us better than anyone, and we rely on them more than we rely on anyone else. When good things happen and when bad things happen—these are the people we want to tell.

While this all looks very neat and organized "on paper," the reality is a bit more complicated. This is because there are different ways of "being close" to someone. I can be close to you because of my affection for you, or because of my commitment to you. We can be close to each other because of the frequency and content of our communication. It is important to keep this in mind. I may see Charlie every day; we have tremendous affection for each other, and we are very free and open in our communication. Drew, on the other hand, I see less often. Yet there is a history between us that powerfully unites the two of us. I may in fact enjoy Charlie's company more, and though I see him much more often we will likely never have the bond that exists between Drew and me.

The closer we are to someone, the greater the solidarity between us. But as I have said, there are different ways of being close. A married man I know keeps a little thimble on his desk. Every now and again he points to it and says, "That represents everything I understand about women." He is kidding, of course. But the thimble serves as a way of reminding him that his wife sees things from a different perspective—from the feminine perspective. He loves his wife dearly, and they are a great couple and excellent parents. While he understands *that* his wife sees things in a particular way—he does not always understand *why* she does. That, in part, is because he is a man and she is a woman. There is a solidarity among friends of the same gender that, in some ways, enables them to understand each other more easily. It is good for us to have friends in our lives besides our spouses. Guys need guy friends, and girls need girl friends. As the circles get smaller, the friends who comprise them are closer to us. We have a few we call our "best friends," and each of us may have one we call our " very best friend." Our best friend might not necessarily be our "favorite friend." I say "favorite" in the sense that someone can be a lot of fun to be with, even if he or she is not a particularly devoted friend. The one who is our best friend is the one who does best the things that friends do. One would expect a "best friend" and "favorite friend" to be the same person. But I could envision someone saying, "No one is a more devoted and loyal friend than Bill, but I happen to enjoy Adam's company better."

We occasionally hear of two friends who relate to each other as "their other self." Two friends in the Old Testament, David and Jonathan, were of this sort. Jonathan was the son of King Saul. But when Saul took up arms against David, Jonathan sided with his friend and not with his father, the king. We read that Jonathan loved David *as he loved his very self.*[45]

The Sympathy of Friendship

Often when people think of sympathy, the first thing that comes to mind is the sorrowful feeling we have for someone who is facing a hardship—which occasions the sending of a sympathy card. But sympathy is broader than that. Depending on the circumstance, it includes the feelings of either happiness or sadness, and it arises from our mutual understanding of each other. It is sympathy's connection with the intellect—rooted in our understanding of the other—that gives it a stability that emotions by themselves do not have.

Sympathy is feeling *with* another, generating an emotional identification with someone. I am happy because you are happy; I am sad because you are sad. We can have sympathy for people with whom we are only slightly emotionally connected, but it is particularly noticeable in relationships with those with whom we have strong emotional bonds.

Sympathy enables me to feel that you are on my side. It does not mean that you agree with me, but you are at least emotionally standing with me, supporting me. Imagine a husband and wife where he is a school principal and she is a teacher at another school. He tells his wife he has had to terminate an employee. She is able to communicate effectively to him that while she would not have made the same decision, she nevertheless appreciates the fact that it was a difficult, stressful decision to make and that she supports him and stands with him as he makes the decision and lives with the consequences.

Sympathy is important in a relationship—especially in a marriage. If I do not feel that you sympathize with me, that you are not really emotionally on my side—or worse yet, that you regularly seem to side against me—then the only thing holding our relationship together is the strength of our wills. It is possible to do that, but such friendships and marriages are experienced more as a duty and a burden than as a joy.

Hopefully we have many friends, and some will be closer to us than others. To expect every friend to be like a best friend would clearly be unreasonable; nevertheless, friends that *are* particularly close seem to have a chemistry between them that enables their thinking and feeling to run along the same paths. It is sympathy that enables this to happen. They think alike. They feel alike. It is the opposite of being contrary—the pattern of contradicting or correcting everything that is said. Did you ever notice how some people always seem to be in a bad mood? They are crabby, cranky, curmudgeonly. They may hang around other cranks—and may even revel in their crankiness—but it is not hard to see why these folks have a hard time making real friends. The pattern of communicating and relating does not generate any sympathy. Their crabby manner makes it hard to believe they are genuinely interested in anyone other than themselves.

Sympathy generates goodwill. If we have frequent contact with people, we are able to see their defects—and we all have them: physical, moral, emotional, and relational defects. How is it that we are able to completely overlook the sometimes serious and chronic defects of some of our friends? It is because of sympathy. Sympathy breeds sympathy. If I believe that you take an interest in me, that you genuinely care about me and that you desire my well-being, I will overlook your defects—and I do so in part because I know that you overlook mine. It makes forgiveness easier.

Like any feeling, sympathy is fragile. And as with other fragile things that we value, sympathy needs to be treated with care. The things we say and do, the things we fail to say and fail to do, all help to build up sympathy or to whittle it away. When you communicate to me that I am important to you and that you value me as a person—as a friend or as a spouse—that in turn builds up my sympathy toward you. We can also do the opposite. I keep leaving messages for you, for instance, but you almost never call me back. I told you something that was really important to me, but I thought your response was completely inadequate—or even cold. You regularly back out of plans we make. All these things wear away sympathy and make one question whether the other values the relationship.

A relationship is in trouble if sympathy dips below a critical level. This is especially true in the friendship between a husband and wife. In a healthy relationship, the individuals know that their love—their friendship—is reciprocated. I care about you and you care about me. This is true for every friendship from marriage to casual friends. The care, the concern, the attention that one gives to the other needs to be reciprocated—or at least come close to being reciprocated. Pope Benedict XVI points this out in his encyclical on love. While it is ennobling and enriching for one to give of oneself, "He cannot always give, he must also receive."[46] If you stop reciprocating, your friend can begin to wonder whether you still want to be friends. Depending on how much sympathy has been built up over the years, the relationship can endure for a time. The relating skills of some people run hot and cold; on again and off again. Those who are friends may wonder where they stand. At times they seem attentive and interested, only to seem the complete opposite the following month. If my sympathy runs out, if I no longer believe that you are interested in being friends, then all those things that I was willing to overlook (because I thought you cared about me) now come back to my mind with a vengeance. This helps explain how people who were so close—such as a husband and wife—can become bitter and hateful toward each other.

We communicate things to others all the time. And we communicate as much by our tone of voice and by our actions as we do by the words we use. We can get a glimpse of what people really think by things they say in passing. Sometimes we choose our words very carefully as when, for example, we are doing an interview for the newspaper or when we are having a serious conversation. Other times the words just come out. When I am not on guard to choose words carefully, you can get a glimpse of what I really think. Positive things said in passing build up sympathy; negative ones tear it down.

The "Four Loves"

When looked at in the most general terms, love is our response or attitude toward something that we perceive to be good. Even when we are mistaken in our judgments and we perceive that something is good when, in fact, it is not—it is nevertheless because we *perceive it to be good* that we respond with love. What we perceive to be good may be a person, a thing, an idea, an event, etc. It really does not matter. All that matters is that we judge it to be good in some way.

Two things follow from this. On the one hand, because the object loved is perceived as good, I see that I stand to benefit from it in some way. No selfishness is necessarily implied, but because of this anticipated benefit, I desire it, using the word *desire* very broadly here. I am in a position to benefit and, indeed, I *want* to benefit. I call this *the love of desire*.

On the other hand, because of the object's perceived goodness, I am moved or prompted to make an adequate response. Goodness elicits a response from me, not only the response of desire, but the response of gift. At the very least, the goodness I perceive in you prompts me to acknowledge your goodness and, still further, to make some kind of return. I want to respond to love with love.

So we have this dynamic of receiving and giving as two modes or responses to a perceived good. When this is applied to persons, the two modes of *desiring* and *giving* combine in various ways to produce the various ways of loving. Lewis identified the four ways of loving—the "Four Loves"—as affection, friendship, *eros*, and charity. While I use the same names for the loves that Lewis uses, my understanding of affection is somewhat different than his, and I see friendship and charity very differently than he sees them.

Affection

Affection is a positive, emotional connection we have with the people we are close to. It is stronger than the feeling of fondness and much stronger than what is commonly meant by "liking someone." The fact that affection is a non-erotic love does not make it less intense than *eros*—a fact that is plainly evident in the powerful feelings of affection that parents have for their children. These emotional bonds of affection give us the feeling of unity and solidarity with those whom we love.

We communicate our affection for another in our words and deeds. We have affectionate ways of speaking—including the words themselves and our tone of voice. We also speak of acts of affection, such as a pat on the back or a hug.

The goodness I perceive in you makes me fond of you. I like you, and I like being around you. There is an aspect of desiring in affection as well as an accompanying motivation to give. Like all of our emotions, the intensity of affection waxes and wanes. Unlike friendship, affection imposes no duties. It is just, so to speak, *there*. And because we cannot count on it always being there, we cannot make it the foundation of a long-term relationship. Long-term relationships need a more solid foundation than the one provided by our emotional responses.

Our expressions of affection should be governed by right-reason and sound judgment. We should ask ourselves whether our actions—or the absence thereof—are appropriate for the context. In our fallen human condition, we cannot count on our emotions to "get it right." They need to pass through the filter of prudence. Aberrations are easy to see in their extremes. Those who are, one might say, emotionally constipated, are unable to communicate (or perhaps even experience) affection. And one can see the ways in which this will complicate the person's life, especially the spousal relationship and the interacting with one's children. But the other extreme, uncontrolled sentimentality and emotionalism, is equally disruptive of normal and functional relating.

Eros

Erotic love is a way of emotionally responding to someone, and it is distinct from affection. It is a particular way of desiring—sexual desiring. It prompts a particular mode of giving and a particular way of receiving, namely, the erotic, sexual way. To be classified as erotic, something need not be explicitly genital. But it involves those things that have to do with "being in love," or the love that is associated with "lovers."

The interaction of two people in love will sometimes be motivated by affection and at other times by *eros*. Not every kiss between lovers is a lover's kiss. The interaction between two people in love can also be motivated by friendship or by charity. This principle of having more than one kind of love motivating and guiding interpersonal interaction is an important one. In happy and healthy marriages, each of the four loves is present since, as most can plainly see, it takes much more than erotic love to sustain a marriage through the years.

Friendship

Friendship, as we have been saying all along, is a *habitual* way of relating to someone. It presumes the friends have the moral qualities necessary for friendship; it is rooted in their mutual interest in each other; and it is lived out in the activities they enjoy doing together. Friendship resembles a feeling because we almost always have fine feelings for our friends, but friendship as a way of loving is distinct from both affection and *eros*. Friends, in a greater or lesser degree, invite each other into their lives, and they share their lives together. They do this freely, willingly, and habitually.

Moral quality is to the friend what athletic ability is to the athlete. It is a measure of one's ability to act well when it is difficult to do so. One who, say, tells a lie when it is convenient to do so, lacks the moral quality that is present in the person who is habitually truthful. One's good moral quality serves two purposes. It makes one attractive—"he is a genuinely good man." It also gives one the ability to fulfill the duties of friendship and to do so cheerfully and generously. This inner moral quality enables one to remain loyal.

In every pairing or group of friends, a pattern of relating is established. I call this the culture of their relationship, and it is the way they say and do things among themselves. The love between the friends takes the form of mutual interest in each other, mutual acceptance and approval, and a willingness to sacrifice in order to bring about what is truly good for one's friend. Friends have favorite activities and common interests where this is lived out. The two of them experience the intimacy of friendship as the relationship unfolds over time, and they increasingly share the hidden matters of their heart.

Friendship, as we said earlier, is not a feeling—it is a habitual way of relating. And it is experienced in a variety of ways. It is experienced in the trust and confidence that friends have in each other; in the security that comes from the expectation that their friendship will endure through the years; and in the warmth of their affection. These friendships endure even during the times when affection is not noticeably present. Using the analogy of a fireplace, the flame of the burning logs initially gets our attention, but it is the red-hot embers underneath that provide the real heat. We enjoy the affection we experience in our friendships, but the friendship itself is something richer.

When two friends are of the opposite sex, there is the potential that the friendship will be experienced as erotic love. If both are open to it, the friendship may develop as such. When it does, the friends are not only lovers but friends as well. Not every erotic relationship began as a friendship. Sometimes the friendship came later. But in every erotic relationship that endures for the long haul, and in which the lovers remain "happy participants," one can see a friendship between the two of them providing a foundation.

Charity

St. Thomas Aquinas said that charity is a kind of friendship with God.[47] It is "kind of like" friendship. In friendship, people share their lives with each other. When we are friends with God, he shares his life with us. It is God's very life, God's very self, dwelling mysteriously within us. It begins the moment we are baptized and remains as long as we are in the state of grace. As with any friendship, we have the power to end it.

In a friendship between two human persons, the intimacy between them gives the sense that each dwells within the other. With particularly close friends, especially in the friendship between a husband and wife, we hear people say things like, "It is as though a part of you is in me" or, "I cannot imagine my life without you in it." In our relationship with God, he genuinely dwells within us. The Divine Indwelling, to the extent that we cooperate and consent, becomes a foundational operating principle in our lives. It affects not only our relationship with God himself, but with everyone who is connected or associated with him—which is everybody.

Other relationships work this way too. I do not know my friend's mother very well, but I am good to her because of my friend. Similarly, sitting next to me at the baseball game is the sister of my friend's fiancée. Again, I treat her well because of the connection I have with her through my friend, knowing my friend would not be happy if I failed in this. There is a parallel here with charity. Because of our friendship with God, we treat all of God's friends the way he wants us to treat them. This love of God dwelling within us, this charity, affects the way we relate to everybody—family, friends, acquaintances, and strangers. Pope Benedict XVI puts it this way:

> Love of neighbor is thus shown to be possible in the way proclaimed by the Bible, by Jesus. It consists in the very fact that, in God and with God, I love even the person whom I do not like or even know. This can only take place on the basis of an intimate encounter with God, an encounter which has become a communion of will, even affecting my feelings. Then I learn to look on this other person not simply with my eyes and my feelings, but from the perspective of Jesus Christ. His friend is my friend.[48]

Understanding charity in this way, it loses the negative connotations sometimes associated with it, such as "charitable giving" to an organization, or doing some good deed that one might just as soon not do. Both of these can be charity, but so are things we very much enjoy doing. Love sometimes prompts us to do pleasant, enjoyable things. At other times it pushes us to make sacrifices.

When charity has the role it should have, it serves as the foundation for everything else in one's life. Everything rests upon it. It has, as it were, a purifying and filtering effect, enabling the other loves to attain their authentic grandeur.

How the Different Loves Relate to One Another

I propose that *eros*, affection, friendship, and charity, relate to each other as blocks forming a pyramid. (On the pyramid, I do not list familial love by itself. In healthy, functioning families, the family members relate to each other in a way that parallels friendship: freely, with mutual interest, affection, etc.) As illustrated in the diagram, the loves that are higher on the pyramid are supported and anchored by the loves beneath it. It is the loves below that provide the foundation. This has two results. First, this allows friendship, affection, and *eros*, to be higher and nobler than they could be if they were, so to speak, standing on their own. Secondly, loves are not only supported and lifted up—they are also secured and anchored, like a hot air balloon being held down by sand bags. The love that is below, both raises up and securely holds in place the love or loves that are above it. This has a purifying effect. It keeps the loves, so to speak, in their proper places, not permitting them to fly off on their own.

Affection and Friendship

What do I mean by raising up a love to make it higher and nobler than if the love stood on its own? Let us look at the loves of affection and friendship. Some people are, by temperament and disposition, more affectionate than others. They communicate affection freely. Some are so free in their communicating affection that they make the recipients of their affection uncomfortable, perhaps in part because the affection seems out of sync with the reality of the relationship. It can seem like empty sentimentalism. This is what I mean by affection "standing on its own" and not as an expression of something larger—like friendship or familial love. When it *is* an expression of something larger, as when affection is communicated in the context of friendship, affection itself becomes something greater than it is capable of being by itself. The *context* in which it is expressed is different. It is represented graphically below.

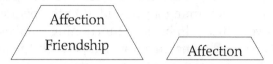

On the left, affection is being elevated by friendship. On the right, affection is standing alone. The same expression of affection means much more when it comes from a friend—especially a dear friend—than when it comes from a mere companion. The presence of the friendship makes the context richer.

Imagine a senior citizen who, for whatever reason, happens to win a football. Not having much use for it, he gives the football to the fourteen-year-old boy living next door. Now imagine the same fourteen-year-old receiving the game ball from his coach as an acknowledgement of his excellent performance during their freshman football game. In both cases, the boy received a football—but the context of each is very different. In the first case, since it was not received on a typical gift-giving occasion such as a birthday, it was a token gesture of kindness by the older gentleman next door. The context of the second case is much, much, richer. Receiving the game ball from the coach has symbolic value.

I use this football analogy to illustrate the significance of *context* in our expressions of love. Affection can stand on its own. But it becomes something more—something richer—when it is an expression of friendship. We will see how this happens with other loves too.

We have just seen how friendship gives affection a fuller and richer meaning than it has on its own. There are two other ways friendship can affect affection. Friendship can push affection forward (upward), or it can hold it back, acting as a restraint. The first of these is seen in Kendra and Marie.

Kendra and Marie have been friends for many years. Kendra's personality is such that she has difficulty expressing and communicating affection. It is not that she is cold; she just is not terribly expressive in the way she communicates her love. The people in her life, who know her well, have learned to "read between the lines" and detect Kendra's subtle ways of communicating her love. But on this particular day, Marie shares with Kendra a grave hardship that her family is experiencing. Marie cannot tell the story without crying. Though it goes against Kendra's natural inclinations, she embraces Marie. Her doing so was sort of half-spontaneous, and half a response to what seemed like the right thing to do at the time because of their friendship. This is an example of friendship pushing affection to a higher level of expression than Kendra's affection—on its own—was capable of reaching.

It can work the other way too. Friendship can act as a restraint for affection, especially spontaneous expressions of affection. Al, who plays softball one evening each week, has a girlfriend named Tara. She comes to the games and watches him play, as do many of the girlfriends of the players. The guys on the team usually go out after the game. Tara would like to give Al a kiss before she leaves—not a lover's kiss, but a kiss of affection. But she knows that Al is somewhat uncomfortable with this, especially in front of the other guys. She knows the guys would tease him about it later. So Tara, motivated by her friendship for Al, restrains her affection.

Affection, Friendship, and Charity

In the last few examples, we have seen the relationship between friendship and affection. What happens when we add charity into the mix? Earlier, we quoted St. Thomas' expression that charity is a kind of friendship with God. It is the word we use to describe a person's intimate, personal interaction with God. As "friendship" is to two human persons, so "charity" is to the individual with God. We should be quick to remind ourselves, as we just stated, that charity *resembles* friendship. Because God actually dwells within us, the union between God and us differs from the union of friendship, but this at least gets our thoughts moving in the right direction.

We saw earlier that affection is ennobled when it rests upon the foundation of friendship, becoming more than it is capable of being on its own. Charity can do the same for both friendship and affection. (Later, we shall see its effect on erotic love.) When charity serves as a foundation for the loves that rest upon it, it raises them to a level they cannot reach on their own, making them part of something greater.

The relationship one has with God reaches beyond simply the individual and God himself. God's love is an umbrella-like tent that embraces everybody, including the people we have never met, and even our enemies. Jesus said that whatever we do to the least of our brothers and sisters, we do to him. But the love of God, which dwells in our heart as charity, also impacts our relationships with those who are dearest to us. Charity can elevate these relationships by transforming them into an aspect of the way we love God. As such, the loving way I interact with my friend, doing all the things that friends do with and for one another, becomes the medium or context in which I love God and live out my vocation. So, at the end of the day, when I look back on the loving way I interacted with my family and friends, I can do so knowing that my love for them has pleased God as well. My friendship is now something *more* than friendship—it is charity.

In some previous examples, we have seen how friendship can, so to speak, push affection forward or hold it back. Charity—functioning as a foundation—can do likewise with any of the loves above it. Suppose you are working for a company that six months ago hired someone who had to relocate to take the new job. This fellow seems interesting enough, but you have the sense that this is a man who, because he seems particularly introverted, struggles to make new friends. Several times you have offered to do things socially, and he has always eagerly accepted. The two of you are becoming friends. Though you do not desire to become particularly close friends, you are motivated by charity to permit this friendship to develop. It just seems like the right thing to do, and the three necessary elements of friendship—sufficient virtue, mutual interest, and some favorite activities—are all present. While friendships such as these can be originally motivated by charity, with the love of God supporting them—they may later be able, as it were, to stand on their own.

Charity can also act as an anchor by keeping our relationships, including our expressions of love, in their proper places. This is the purifying effect of charity. Not every desired expression of love is, in fact, a good one.

In the first illustration below, charity is acting as a foundation for friendship and for affection, raising them higher than they are capable of reaching on their own. In the second illustration, friendship alone is supporting affection. In the last illustration, affection stands alone.

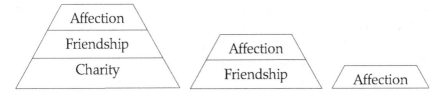

Eros, Affection, Friendship, and Charity

From what has been seen thus far, it should be simple enough to see how *eros*—the love itself, as well as its expression—fits into this schema. While *eros* can exist alone, apart from the other loves, it should not. Just as affection, if it is to be more than empty sentimentalism, needs the other loves to provide a foundation, *eros* needs a foundation as well. Without it, it is merely eroticism. It needs the other loves as a foundation if it is to be an authentic expression of love.

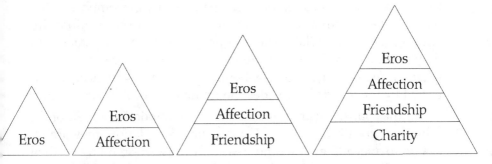

In the first illustration, *eros* stands alone, without a foundation. This represents anonymous sex where people (often after drinking heavily) "hook-up" with people they may not even know.

The second illustration represents what has come to be known as the "friends with benefits" relationship. Though they use the word "friends," these relationships are not friendships. The foundation of the relationship is affection, which presumes a kindness and warmth in the way they relate. The people involved are looking for the excitement of a sexual relationship, but without any real commitment. They are not "boyfriend and girlfriend." It is difficult to sustain this manner of relating because sexual activity brings along with it a natural desire to commit. Unless they suffer from some pathology, they eventually see that the absence of commitment, which they initially saw as *freedom*, in fact impoverishes the relationship. Committed love comes far closer to satisfying the demands of the human heart than eroticism can ever achieve. At some point, they will either become "boyfriend and girlfriend," with the commitment that that entails, or else they stop seeing each other altogether.

The third illustration represents a relationship that is both affectionate and erotic, and it rests upon the foundation of some kind of friendship. The boyfriend/girlfriend relationship is a particular way of being friends. So is being engaged or being married. When people see their relationships, including marriage, as in some way including their relationship with God, then the way they interact will be determined accordingly. By contrast, in this third illustration, it is the couple-relationship itself that provides the foundation. It is different from the relationship where friendship is absent, as was the case in the previous example. It is also different from the relationship where the love of God, or charity, is the foundation. My purpose here is not to make a moral evaluation of these relationships, but simply to point out that the love that provides the foundation for our relationships affects the way we relate. The way people relate and interact, how they express their love, and the manner in which one determines whether one is "playing out-of-bounds"—all these things are determined by the love that provides the foundation of the relationship.

In the fourth illustration, charity is the foundation for all of the other loves. With the love of God as their foundation, they are elevated to a level they could not reach if they were standing on their own. Earlier we saw friendship and affection resting on the foundation of charity. Here *eros*, along with friendship and affection, are an aspect of the individual's love for God and all that that entails. Affection, friendship, and charity will each affect the way erotic love is communicated. Sometimes they will push erotic love forward. The proverbial wife who has a headache may make love to her husband because she is motivated to do so by affection, friendship, charity, or any combination thereof. Other times, affection, friendship, and charity will hold back the expression of *eros*—perhaps because he knows his wife has a headache or the circumstances are not right. But, as with all the other examples, when erotic love rests upon affection, friendship, and charity, that very fact elevates it to a level that it cannot reach without the other loves. It can appear that *eros* is freer when it is not tied down. But the highest does not stand without the lowest. Erotic love is indeed the highest *experience* of love. But the lowest is what provides the foundation. When *eros* is an expression of affection, friendship, and divine love—with all the expectations that these various loves bring—then erotic love communicates something far greater than *eros* itself. All the loves come together at once. This is erotic love that is truly authentic. Pope Benedict XVI wrote: "Evidently, *eros* needs to be disciplined and purified if it is to provide not just fleeting pleasure, but a certain foretaste of the pinnacle of our existence, of that beatitude for which our whole being yearns."[49] It is what God intended *in the beginning* when he created us male and female.

All of our interacting with others, all of our ways of loving, must pass before the loving gaze of our Father God. Our loves are noble and pure when they are taken up and drawn into his love. In Genesis, when God finished his work of creation he looked upon all he had made and found it "very good."[50] May he look upon all our loves and find them "very good." In the final analysis, all our loves should be founded on divine love if they are to achieve their true beauty and splendor.

We have seen how the different ways of loving are related to one another. In the next three sections, we will see three particular applications of this. First, we will see how the loves that serve as a foundation can push us on to give generously of ourselves. Next, we will look at the application of the pyramid of loves to non-erotic friendships between men and women. Finally, we will see how the pyramid of loves gives us new insights into evangelization.

Creating a Culture of Love
Includes Generously Giving the Gift of Ourselves

When we began our considerations of the topic of love, we saw that all love is a response to something we perceive to be good. Two things follow from this. We want to *receive* because we believe that we will be fulfilled in some way. We also want to *give*, to make some kind of return. So we have seen two modes of loving—giving and receiving—and they are ordinarily found together.

Both giving and receiving love are essential aspects of our human nature, and it is by giving and receiving love that we experience fulfillment. Of the two modes of loving, giving and receiving, the former is the more noble. We all know people, either personally or by reputation, who consistently live this way. Many of us would say that our parents are like this. The ability that some people have to live their lives *for others* is what Pope John Paul II called "living in the dimension of gift." And the idea that one could live this way develops during adolescence. When a person reaches this stage of life, changes take place that go beyond physical and sexual development. People begin to discover a way of relating that had previously not occurred to them as they discover new ways to give of themselves.

Looking at little children and at the way they interact, we see them willing to do good things for others, but they expect something in return. At the very least they expect to be praised. But with the changes that occur in adolescence, children begin to discover that they could, in fact, do things for others without the expectation of a reward. It is a huge discovery. One begins to see the potential for real loving and real greatness. We all want and need to be loved and to experience love. We enjoy being on the receiving end of it. And although giving and receiving love often go together, it is possible to give without the expectation of receiving.

A maturing person may look at his or her life and see that it would be possible, and perhaps desirable, to live more generously. I think we all like to think of ourselves as living generously, at least as regards the people we love the most. But we are also aware, or should be aware, that we are weak, and we let opportunities for generosity pass us by.

Generosity, as I am using it here, is the giving of one's time, attention, affirmation, etc. It is not a matter of giving money or things, but a giving of oneself. This is one of the qualities—one of the virtues—that is a factor in one's capacity for friendship. We do not have to be perfect to be a friend. But the greater extent to which I am capable of generously giving of myself, the better friend I am capable of being.

Generosity, like every other good quality we have been discussing in this book, is easier when we see it modeled by the people we admire. We discover love by being loved. Living in an environment where we know that we are accepted and loved gives us the internal freedom to open ourselves to others. Providing this environment, where people feel free and feel safe, is a tremendous gift we can give to someone. This is what I mean by *creating a culture of love.* We should never underestimate the transforming power of love. Giving someone the gift of your love—by giving your time, your attention, your affirmation—can change a person's life. Whether it helps a woman who feels isolated to feel more connected, or inspires a very good man to give of himself heroically, the experience of generous love always enriches.

Experiencing Generosity and the Effect it Has on Us

Many people go through life feeling disconnected. In chapter one, I referred to a sociological study that reported twenty-five percent of the population has no one to talk to about important matters. Perhaps their experience of life would be different if the people around them generously gave of themselves and created an atmosphere of acceptance and trust.

Knowing that there are many people who feel disconnected, perhaps even people with whom we have some regular interaction, is there something we can do about this? We like to think of ourselves as being approachable and easy to talk to, genuinely caring about the people in our lives. But is that, in fact, the *environment* we create? The people who have difficulties relating typically have had insufficient and inadequate experiences of being loved. We might ask ourselves the following questions:

- What kind of atmosphere do I create with the people in my life?
- Am I creating a culture of love, an environment where people feel they can safely talk about important matters?
- Do my patterns of speaking tend to build people up?
- Do I effectively convey to my family and friends that I am genuinely interested in them?
- Can I be relied upon to keep people's secrets?

Clearly, this is not an exhaustive list. But it can spark our thinking. Some people are especially good at creating this culture of love we have been talking about. Perhaps you know people, as I do, whose way of interacting is powerfully uplifting. I can recall a lady in her nineties that, as a young priest, I would visit in the nursing home. She has long since gone to God. Visiting her was almost like making a spiritual retreat, and I always looked forward to those visits. It was always an uplifting experience for me. Her mind was alert, but her body had deteriorated to the point where she was bedfast. I think she spent the entire day in conversation with God. When I entered the room, she always seemed very happy to see me. When I would ask her how she was, she would respond with an outpouring of gratitude to God for all that he continued to do for her. She was, in fact, in physical pain all the time. She was interested in me and in my life, including the members of my family. And I knew that her interest was genuine by the fact that she would remember little details of our previous conversations. I went as a priest making a pastoral visit to the sick; yet our time together was so much more than that. I always left with the feeling that I was somehow on the receiving end. I have often thought that the holy people we read about in the *lives of the saints* must somehow have lived like she lived. I find it insightful that I cannot adequately describe my experience with this holy woman. If we can only, with difficulty, describe what holy people are like, is it any wonder that it is impossible to describe God—of which the saints are but a dim reflection? We fumble about, trying to find the right words, and in the end, we must attribute these experiences of love to the mysteriousness of God himself—who is Love.

Being in the presence of people like this is inspiring. And if we do not personally know such people, at least we can read about them. The saints were people who, one way or another, reflected the love of God in their lives. I am personally inspired by the lives of people like St. Maximilian Kolbe and Bl. Teresa of Calcutta (Mother Teresa). In their own way, in the midst of ugliness, hatred, and evil, they managed to create something beautiful. Where they did not find love, they put love. They did not escape the world, but created a culture of love that they carried with them everywhere they went.

This kind of loving, the kind we see in people like St. Maximilian Kolbe and Bl. Teresa of Calcutta (Mother Teresa), requires great inner strength. It is difficult to look at their lives and not conclude that we are too weak to love as they loved. But though we perhaps cannot love as they loved, we too can create a culture of love. God calls us to do so in the environment into which he has placed us. Married people, in particular, are called to create such an environment within their families. Those who have the vocation to celibacy, such as priests and religious sisters and brothers, are called to create such a culture of love more broadly and in a way that includes more people—such as an entire parish. And of course, regardless of our state of life, we can also create such a climate in our friendships.

While these images of generous loving are inspiring, the experience some people have of their own emotional neediness prevents them from loving in this way. One man described his emotional pain like this, "It is like having all of the fingers of your hand broken and throbbing, and then trying to go about daily life, trying not to think about it. When it hurts all the time, it is hard not to think about it." It is not that they do not want to love generously—they do. And, indeed, many emotionally needy people are quite generous. But it is often difficult for them to get their minds off of themselves. But that is precisely what they need to do. People suffering from emotional pain develop friendships just like everybody else—by having good relating habits, having a mutual interest in each other, and favorite activities where they live out their friendships. We are all wounded in one way or another. And some are wounded deeply. If they remain unable to get their attention off of themselves, no real friendship can develop. But if a genuine friendship is *established*, they then have a context in which they can, among other things, talk about their emotional pain. We talk to a friend differently than we talk to a counselor. From a counselor, we want understanding and advice. But from our friends, we want acceptance and love. We all need friends; and some need counselors. But the way we relate to each of them is very different. This is why people suffering from emotional wounds must struggle to establish genuine, vibrant friendships—just like everyone else does. Once they have been established, in the context of a friendship where they are aware that they are loved, many such people experience healing. It does not happen overnight. But love does have a healing and transforming power that enables wounds, sometimes decades old, finally to heal.

The Benefit That Comes to Us When We See Generosity in Others

Besides the experience of a loving environment, we also need to have good relating habits modeled for us. Seeing someone love heroically can inspire us to love better and to give more of ourselves. It can inspire a conversion—not a religious conversion as such, but a real change in the way we see ourselves and the way we relate to the world around us. Consider the following.

Tracy and Luke have been married for fifteen years. They married in their early twenties, and they now have a ten-year-old son. Tracy, by most standards, is a good wife and mother. But Luke, for his part, is rather self-absorbed. He genuinely wants to be good, and by in large is he is good. But he sees goodness in terms of "not doing bad things." He has never been introduced to the notion of living in the *dimension of gift*, and the concepts of generosity and self-giving have never really crossed his mind. He sees his life in terms of doing his duty. And he *does* fulfill his duties quite well. No one could accuse him of not doing what he was "supposed to do." At this stage in his life it would require something dramatic to significantly change the way he looks at life. His patterns of thinking, judging, and respond-ing are well established by now.

Sometimes dramatic events do happen that prompt a real change in one's way of thinking. Getting back to our couple, suppose their ten-year-old suffers from kidney failure and has to receive hemodial-ysis three times a week. They live in an out-of-the-way place so they have to travel some distance to do this. The father, Luke, usually takes their son, but this has been going on for six months now, and Luke is becoming embittered by it all. He is not mad at anyone, neither God nor his son, but he resents the imposition this has had on his life. It is evident in his personality, and he is increasingly irritable.

Over time, Luke and his son recognize the other patients and the family members who accompany them for their treatments. Luke is particularly struck by one of the dads who is there with his daugh-ter. There is a serenity about him, and he has a cheerful way of in-teracting with her. As the two fathers converse while the children have their treatments, this other father communicates to Luke that while he is often frustrated by the feeling of powerlessness over his daughter's illness, he nevertheless tries to use it as an opportunity to be generous with her and to give her extra attention, since her treatments require her to miss out on peer interaction at school. He says, "It is not that I do anything spectacular; I just try to make her feel special. Because she *is* special—she is special to *me*."

Luke is intrigued by this and somewhat inspired. There is an opportunity here for conversion. His being moved by the apparent selflessness of this other father may prompt him to rethink some of his own way of thinking and evaluating. Like all the opportunities and grace-filled moments in life, Luke may *see* the opportunity and the beauty of another way of approaching life, but in the end he will have to *choose* to respond. It will not happen automatically. As this story illustrates, we can discover new and better ways of relating by witnessing generosity in others.

Friendships between Men and Women

What about friendships between men and women? Is it even possible for a man and a woman to *just be friends*? Of course they can. And I am not referring to those friendships that resemble the mother/son or father/daughter relationship. But men and women, who wish to remain friends in a non-erotic relationship, must understand the way the different loves interact with each other. We need to look at the boundary between friendship and *eros*. Recall that when I use the word "*eros*," I am using the word generically. It refers to the entire category of romance and the interaction between people who are "in love." *Intimacy*, or the sharing of one's life in a personal way, does not presume the presence of *eros*. There is, for example, the intimacy of friendship, which we will explore in subsequent chapters.

Male–Female Interaction in General

Before we look at the difference between friendship and *eros*, let us look first at affection and *eros*. Both of them are a particular way of feeling and experiencing a person. These two loves, affection and *eros*, seem to be ways of responding to internal stimuli in ways that friendship and charity are not. It is as though we experience affection or *eros* welling up within us. Friendship and charity both require an active participation on our part, and the engagement of our free will. You cannot be friends with someone *against your will*, but you can be attracted to someone or fall in love against your will. We can imagine someone saying, "I wish this were not happening, but I think I am falling in love with her." But it would be very odd to say, "I wish this were not happening, but we are becoming friends." That is because friendship imposes duties—duties that are freely and willingly assumed. This is the free will element of friendship, and we assume those duties because we choose to. It is not something that spontaneously happens to us.

A moment ago, I said that the experience of *eros* is a response to internal stimuli. Someone can say or do something that strikes a chord within us, and we experience the stirrings of erotic, romantic love. It can be slight, or great, or anywhere in between. Sometimes a person will intentionally try to elicit such a response, as for example, a man looking into a woman's eyes and telling her she is beautiful. But reactions can be difficult to predict, and not every "smooth move" gets the desired response. And sometimes we elicit a response unintentionally. It is all part of the mysteriousness of the human person and interpersonal interaction.

Now, we know, of course, that there is a difference between friendship and *eros*. We certainly experience them differently. But beyond our internal experience, what is the difference between friendship and erotic, romantic love?

Lewis wrote in *The Four Loves*, that lovers stand face-to-face, friends stand side-by-side. Erotic love (the committed type of which good marriages are made) entails one person saying to another, "I want my life, in a certain sense, to be about you. Much of what I will do, I will do for you—we will make and live our lives together." Using the language of vocation, we would say that the other person becomes a primary focus of one's life. A husband, cooperating with the loving plan of God, organizes his life around his wife. They do not just live *with* each other—they live *for* each other. In their thinking and choosing, spouses look to do more than *please* their spouses; they *serve* their spouses in a way that helps them become the person they are capable of being. A good husband does his part to help his wife become a good wife and mother. And she does the same for him, helping him to become a good husband and father. They want everything they do to build up their family, fulfilling their responsibility to build up the Kingdom of God. This is what I mean in saying they live for each other, and in saying they stand face-to-face.

In friendship, people walk side-by-side. They share with each other their joys and sorrows. Depending on the depth of the friendship, they may reveal their deepest secrets to their friend. But our friends are not the *primary* focus of our lives. Our lives are not *about* them in the way that spouses' lives are about each other. This helps us see why it is so important that we understand the concept of *vocation* and come to see our own specific vocation. It is what God calls us to do with our lives. Our friends are part of it, but not in the same way as our spouses. So the difference between friendship and erotic love is not a matter of greater or lesser closeness—rather it is *a different kind of closeness* that is based on the fundamental orientation of our life.

Many people who are not yet married are still in the process of sorting out what it is that they are to do with their lives. Some unmarried people, such as priests and religious sisters and brothers, have committed themselves to celibacy for the sake of the Kingdom of God. Celibate priests are not bachelors; they are committed and promised to another. The primary focus of a priest's vocation is to be the spiritual father of the people entrusted to his care. Friends play an important role in his life as they do in any person's life. Within the life of a priest, as in the life of a married person, friendships are indeed an important aspect of his vocation—but not the primary focus.

Discerning an Ethic

So let us put all this together in a way that enables us to see an ethic for interaction between men and woman who are just friends. If two people wish to keep their relationship at the level of friendship, several safeguards need to be in place. They should not say or do things that are likely to elicit an erotic response. And if they notice an erotic response developing in themselves, they should not pursue it—not even in their own minds. This is what spiritual writers mean by the phrase "keeping custody of one's heart." If they do not want a romantic relationship to develop, they should not daydream about what a romantic or erotic relationship might be like.

So let us imagine four friends, Felicity, Todd, Matt, and Karen. They work together, and they have the three essential elements of friendship. Namely, they have good relating skills; they are all mutually interested in each other; and they enjoy their work, which is the way they live out and experience their friendship.

Matt and Karen each have a spouse. Todd seriously dated a girl named Tanya for about a year, but that relationship has recently ended. Felicity is not dating, but is interested in pursuing such a relationship with Todd, now that he is no longer in a committed relationship.

Matt very much enjoys the company of Felicity and Karen. They have a great working relationship, and they have a lot of fun together. Sometimes Matt and his wife do things socially with them. When Matt interacts with Felicity and with Karen, because he is a married man, he is careful to speak and act appropriately. He does not want to give the impression that he is looking for his relationship with Felicity and Karen to be something more than friendship. He happens to think both of them are attractive, but he does not let his mind pursue romantic or erotic possibilities. He knows that nothing good could come from such musing.

As for Felicity, she and Todd have been friends for a long time, and she had always hoped that circumstances would enable her relationship with Todd to develop into more than friendship. While she had the inklings of a romantic relationship with Todd, she resisted the desire to permit it to develop. Even in her own mind, she resisted the interior promptings of erotic love because she knew that such a relationship was not possible at the time because of Todd's relationship with Tanya.

It is commonly done, but is it appropriate to attempt to woo or steal away a person who is already in a romantic relationship? (Some television shows make it out to be some sort of game to be played, a game of catch-as-catch-can.) Committed relationships entail some sort of promise. The highest of these is the commitment of marriage, wherein one makes a solemn vow that reaches far into the future—"until death do us part." Engagement entails a promise to marry, but it is not an absolute promise. People sometimes break off an engagement, and they can be justified in doing so. When a couple is dating, they make a commitment to each other—the commitment not to date anyone else. The commitment reaches into the future, but not very far into the future. Their promise is for the foreseeable future. Both parties know that the relationship may be terminated.

Felicity might have thought to herself, "Todd would be much happier with me than he is with Tanya. I will pursue a relationship, and Todd can decide for himself." And maybe Todd *would* be happier with Felicity. But she finds it distasteful to try to break up an established relationship. And her decision is made, in part, because of her *friendship* with Todd. Now that Todd is no longer in a relationship, Felicity is interested in pursuing one. And Todd will have to decide whether he is presently interested in entering into a dating relationship, and whether he is interested in doing so with Felicity.

If we look carefully at the experience itself, we see that while both affection and *eros* can be, as it were, harnessed or restrained, it is always something other than affection or *eros* that does the harnessing or restraining. Affection cannot hold itself back. Neither can *eros*. But they can be restrained by something else. (They can also be pushed forward, where they do not really want to go—like when your mother made you give Uncle Charlie a kiss, a token of affection that you would have rather skipped.) The fact that the loves of affection and *eros* can be restrained or held down is an important principle.

But it is not just their *external expression* that can be restrained; their internal experience can be restrained too. When two people have the potential for having a romantic interest in each other, they might simply let *eros* develop on its own—or they might choose not to let that happen.

So men and women can have close, meaningful friendships—relationships that are not a watered-down version of erotic love. With prudence, refinement, and a healthy dose of common sense, we can enjoy lifelong friendships with members of the opposite sex.

Friendship and Evangelization

The word "evangelization" means different things to different people. The most basic, fundamental meaning of the word is to proclaim the Gospel by one's words and by one's life. Being a priest, I am in the evangelization business. But the work of evangelization is both the right and the obligation of all the baptized. All are called to labor in the Lord's vineyard, but the way in which we do so varies from vocation to vocation.

Many people, when they think of evangelization, think of traveling to a far-off land where the people have never heard the Gospel. That is one kind of evangelization, and some in the Church have that calling. But we do not need to go to a far-away place. And evangelization is not limited to those who have never before heard the Gospel. It is about communicating the love of the Father, the Son, and the Holy Spirit to the people we encounter in our daily lives—especially to those closest to us. Charity begins at home.

When people have the experience that they are loved, appreciated, and valued, something powerful happens in their lives. It gives them the ability and the desire to open themselves more fully. It is the experience of giving and receiving love, which is the opposite experience of being withdrawn and isolated. We need not go far to do this. It can happen right in our own backyards, in our living rooms, or at work. When we are in an environment where we feel accepted and appreciated, we are disposed to opening our hearts and sharing our personal stories. This is an ideal context for sharing our faith. Friends often talk about personal matters and the things most important to them. If our relationship with God is important to us, we will not be afraid to talk about it. We talk about everything else, why not talk about that?

Sometimes evangelization is done by one who is in a position of authority, such as the day-to-day activity of a priest or a teacher. It is done in a different way when it occurs among friends. In that context, it is not a matter of preaching or teaching, but of sharing. We relate what our relationship with God means to us. In those moments, we let our friends see *why* we live our lives the way we do. Our friends know us; our good friends know us well. They see what we are like, for better or worse, in season and out. In the difficult times, the authenticity of one's faith is seen for what it is. We do not have to be living heroically good lives to be effective evangelizers. Whether we are novices, or have spent many years in the Lord's vineyard, there is a real value in sharing our faith with our friends. St. Josemaria Escriva put it this way:

> You have had the good fortune to find real teachers, authentic friends, who have taught you everything you wanted to know without holding back. You have had no need to employ any tricks to *steal* their knowledge, because they led you along the easiest path, even though it had cost them a lot of hard work and suffering to discover it. Now, it is your turn to do the same, with one person, and another—with everyone.[51]

Some of the greatest work of evangelization can be done with the people closest to us. They can experience the love of God through our love for them. Perhaps this could serve as a motivation to try to be a better friend to the people in my life. Even if our friendship skills are finely tuned, we could all improve. No one is a perfect friend. It might not be a matter of doing *more*, but of doing some things *better*. Throughout this book we have been looking at the virtues that make for good friendships, such as attentiveness, responsiveness, generosity, and loyalty, just to name a few. If we were to make even a slight improvement, it can be experienced by the people in our lives as an even greater, richer culture of love.

Questions for Philosophical Consideration and Personal Growth

1. What can friends or spouses do (or avoid doing) to increase the sympathy in their relationships?

2. Suppose you have a co-worker that you have known for many years. You like each other and trust each other, but your co-worker is moody. At this point, you have simply accepted the fact that this is the way he or she is. But you can tell that your co-worker is a lonely person. If the opportunity presented itself, how might you address this issue with him or her?

   What if it is not a co-worker, but your son or daughter? What if it is your spouse? How might you address this issue?

   If someone close to you thought you were moody, would you want this pointed out to you?

3. Think of the people whom you encounter in your daily life. What specifically (if anything) do you do to communicate "You matter to me"? Can you think of some people whom you know who are particularly good at this? How might you begin to pattern some of your interaction after theirs?

4. What role does affection play in a friendship? What about in marriage and family life?

   Some people suffer from a chronic inability to communicate affection—even to their own children. Why do you think this is? In your judgment, what effect does this have on the children over the long term?

5. What does it mean to say that affection, on the pyramid of loves, is *higher* than friendship—and that friendship is more *foundational*?

6. Give examples of the following:
   - Affection elevating *eros*
   - Affection securing *eros*
   - Friendship elevating *eros*
   - Friendship elevating affection
   - Friendship securing affection
   - Friendship securing *eros*
   - Charity elevating *eros*

- Charity elevating affection
- Charity elevating friendship
- Charity securing affection
- Charity securing friendship
- Charity securing *eros*

7. How would you explain to someone that our loves are freer to be what they are capable of being, not when they stand alone, but when they are secured by other loves, especially charity?

8. Though we have heard it said it many times, *why* is it better (more noble) to give than to receive?

9. When speaking with others, do your patterns of speech build people up? Or are you one who perpetually corrects whatever is said?

   When someone shares good news with you, how do you respond? Do you share their joy? Or are you dismissive? Do you typically find something negative to point out?

   How do you communicate to others that you are genuinely interested in them? Of all the people in your life, which ones are particularly good listeners? What makes you think that? How do they let you know they are really *hearing* you? What about you? What would others say about your listening skills?

   How frequently do you communicate approval to the people in your life? What specifically do you do to communicate approval? When was the last time you did this?

   All of this speaks to the issue of the kind of atmosphere you create with the people in your life. Suppose you were going to make one or two resolutions regarding these matters. What would they be?

10. Having good relating habits modeled for us is important. Who are the people that, in your opinion, have ways of relating that you would like to model? In particular, what do you find inspiring?

11. What would you consider to be appropriate interaction between your spouse and someone of the opposite sex? What would you consider inappropriate?

12. Think of the great evangelizers of history. Naturally, what made them great evangelizers was the grace of God. But what were they like *humanly*? What do you suppose their relational

skills were like? When, for example, Pope John Paul II had dinner with the members of the Pontifical household, how do you suppose he interacted with them? What insights can you draw regarding friendship and evangelization?

Chapter Five

The Intimacy of Friendship

We embrace very many with every affection,
but yet in such a way that we do not admit them
to the secrets of friendship,
which consists especially in the revelation
of all our confidences and plans.
Whence it is that the Lord in the Gospel says:
"I no longer call you servants but friends";
and then adding the reason
for which they are considered worthy
of the name of friend:
"because all things,
whatsoever I have heard of my Father,
I have made known to you."
And in another place Jesus says:
"You are my friends,
if you do the things that I command you."
From these words, as St. Ambrose says,
"He gives the formula of friendship for us to follow:
namely, that we do the will of our friend,
that we disclose to our friend
whatever confidences we have in our hearts,
and that we not be ignorant of his confidences."

From *Spiritual Friendship*[52]
St. Aelred of Rievalux, Twelfth Century

What Is Intimacy?

As we continue our conversation about friendship, about the relationship between two people who genuinely care about each other, we turn now to the topic of intimacy. In a certain sense this book, more than anything else, is about intimacy. When any two people enter into each other's lives in such a way that the experience for each of them is not "I" and "thou," but rather "we," they have at some level established intimacy. We know that we cannot be fulfilled by ourselves. Only by mutually entering into the life of another, or others, will that love for which we were made begin to be realized in us.

The word *intimate* comes from the Latin word *intimus*, which is the superlative of *intus*, meaning "within." *Intimus* is that which is deepest within me. Intimacy is about sharing your life and letting another see what you are really like on the inside—your joys and hopes, your fears and anxieties. The idea of letting someone get to know me "on the inside" can be frightening inasmuch as it makes me vulnerable. But this interpersonal sharing of people's lives is what gives depth to our loving. It is part of our human nature that we desire to be loved, to be accepted, and to be appreciated. If I am to be loved deeply, I must let myself be deeply known. This is what intimacy is all about.

Intimacy, properly speaking, is more than an emotion. It is a spiritual reality inasmuch as it involves the union of two persons. The degree to which two people are intimate with each other is measured in terms of how much they enter into and share each other's lives. If we open ourselves to each other, we know how the other thinks and feels. If we can reveal the secrets of our hearts to each other without fear, and if this relationship has endured over time, then we have an intimate relationship. There will be moments when this intimacy will be felt—moments when I *feel* particularly close to you. It is an experience of oneness, of union, of *interpersonal* union, and this experience of intimacy is a profoundly positive one. Some would argue it is *the most positive experience one can have*. "I feel connected with the one I love. I am not alone."

But the intimacy itself is something larger than the *feeling* of intimacy. When two people intimately share their lives the relationship is, in fact, an intimate one. Sometimes the intimacy is felt, and at other times it is not. A few parallels may help to illustrate this.

There is a difference between *being* sick and *feeling* sick. Suppose you wake up in the morning, and you just do not feel right. The barometric pressure is low and you did not get as much sleep as you needed. You are not sick; you just do not feel very well. Compare that with the man who feels fine but has some peculiar symptoms. He goes to the doctor and is told he has cancer. He feels fine, but he is not fine. He is sick.

A mother gets a phone call at midnight from her son who is calling from the county jail. He has been arrested for drunken driving. The mother is angry, she is hurt, she is embarrassed. She does not love her son any less at this moment, but she does not *feel* particularly close to him *right now*.

It works the other way too. Two people can relate physically, sexually, in a very intimate manner and in a way that carries with it very highly charged intimate feelings. Yet there may be very little true intimacy between them. It feels very intimate, but the feeling is an illusion. There is an insight here. What we want is real intimacy.

People differ in the way they communicate and experience intimacy. It seems that some of this is determined by one's temperament, as well as by one's maturity and life experiences. Some connect very quickly with people. They are inclined to trust and to communicate freely. We get to know them much more quickly than those who are more reticent and taciturn. It may take a long time to get to know them because they are not inclined to reveal much of themselves, at least not right away. But, generally, the more one experiences acceptance and love, and the less one has the feeling of fear and anxiety, it is increasingly likely that he or she will be open to the self-revelation that is integral to intimacy.

The sense of connecting with another can be experienced in a variety of ways. It can happen through our conversations, or in the things friends do together. When a friendship is firmly established, any common activity they do together has a way of uniting the friends. This is true of spouses as well. Suppose it is Memorial Day weekend. Jake and Anne spend the day working outside in the yard, mowing the lawn, trimming the hedge, and planting flowers for the summer. The nature of their activity was not, in itself, intimate. But two things enabled them to experience solidarity. First, a foundation had already been established in their relationship—in this case, they are happily married. Secondly, they had the sense that they were doing something *together*, not simply doing things at the same time.

In a relationship, people experience the unity of intimacy by being aware that they each, to one degree or another, assumed responsibility for the other. They have a shared history and will share an anticipated future. This plays a large role in people feeling connected with one another. Even when people have rather infrequent contact, strong bonds forged years ago can continue to bind them together. It is not just our past that binds us; we also are connected to people by our confidence about our relational future. As I look at my life, imagining how each of us will continue to assume the responsibilities of friendship—that awareness of our future gives me a sense of our unity here and now. This is clearly the case in the commitment-for-life of a husband and wife.

At the beginning of this section we saw that the word "intimate" comes from a word meaning "within." It is essential to intimacy that, in some way, I communicate to you the matters of my heart—and that you respond appropriately. We communicate a great deal through bodily language—through a pat on the back, playful activity, a hug, a kiss, or love making. And the things we do *for* each other communicate our love as well. But the ones who really seem to flourish in their intimate relating also have the ability to communicate their love verbally. Conversation is an important part of intimacy. Not surprisingly, those who have difficulty communicating verbally often experience relational inadequacy as a result, wondering whether their loved-ones really know just how much they are loved.

How Does Intimacy Develop?

There are things we can discover about a person by having a five-minute, causal conversation. This is the knowledge we have of our acquaintances—the people with whom we are *acquainted* but with whom we have no relationship, not even companionship. Companions are more than acquaintances. We know them better. Our companions are our classmates, teammates, co-workers, and neighbors. They are the people who simply happen to be in our lives. We may see each other very often—even daily. Companions who are co-workers know about each other's work, whether they are married, how many kids they have, and where they like to vacation. They have a general understanding of each other's personalities and may have a casual knowledge of the things that are happening in each other's lives—the kind of information one might share in the employee lunchroom. But they have not chosen to share their lives very deeply with these people. This is why they have remained companions but are not (yet) friends. Our friends, on the other hand, are distinguished from our companions in that we let our friends get to know us personally and privately. We tell them things about ourselves that they otherwise would not know, and the degree to which we do this is a significant indicator of the depth of our relationships.

Intimacy is about trust and trust takes time. It does not develop overnight. Imagine that you were going to go on vacation for a month. If you have some neighbors you do not trust, you will hope they do not notice that you are gone, and you certainly would not advertise the fact that you will be away. You would not want the message on your answering machine to say, "Hi, I will be gone for the month of July . . ." You would just be asking for trouble. Some people cannot be trusted with that kind of information, and if they have it they may well use it against you. But there are others that you *do* trust. You tell them of your vacation plans and ask them to keep an eye on your home. You might give a key to a trusted neighbor of many years, asking him or her to look in every few days. One who is in your innermost group of friends, what some call an "*intimo*," could come and go as he or she pleases.

Now suppose a family moved in next door and has been living there for a couple of months. You may have spent time with them, and your children may go to school together and play together. But to give them a key to the house would be imprudent. This relationship with the new family next door has not been "time tested." They may seem like nice enough people, but looks can be deceiving. Some dishonest people make a very good impression. And even people who do not intend to do harm can, at times, hurt people by their poor judgment or lack of attention. The things in my heart are much more valuable than the things in my house, and if it will take time to trust you with the latter it will certainly take time to trust you with the former.

Recall that we have seen a "relational continuum" that has the stranger at one end, and those closest to us at the other, as illustrated below.

Stranger	Acquaintance	Companion	Casual Friend	Friend	Dear Friend

Intimacy begins here, and increases
as one moves to the right.

- "Strangers" are people we have never met, though we may recognize them.
- A relationship begins when we first meet a person, or as we used to say, "make their acquaintance."
  We have met them, but they do not have enough of a role in our lives to qualify as a "companion."
- The arrow pointing to the right indicates that, in theory, there is no limit to how close two people
  can become.

By definition, the relationship of companions is not an intimate one. That is why they are companions and not yet friends. Once there begins to be sharing of personal information, once one begins to share his or her life in a personal and private way, the two people begin a casual friendship. The friendship is a causal one because the information, while private, is not terribly deep; and there is not yet the mutual, personal commitment that is characteristic of genuine friendship. Both companionship and casual friendship can develop into a deeper friendship, an intimate friendship, if certain things fall into place. These things often do not fall into place. But when they do, it is because the individuals involved have both the ability and the desire for such a relationship. That will only happen when they trust each other and are willing, at some level, to reveal themselves to each other and to affirm each other. If we look at the number of people that are a part of our lives—and for some that is hundreds or even thousands of people—there are comparatively few to whom we give the gift of intimate friendship. These are the people with whom we share our lives. We are *there for them*, and we want them to be there for us. We experience joy and freedom in our interacting. When we think about them and the role they have in our lives, our attitude toward them is "It is good that you exist."

The first ones with whom we have an intimate relationship are our parents or primary caregivers. They help the child feel safe and loved. The intimacy experienced in pre-adolescent childhood is not characterized by intimate conversations as much as it is by the trust and confidence that produces the general sense that *I am at home in the family home*; I am wanted, valued, and protected by mom and dad. They support me and keep me safe. If the home environment is "normal enough," this relating with mom and dad goes smoothly.

The typical boy or girl is not aware that this is going on, nor should they be. In their minds it is just "regular life." Their minds are occupied with the various and sundry things that occupy the mind of a child.

Peers, including siblings, enter one's life in childhood. Peer relationships in childhood affect how one relates intimately later in life. No one has a storybook life. Our lives do not begin "Once upon a time," and they do not end "and we all lived happily ever after." Bumps and bruises are part and parcel of every life. With that being said, it is nevertheless a fact that a child's experience of life includes the general sense of either being accepted by his peers or rejected by them. We do not need to be accepted by everyone—but we need acceptance from a few. We all want to know that we fit in somewhere and have some group that we can call our own. When this does not happen, a sense of sadness and personal inferiority can develop, which will later make intimate relating difficult. Peer relationships affect the way I think about myself. To a large degree, those around us tell us who we are. If my experience is one of rejection, I will then, as it were, position myself accordingly, becoming actively or passively defensive. Perhaps you have noticed people who, in their relating with others, are always defensive. They have the sense, rightly or wrongly, that they are not accepted by those around them. They put up an invisible wall around themselves that prevents them from being hurt—but one that also keeps them isolated. As long as that protective wall stays up, they will not experience intimacy. For many, emotional healing is necessary, without which their persistent fear of rejection will prevent them from letting people very deeply into their lives.

Our view of who we are and how we can relate to others changes with the onset of adolescence. Before adolescence, life was much simpler. The most profound changes that accompany this period are not biological but relational. Eighth graders see friendship differently than fourth graders. A fourth grader (who is typically nine-years-old) sees friendship more or less in terms of having a playmate. "We do fun things together." The change from fourth to eighth grade brings with it a new understanding of what it means to be a friend, and what it means to be loyal and to keep another's secrets. The thirteen-year-old is very new at the game, but the capacity for intimacy is budding.

The growth in the next four years is equally dramatic, as evidenced by the late teens' growth in self-understanding. They are beginning to have a sense of what it means to share their lives and what it means to let someone into their hearts. They have secrets, and they share them both with same-sex and opposite-sex friends, and they expect their secrets to be kept. This is an important time, because if these first experiences of sharing themselves go well—if they work through the awkwardness of *revealing* and *receiving* personal information, and they keep each other's secrets—then they will be in a position to continue that kind of intimate, personal relating. But if these first attempts at opening up do not go well, if their experiences are ones of being betrayed or humiliated, they may find themselves, as it were, *gun shy* and unwilling to take that risk again.

The period of youth is an important time in one's life—a treasure—when childhood is left behind and the full maturity of adulthood has yet to be reached. Pope John Paul II wrote in his *Letter to Youth*, "The period of youth is the time of a particularly intense discovery of the human 'I' and of the properties and capacities connected with it."[53] It is a time when there is a particular desire for meaning in life. And it is a time when people realize that the path of life runs alongside and, indeed, is inseparable from the path that is the life of the other persons whom God has put into their own lives.

In the world of interpersonal relating, some bloom early, some bloom late, and a few never bloom at all. Certainly one would expect to see some capacity for intimacy by the time one is a high school senior. But many are out of high school before they begin relating in this way—either because the ability to relate this way is still undeveloped, because they are afraid, or because they simply are not yet interested in it. Most people realize at some point, however, that they could share what is going on in their private lives with someone else. These first steps into interpersonal relating can cause more than a little anxiety. Relating intimately is an art, and like all such things it does not always go well on one's first few attempts. But when it does go well, it brings with it its own reward—the experience of sharing one's life. Perhaps it is the high school boy who tells his teammate he is saddened that his father does not come to watch him play, or the college girl who admits to a friend that she has an eating disorder. When private information is revealed and is received positively, people have the experience that their lives have been shared. They have started to let someone into their lives. They are no longer alone.

Such sharing is an experience of *interpersonal union*, of intimacy, of closeness. But it is just a start, and there are many more skills yet to be acquired. One must learn when such conversations are appropriate, how much should be revealed, and to whom. We learn as we go. If we make the mistake of revealing too much information at once, the listener may feel overwhelmed and not know how to respond. If we have something particularly delicate to discuss, it is a good idea to prepare the listener by saying something like, "I have something that weighs heavily on my mind, something rather personal, and I would like to talk to you about it if that is okay." The conversations we have where we share our personal lives need not be emotionally intense or dramatic. They need not be long conversations. What makes them intimate is the fact that I tell you something about my life that I consider personal and private—something I tell to few others. We also learn by experience that some people cannot be trusted with personal information—they blab. Sometimes it is done innocently or inadvertently. Other times it is done maliciously. Either way, we learn whom we can talk to and whom we cannot.

By the early twenties, it is common to have established the habit of interpersonal, intimate relating, though people differ in their capacity and desire for it. College seniors, twenty-one-year-olds, should be able to distinguish a friend from a companion, though they likely do not use this vocabulary. They know that the many people with whom they interact in the dorm and in class are not, properly speaking, "friends," though some of them are. They should further understand that among those that *are* their friends, these friendships exist in varying degrees, from the casual friend to the very close personal friend. How much will they reveal? That depends on a number of factors. One's capacity for intimacy is a big factor, but even when there is the *capacity* for it, I still must desire it, and I must desire to relate in this way with some specific person. This "specific person" must in turn be open to such relating and reciprocate in some way. If you do not in some way reciprocate, in some way open up to me, then you are more like my counselor than my friend. Yet when there is reciprocity, the intimacy and experience of *union* between the two people grows. It builds upon itself, and if I feel safe and supported, I am inclined to reveal more.

From the very beginning of this process, discernment is taking place. How much do I trust you? How much do I like you and sense a certain connection with you? To what extent do I want to share my life with you? As a relationship unfolds, I begin to experience a sense of union with the other. It comes about because I sense, in certain important ways, that we understand each other and feel accepted by each other. You are interested in me and in my life, and I am interested in you. We can speak freely with each other.

With the passage of time, as the years go by, the intimacy can continue to deepen. Relationships never go perfectly smoothly, and the manner in which the bumps along the way are handled determines how close the two will ultimately become. In theory, there is no limit to it. One could think of two sisters who since childhood have shared everything about themselves, and who do so happily and eagerly. Some are blessed with that friend who is like their "other self." Husbands and wives should view this as an ideal to strive for, even as they see that they have much room for growth, and should not be discouraged by the fact that their love is seldom what it might be.

The *interpersonal union* for which we long takes time to develop. If we are patient, if we struggle to overcome our fears and anxieties, and if we are willing to "put out into the deep and let down our net for a catch,"[54] then Jesus—who gives us our friends—will put people into our lives. It is something worth praying for.

Nobility of Life Is Required for Intimacy

By "nobility" I do not mean highbrow or aristocratic, but a certain goodness of life without which friendship cannot even take root, much less flourish. When the ancients spoke of friendship, they did so in the context of virtue. Josef Pieper once wrote, "Virtue is the utmost of what a man can be; it is the realization of the human capacity for being."[55] Virtue is not a guarantee of friendship, and it is not a guarantee of the experience of intimacy. But without virtue, sustained intimacy will elude us.

Sustained intimacy presupposes a number of virtues. While much of what follows is simply common sense, the presence of these virtues is not as common as it might be. When virtues are present, our lives begins to resemble the divine; when they are missing, it is barely human.

Selflessness is part of a virtuous, noble life. On the continuum that has self*ish*ness at one end and self*less*ness at the other, it is not hard to see where the noble man or woman spends most of his or her time. It is rare to find someone who is selfless nearly all the time, though such people do in fact exist. Perhaps you are blessed to have a few of them in your life. We would all like to think of ourselves as selfless, and most of us have moments when indeed we are. Yet it is part of our fallen human condition that we are susceptible to putting our own interests and desires ahead of others, and some do this habitually. To the extent that I put myself first and my life is marked with a general self-centeredness, I will necessarily struggle to make and keep intimate relationships. Why is this? Because at the root of genuine love is the authentic commitment people make to each other, and not merely the pursuit of one's own interests.

Honesty

The first of these virtues is honesty. I list honesty first because if we are going to have any kind of personal relationship, I have to be able to trust you. I have to believe what you say and believe that your intentions are sincere. One who is honest is a person of conscience and a person of principles. Credibility inspires trust. These are integral aspects of one's personality, and in a particular way determine who a person is. This fundamental attitude toward truth, which is developed in childhood, limits the field of potential candidates for one's friendship. Parents are well advised to establish a culture or climate of truth and honesty in their homes, where mothers and fathers speak honestly with their children and parents appropriately punish their children for not telling the truth. (In many homes, conscientious parents punish their children more for lying than for the infraction the child lied about.)

If we think back on the days of our childhood, perhaps we can recall, with a greater or lesser degree of clarity, those who were our earliest classmates. There were some that we kept away from—not because of their personalities—but because we did not trust them. We may even have said to ourselves, "Mom would not let me go to his house." Whether consciously or not, we size people up when we meet them, and the criteria we use in our assessment says as much about us as it does about them. We look at the way they have chosen to live their lives, and we discern whether we want them to be a part of our own lives. As moral theologians say, "We determine ourselves to be the persons we are by the choices we make." At the deepest and most profound level of our personhood, whether we are noble or ignoble, whether we are great saints or miserable wretches, or whether—like most people—we are somewhere in between, we are who we are because that is who we *choose* to be. People are honest by choice.

Honesty, like many virtues, is seen most distinctly when life is not going well. What is a person like when she is stressed, when she feels as though she is in a pressure cooker? At that moment (as far as honesty goes), you see one's true colors. If there is a degree of duplicity in one's way of relating—one fudges the data or tells an outright lie—one will not attract honest friends. One may have plenty of companions or a certain semblance of friendship with others who are similarly dishonest. Discovering that someone is less than honest inclines one to maintain a cautious distance in personal relating. We do not trust people who do not tell the truth.

Loyalty

Related to honesty is the virtue of loyalty. When we are loyal to people, we take their side and we stay on their side. I do not have to agree with you to be loyal to you.

Perhaps you have met people who always seem to agree with everything that is said, including negative things said about others. You might well wonder what they really think. Rather than honestly saying what they think, they go along with whatever is said, in a superficial spirit of friendliness. But being loyal to you means I will not speak ill of you, nor let others do so in my presence. Sometimes we need to be straightforward with people who are speaking ill of our friends and simply say something like, "Dan is a friend of mine—I think we should talk about something else."

Tact and discretion are important virtues as well. In both personal and professional relationships, learning to express disagreement in appropriate ways is an invaluable skill. Those who have not acquired this skill or who only practice it at rudimentary levels will suffer because of it, and they will make others suffer along with them. People who love each other can and do disagree and disagree strongly, even loudly. If two friends cannot express disagreement without fear of rejection, their friendship is still at an elementary level. Learning how to express disagreement in a respectful and helpful way is a fundamental, basic relating skill. We may need to look at the way we respond to people when we disagree with them, when we are tired, or when we are angry or frustrated.

Being honest with people does not mean that we must express every thought that comes to mind. Someone once said: "God gave us two ears and one mouth—we should take the hint."

Sharing Each Others' Sorrows and Joys

When we love people, we share our lives and experience *intimacy*. In a particular way, we share each with one another our joys and sorrows. Even small children do this. *I am happier because you are happy with me.* This is a phenomenon that remains all through life. St. Paul said, "Bear one another's burdens, and so fulfill the law of Christ."[56] When another helps us to shoulder our crosses, it lessens our burdens and lightens our loads. Not everyone can speak eloquently or find just the right words for every occasion (which is why we often let greeting cards do the talking for us). But we communicate as much in the tone of our voices and the looks in our eyes as we do with the words themselves. Even if "just the right words" seem to escape us, our attentive presences, the looks in our eyes, and the tone of our voices communicate more than we may realize.

Simply knowing I am in the presence of someone who loves me diminishes my sorrow, for at least I know that I am not alone. In Our Lord's final hours he was betrayed by Judas, thrice denied by St. Peter and abandoned by every other Apostle save one. It must have been a tremendous comfort to Our Lord to have St. John there with him at the foot of the Cross along with Our Lady. Both Mary and St. John must surely have had a sense of helplessness, of impotence, wanting to do more—wanting to do *something*—for the one they loved. Simply their presence there did a great deal. Simon of Cyrene helped Jesus to carry his Cross, but so, in a different way, did his Mother and St. John. Having a friend that stands with us in our time of sadness is a great gift. When our friends stand by us in our time of sadness, our love and appreciation for them grows exponentially. This attentiveness gives our intimate relationships a certain charm because it is a way of communicating "You are an important part of my life. You matter to me."

The Pursuit of Generous Loving Is More of a Process Than a Goal

Different images come to mind when we think of loving with a noble and generous love. One such image is given by St. Paul in his First Letter to the Corinthians. He wrote,

> Love is patient and kind; love is not jealous or boastful; it is not arrogant or rude. Love does not insist on its own way; it is not irritable or resentful; it does not rejoice at wrong, but rejoices in the right. Love bears all things, believes all things, hopes all things, endures all things. Love never ends.[57]

Looking at St. Paul's words, and reflecting on all the things that go into the making of a noble life, one could ask, "Who could ever do all these things and do them well?" No one does them perfectly, but with effort and struggle we can all love a little better than we do now. I find it helpful to use the analogy of a committed athlete. Ask college or professional athletes if they are satisfied with their games. They are extremely gifted athletes and they perform well. But they are *never* satisfied with their performances. The true athlete is always striving to improve his or her game and will never rest in the pursuit of excellence. They are aware of the fact that they are talented, yet at the same time they know their performances and execution could always be better. That is exactly the attitude we want to have in our interpersonal relating. We know that we do some things well—perhaps very well. But if our goal is to love in the way St. Paul describes, if we desire to be heroic in our loving, we must continually strive to love better and to live in a more virtuous manner. It is a matter of coming to the sober realization that loving is difficult, especially loving well, but I can improve the quality of my relating and may even someday love heroically. But I will never do so without serious effort and that "dying to myself" repeatedly mentioned in the Gospel. One can be motivated in the struggle by remembering that the greatest gift you can give to someone is the gift of a better *you*.

Six College Seniors—An Illustration

People experience intimacy on a variety of levels. And, for a variety of reasons, we also experience alienation. Both of these manifest themselves in different ways, but most especially in the way we try to relate to others. In the following illustration, six college seniors live in the same dorm, and they interact with each other with varying degrees of intimacy. Their names are: Frank, Ed, Dan, Chuck, Brian and Andrew; and the story shows varying levels of intimate relating. For the sake of simplicity, in the stories below they are listed alphabetically, with each succeeding person having a greater capacity for intimacy than the previous. Frank has the least capacity for intimacy, while Andrew has the greatest.

These men have known each other since their freshman year, and all six of them were accepted to the university on their own academic merits. Frank and Brian are the brightest of the group, while Dan has to work very hard to compete academically at this level. The other three—Ed, Chuck, and Andrew—are about average for a student at this university.

We begin with *Frank*. He and Ed are roommates. Having known each other since grade school, the two of them decided four years ago, when they were high school seniors, that they would room together when they got to college. From time to time they both experience some frustration with each other, as is typical of college roommates, but neither has ever mentioned that fact to the other—though Ed occasionally complains about Frank when he is with Dan. While Frank is particularly bright academically, socially he is a loner. Fear and anxiety keep him from anything but the most basic interacting, and he has struggled in social settings from the time he was a youngster. He and Ed chitchat in the room, and he can hold his own when discussing academic issues and sports, especially college basketball. He cannot (or will not) discuss anything personal. It is a stretch to call him insecure because, except for his family, he is not really connected with anyone—securely or otherwise. When he talks to people, he looks over their shoulder or at their mouth, never their eyes. He did not date in high school and never seriously entertained the possibility thereof. He is fortunate that Ed offered to room with him. Were it not for Ed's social connections, Frank would not interact with anybody.

Ed, for his part, fares somewhat better in social settings than does Frank, and though not as academically gifted as Frank, he is capable of some basic interpersonal relating. The group of guys goes out fairly regularly. Ed enjoys this, and as a rule they enjoy him. Ed's childhood and early adolescence were a difficult time, and those struggles have had an effect on Ed's present way of relating. Ed would not describe himself as angry, but, in fact, his high school experience left him with a sense of having to prove himself to others; there is a visible anger when Ed intellectually bullies other students. Ed lives with a nagging sense of personal inadequacy that prevents him from talking about personal matters. He will never show weakness. His strategy is to attract people to himself by impressing them with what he knows and with what he has. At this point in his life, he is more sophisticated in this than he used to be, but his know-it-all way of engaging people in conversation is more than a little annoying. While Ed makes an impressive first impression—he is good-looking, articulate, well-dressed, and seemingly bright—Brian and Andrew, who know Ed better, can see that behind Ed's superficial pattern of relating is a deeply lonely man.

Ed wants people to like him; he wants to have more serious friendships. The great irony is that the more he tries to impress, the less impressed people seem to be. In one-on-one conversations, Ed sticks with topics that he considers to be safe. He avoids revealing personal information—even with people he has known for years—and when others try to talk to him about their own personal matters, they sense a certain discomfort in Ed. He has done a bit of dating in college, but things never really came together in that area of his life. He tries to impress the girls, but they are turned off by his superficial and immature manner and find his attempts to impress them with "manly" behavior to be boorish.

Ed fears intimacy. He does not want others to see what he is like on the inside, for he thinks if people saw what he is really like, they would reject him. Without realizing it, he keeps a "safe distance" from people. He will not let anyone *in*. He does not really know anybody, and nobody knows him. Ed thinks he has many friends, when in fact he has none, though he is fortunate to have a number of *companions* who are somewhat fond of him.

Dan is the third member of the group. Being an underachiever in high school, Dan was fortunate to be admitted to the university, and his general lack of interest in academic matters makes it questionable whether he will graduate. He goes to class about half the time. Originally he had wanted to be an engineer, but after his first semester he changed his major to something much less ambitious. Chuck teases Dan mercilessly for spending the few hours of the day when he is awake either playing video games or watching ESPN. High school had been uneventful for Dan, and by most people's standards, normal. He excelled in sports, and for most of his junior and senior year he had a girlfriend. In college, he plays intramural sports and has had the same girlfriend, Colleen, for two years. If pressed, he will admit that he will probably marry her someday, but he honestly does not give it a lot of thought. Colleen is a very attractive college junior who really struggles with her own sense of confidence in personal relationships. She has a hard time believing that someone would want to be with her for the long haul. She admits to her friends that she often finds Dan boring. Colleen and Dan spend most of their time together watching TV. Occasionally Colleen tries to engage Dan in serious, personal conversation to which he often responds with "Not that kind of talk, not tonight."

Dan genuinely cares about Colleen and shows it more in what he does than in what he says. Colleen's grandmother lives about an hour away from campus and Dan willingly spends one afternoon a week taking Colleen to see her. He has strong feelings for Colleen, both affectionate and erotic feelings, but his feelings for her are not matched by a willingness to open up with her. Dan's lack of interest in romance saddens Colleen, but at this point she is resigned to it. "You cannot have everything," she tells herself. In many respects, Ed is in a better position than Dan. If Ed's self-hatred and sense of inadequacy were healed, he would quickly surpass Dan who, rather than fearing intimacy, simply has no interest in it.

Chuck and Brian have a closer friendship with each other than either has with the rest of the men we have seen thus far. Brian's parents live too far away for him to drive home for weekends or breaks, though he does drive home for Christmas. During their junior year, Chuck invited Brian to his family home for Thanksgiving. The invitation was graciously accepted and those few days they spent together were the occasion for their friendship to deepen. In contrast to Brian, whose personal confidence and capacity for intimacy have always been high, Chuck very much struggles in this area. A year ago, one would have described Chuck as a deeply lonely man who attempts to disguise his loneliness with comedy. The fuel feeding his loneliness was fear—fear of interpersonal relating and intimacy. Thinking he did not have much to offer and not wanting to be rejected by his peers, he would play the role of the comedian. Comedy was Chuck's answer to everything. He is genuinely funny, and people like having him around. There is a joviality about him that makes him the life of a party.

Chuck will talk about matters that are of no personal consequence—politics, sports, and movies are his favorites. But at the
time, he suffered from a chronic inability to be serious and engage
in meaningful conversations. When someone would try to move the
conversation in that direction, he would deflect it with a humorous
comment. Chuck knew something was missing in his relationships.
He could see the way Brian and Andrew were able to talk about
things, and he greatly admired their sense of confidence. But he was
simply too fearful to reveal much about himself. And while humor
does give him a social role—people do in fact enjoy being entertained
by him—his feeling of isolation continued.

This all began to change about a year ago because of his friendship with Brian. Brian's kind and gentle manner has a way of putting
others at ease. He is a sensitive soul whose confidence never gives
rise to arrogance. He is genuinely interested in others—in their happiness and their well-being. Both by what he says, and the tone and
manner in which he says it, he has a way of building people up and
eliciting their trust. With complete naturalness, he manages to get
the message across, "I believe in you." All of this has had a powerful
effect on Chuck whose self-confidence has always been low.

A year ago, during Thanksgiving break, Chuck finally opened up
and began to discuss personal matters in a way that he had never
done before. Chuck knew he was taking a risk, but he was tired
of being lonely. His risk paid off. These conversations went better
than Chuck expected, and throughout the year his fear has steadily
decreased. The others in the group find him opening up more and
more. When Chuck is nervous or anxious, he still reverts back to
his comedian role; that is happening less as time goes by. But he is
hopeful. His interaction with Brian has had a very positive effect on
him; while he knows he still has a long way to go, he is encouraged
by the progress he has made. His willingness to begin to let others
see him as he really is has brought a decrease in fear and an increase
in his capacity for intimacy that is having its effect on all his personal
relationships.

Brian, for his part, is a relationally-gifted man, and those who
know him consider themselves blessed to have him in their lives.
He is a multi-talented person who, for all his talents, is known most
of all for his kindness. His genuineness has a way of putting others at ease. He is free from the anxieties and fears that burden the

lives of the others we have seen. His conversation is a healthy mix of showing genuine interest in those he is with and appropriately commenting on the happenings in his own life. It is all done with complete naturalness. Today, for instance, he is at the lunch table with the gang. He talks about himself, not in an egotistical way, but in a way that is appropriate for the context and that displays a sense of trust in the guys he is with. Brian's history class met this morning. He had had high hopes for the paper that was due today, but he knew his paper was a little better than mediocre. He talks about his disappointment:

> My history paper was due today, and I do not think I am going to get the 'A' that I was hoping for. It just did not come together like I had hoped it would. But it was due today, so I had to hand it in. It is not horrible—but it certainly is not my best performance either. We will see what happens.

In the context of the lunch table, this is appropriate self-revelation. This capacity for letting others into his inner life, sharing with them what he thinks and how he feels—this capacity for intimacy—will serve him well in all his personal relationships. He will likely have a better marriage because of it.

The last member of the group is *Andrew*, whose capacity for intimacy is the greatest of the six of them. Andrew spends more time with Brian than with any of the other five. He is willing to go out with the whole gang, but he much, much prefers one-on-one gatherings that afford him the opportunity to talk. Andrew loves to talk and he loves to listen. He is not a chatterbox. Superficial conversations bore him, especially "bar talk" where, as he puts it, "Guys sit around for hours and talk about nothing." He likes real, substantial conversations that, though not necessarily intense, are conversations *about something*.

Andrew is intensely loyal, and he exhibits a conviviality that makes him enjoyable to be around. His circle of intimate friends includes Brian (from the group) and Sara, the girl he will probably marry. They know him very, very well, and he is fiercely loyal to them. Andrew's friends know that those deep relationships are what his life is all about. His life is about people, including God. Andrew is observant of the norms and obligations of his faith, and since adolescence, he has seen discipleship as a call to a relationship with each of the three members of the Blessed Trinity and with the Blessed in Heaven.

Andrew is aware of the "restlessness" of which St. Augustine writes. He experiences the intimacy—the connecting—coming and going, as it were, in waves. His heart is never satisfied for long, and he longs for ever greater and deeper intimacy. But he has come to have realistic expectations. He often reminds himself that *being* united is not the same as *feeling* united, and that of the two, the former is far more valuable. It took Andrew a while to realize that the intense and sustained intimacy for which he longs only happens in Heaven. There his heart will finally be at rest.

All the men in the illustration (which just as easily could have featured a group of women) are fictional, but they typify the way people differ in their capacity for intimacy. At times, their traits were presented in the extreme for the sake of illustration. But the characteristics presented are real, and readers may find similar traits in themselves, or in those they love. The important thing to see and understand is that one can grow in the art of intimate relating, and that it is not something that only occurs in the context of a male-female relationship.

Increased Self-understanding
Increases the Capacity for Intimacy

People vary widely according to their capacities and their desires for intimate relating. Some seem incapable or uninterested in establishing close personal relationships. Their relating skills are weak, and they do not seem to engage people. On the other hand, others show a deep capacity for intimate relating. They thrive on it when they find it. How do we account for this?

More than anything else, intimacy comes about by communicating (sharing) my inner-self with someone. Two things prevent this from happening, the first of which is *fear*. If we return for a moment to the illustration of the six college seniors, we see that the first two men, Frank and Ed, were possessed by a fear that prevented them from revealing matters of their inner lives. And because they did not want others to see their inner selves—because they were afraid—intimate relationships eluded them. Besides the fear of revealing, one may also have a fear of receiving. They do not want to hear someone's personal story because they feel awkward and do not know how to appropriately respond.

The second thing that prevents intimacy is an insufficiently developed *self-understanding*. This was clearly the case with Dan in the illustration above. Dan was not afraid to talk about things—but his lack of self-awareness meant that he really did not have anything to talk about. Dan was presented as a rather shallow man who does not think much about anything, except perhaps his hobbies. He certainly does not reflect much on matters of his inner life. This is why I said earlier that if Ed were to overcome his fear, he would quickly surpass Dan in the pursuit of intimacy.

If intimacy is the art of communicating that which is deepest within me, then increased self-awareness will bring increased capacity for intimate relating. It is a quality of the soul that is developed and deepened over time. Through the process of inner reflection, we look introspectively at our lives, and we develop a sense of self-understanding. Naturally, this self-understanding grows through the years. The twenty-year-old understands herself far more deeply than she did when she was ten. Another twenty years hence, we hope she will, as a forty-year-old, have a corresponding increase in her self-understanding.

As we grow, we discover that we have an inner life. It is an integral aspect of our *personhood,* and it is what we have in common with the three divine persons—Father, Son, and Holy Spirit—and with the angels. And even though a man or woman's self-knowledge increases over time, we still remain at our deepest and most intimate core a mystery even unto ourselves. We never completely and absolutely understand ourselves. "Why do I like this?" "Why am I attracted to that?" "Why do I find this interesting?" These are questions we may never be able to answer.

In humans, this inner life is marked by a sense of *striving* and a sense of *valuing*. We have an inner *spiritual* life which cannot be reduced to physiology or psychology, enabling me to relate to another as person-to-person. Because of our free will, this inner life is marked by *self-determination*. By the exercise of my inner freedom—by my own freely made choices—I existentially become the man I choose to be. This, for good or evil, is my true self. It is, as it were, the man I am on the inside. As I discover these things about myself, my sharing them with others creates intimacy. Deeper awareness creates a greater capacity for intimacy.

Sometimes we are prompted to grow because of qualities we perceive in people we admire. This awareness of the ways in which my life falls short increases my own self-understanding and self-awareness. Simply seeing where I am, and seeing what I might be—that, in itself, adds depth to my inner awareness. We are somewhat wiser because of it. All of this adds depth to one's personhood, making deeper and more meaningful interpersonal communication possible. If I have no (or very little) awareness of the matters of my inner life, I cannot communicate them to others.

Some are naturally more self-reflective than others. Reflectiveness is, in a certain sense, an inquisitiveness regarding one's inner world. Pondering in one's heart the serious matters of our inner lives adds depth to our souls and brings an accompanying wisdom. St. Luke speaks of Our Lady who, after all the events surrounding Jesus' birth, "kept all these things, pondering them in her heart,"[58] reflecting on what they would mean for her life.

It is said of some people that they are shallow. They are not referring to intellectual inferiority, but to a certain lack of interior reflection. Being occupied with the external things of life, the finer details of their inner life seem to escape them.

As we reflect on our lives, we naturally desire to share—with carefully selected persons, and in ways that seem appropriate—the private, intimate aspects of our lives. "I want to share myself with you—I want you to see what I see." We inwardly desire to know others, and to be known by them. This mutual sharing of our inner lives create intimacy. Not surprisingly, those who have this capacity and desire for intimacy typically seek friendship with those who are similarly inclined. St. Augustine was one such person. His autobiography, *Confessions*, is an outpouring of self-revelation. He was one who seemed to have a deep capacity and a longing for intimate relating, and connecting with those he loved. Writing to his clergy he said:

> Preserve, my sons, that friendship which you have begun with your brethren, for nothing in the world is more beautiful that that. It is indeed a comfort in this life to have one to whom you can open your heart, with whom you can share confidences, and to whom you can entrust the secrets of your breast. It is a comfort to have a faithful man by your side, who will rejoice with you in prosperity, sympathize with you in trouble, encourage you in persecution. What friends were those Hebrew youths whom even the flames of the fiery furnace did not separate from their love for each other.[59]

Many are acutely aware that such relating is possible, and are saddened by the fact that their own relationships are not what they would like them to be. They read St.Augustine saying, "It is indeed a comfort in this life to have one to whom you can open your heart, with whom you can share confidences, and to whom you can entrust the secrets of your breast," and they wish they had such a friend. But they do not. I cannot offer a panacea for overcoming the experience of being disconnected from others. But there are a few things one could consider. I think one should "start at the top," and work one's way down. If my relationships are not as intimate as I would like, I might try deepening the *friendships* I already have. As we have seen, this process happens by slowly revealing the matters of one's heart. If that option is neither possible nor desirable, I might seek to pursue a friendship with someone who is already my *companion*. We make friends with our companions, not with strangers. Since our friends nearly always began as our companions, we could try to deepen a relationship with someone who already happens to be in our lives. Finally, we can expand the group of people who are our companions in the hopes that one of them may one day become a friend. By becoming more involved in community, fraternal, and service organizations, we increase our contact with people.

We all desire intimacy, to connect deeply with others. But genuine intimacy takes time. Our ability to relate intimately must develop, as well as the relationships themselves. The experience of being disconnected tempts some, in their impatience for satisfying relationships, to "force" the relationship. We see this in those who want to experience closeness *now*, so they settle for imitations of intimacy that never really satisfy the longings of our hearts. In male-female relationships, this attempt to rush intimacy through sexual experiences can hinder one from acquiring the important—though difficult to master—relationship skills they will need later on. As Pieper puts it, "Those who love young people cannot share the delight they seem to feel in (as it were) lightening their knapsacks and throwing away the basic rations they will eventually need when the going gets rough."[60] It can create, as John Paul II put it, an "illusion of intimacy." They are not so nearly united as their experience leads them to believe. That is because real intimacy takes time, and it involves being vulnerable with the ones I love—opening to them my mind and my heart as I let them into the deepest recesses of my life.

We naturally desire true human closeness and unity with others, knowing that this is the only way of overcoming loneliness and disconnectedness. Only real love, real intimacy, can achieve this. There are no shortcuts. Our hearts long for the intimacy that is the fruit of a relationship where we connect with another because of our mutual self-revelation, mutual self-gift and mutual acceptance. Relating this way, we have the confident assurance that we are committed to each other—a reciprocal relationship where it is no longer "I" and "thou," but "we."

This discovery of intimate, interpersonal relating enables one to understand more fully the intimacy of marriage and the intimacy we have with God. How could it be otherwise? Those who have experienced many years of a happy and satisfying marriage are the same ones who grasp what real friendship is all about. Great spouses have the qualities that make for great friends—and *vice versa*. And it is similar in one's relationship with God. This is because *intimate friendship is the fundamental and primordial interpersonal relationship*. Is it any wonder that the great lovers of God are the ones who speak most eloquently of the love of friends and the beauty of friendship? How delightfully St. Augustine wrote about the intimacy of friendship, as the following passage shows:

> What is a friend but a partner in love, to whom you conjoin and attach your soul, with whom you unite and desire to become one, to whom you commit yourself as to a second self, from whom you fear nothing, and of whom you ask nothing wrong for the sake of your own advantage. Friendship is not materially lucrative, but is full of seemliness, full of grace. Friendship is a virtue, not a way of making money. It is acquired, not by money, but by favor; not by offering a price, but by mutual rivalry in good will.[61]

In intimate friendship, we first learn what it means to enter into the life of another, sharing the things of our hearts. Ideally, it is the love we hope to find as the foundation of every marriage and at the heart of our relationship with God.

Questions for Philosophical Consideration and Personal Growth

1. Give examples of someone being either actively or passively defensive in his or her relating. What effect does this have?

2. Some people are what one might call "morbidly shy." What effect does this have on relating, especially as regards intimacy? What practical suggestions would you have for someone like this?

3. Suppose you were speaking to a group of eighteen-year-olds. What practical suggestions would you offer on becoming less selfish and more selfless? In your own personal struggle, where does selfishness show itself?

4. Do you think that "being honest with someone" means that I say whatever happens to come to my mind? How does one balance the virtue of honesty with things such as tact and refinement?

5. The tone of our voices is as much a part of communication as the words we use. Have you noticed how some people regularly sound impatient, cross, or irritated, while others habitually seem the opposite? In either case, what effect do you suppose this has on their relating? Are you aware of the tone of voice that you use—or is it simply dictated by your mood?

6. Sometimes it is said that we should be able to completely "be ourselves" when we are at home—that we need not "mind our manners" in our own homes. But should not the members of our households—the ones we love the most—see us at our best? How does one balance this?

7. Imagine someone with whom you regularly interact telling you that you are his closest friend. On the one hand, you know that you probably *are* his closest friend. And yet you are also aware that, for his part, he relates only superficially. You like this individual and you are good to him—because you believe that this is the right thing to do. But you clearly do not consider him your closest friend. As you see it, he is barely capable of friendship. What approaches might you take to help him grow? (This is not an easy question.)

8. Think about the many people who are a part of your life. Perhaps you can see varying degrees of the capacity for intimacy. Regarding those who seem relationally handicapped, what specifically do they do in their interacting with others that enables them to

avoid intimacy? Some very intelligent, competent, and professionally successful people have relating skills that are underdeveloped. How do they arrange their environments so that they can avoid intimacy?

9. Give some examples of people, perhaps public figures, whose ability to connect deeply with people dramatically improves their professional lives.

10. How does it change the work environment when those in management are able to connect and identify with the people they supervise? What are the advantages and disadvantages of this? When supervisors do not personally connect with others, what do they do instead in their managing role?

11. Consider fathers and mothers who do not connect very well with their children (or with each other). Describe the environment of the home.

12. What limits your own growth in this area?

13. What is meant by the "illusion of intimacy"? In what ways is it defective, i.e. how is it different from genuine intimacy?

14. How does the intimacy of friendship prepare one for marriage?

Chapter Six

Intimacy between Men and Women

"...And after all these years,
he still plays beautiful music on the strings of my heart."

Anonymous

The Love between the Sexes

Intimacy, as we have seen, is a matter of sharing one's personal life and thus creating a bond with another person. It is about interpersonal union that arises when two people enter into each other's private and personal life. This relational bond turns companions into friends. And as it increases, it turns friends into dear friends. What develops in the male-female relationship is a particular type of intimacy. Ideally, the relationship between a husband and his wife is the most intimate relationship that spouses have. *Ideally* because of the seemingly obvious fact that many marriages are not what they might be. What began as an intimate relationship later devolved into something else.

Intimacy in the male-female relationship involves the broad category of *erotic love*. It is said "Male-female relationship" to indicate relating between a man and woman where the two of them are relating to each other not merely as two friends, but as *man to woman*. The relationship is qualitatively different from friendship, though romantic/erotic relationships often begin as a friendship. Or a man and a woman may begin as companions and move rather quickly into a male-female relationship with only a brief period intervening when they were simply friends. Imagine Molly and Jerome who are two college students on a school-sponsored trip to Europe. They had never met each other before their trip. But during those two weeks they rather quickly established a connection with each other and returned to the United States as girlfriend and boyfriend.

This type of love we are considering often arises as an erotic *interest*. This interest may be present in one, long before it is present in the other. It may not, at first, manifest itself as a sexual interest, but may take the form of a certain fascination with the other person. And there arises the awareness that the other could complete what is lacking in me. Masculinity seeks completion by femininity, and *vice versa*. The two of them together form, as it were, the complete person. The masculinity of the man is attracted by what he perceives as the femininity of the woman. And she is attracted to him, not insofar as he is a person, but insofar as he is a man. At a certain point, what began as an erotic fascination begins to be felt as desire for the other—a sexual desire—which seeks fulfillment in the *one flesh union* of sexual intercourse. Having felt this desire, one begins to consider the possibility that this is indeed the one with whom they wish to spend the rest of his or her life, as a spouse. Their mutual love is prompting both of them to make a commitment to love in the future.

Love Creates Expectations

The intimacy experienced in personal relationships is one of the great joys of life. But along with its joy, it brings with it the potential for sadness and heartache. The reason for this is simple enough: along with intimacy comes expectation. Sometimes our expectations are reasonable and realistic, sometimes not. Either way, when expectations are not met, we experience disappointment. We can be disappointed by what happened—by things that were said or done—or we can be disappointed by what did not happen, contrary to our expectations. This gives us the feeling of being let down by the one whom we love.

To the extent that our relationships are intimate ones, to the extent that we let others into our lives, we have corresponding expectations that follow. Intimacy and commitment should run along parallel tracks. When one out-paces the other, we have a recipe for disaster. People are hurt when one fails to live up to the commitments that naturally follow from their intimacy. If we are close friends, but you ignore me at a dinner party, I will naturally wonder why. One reasonably expects that those with whom they share a degree of intimacy will have a corresponding degree of commitment and that they will act accordingly. It is, for example, precisely because he believed she was committed to him that he opened himself up to her and revealed the secrets of his heart. If afterward, she turns out not to be genuinely committed to him, he is hurt. Depending on the depth of their intimacy, he may feel not only hurt but also bitter, embarrassed, abandoned, used, violated, etc. This does not just happen in male-female relationships. It happens whenever one person presumes (rightly or wrongly) that another is committed, but the commitments are not kept.

The only way to avoid these disappointments altogether is to have no expectations of anyone. But that is hardly a desirable solution and does nothing but resign one to a life of isolation where one has only casual relationships—friendly with everybody, but close to nobody. Disappointments are part of life. In healthy relationships, we can tell our loved-ones that they have let us down—and they may tell us, in turn, that our expectations were unrealistic.

Perhaps our expectations are unreasonable and unrealistic. Or, perhaps our expectations are reasonable—but we have not communicated them very well. What is obvious to one person may not be obvious to another. Love is a matter of *union*, not *fusion*. Even when we try to be attentive and responsive, we nevertheless remain separate individuals—we cannot read each other's minds.

In our personal relationships, we rightly expect people to keep their commitments. If, for instance, Matt and Kelcie have made plans to have dinner, and Matt backs out at the last minute, just because he does not feel like going out, Kelcie is justifiably irritated. This insensitivity on Matt's part, which may be due more to immaturity than to anything else, is a relational obstacle. (If Matt is immature, it does not occur to him that backing out at the last minute will hurt Kelcie. If he is a narcissist, it does occur to him that she will be hurt—but he does not care.) If Matt establishes a pattern of backing out on commitments, he can expect to have few friends. He is not dependable, and he lets people down.

The degree to which people keep their commitments in personal relationships is, to a large extent, the degree to which they love us. Why do people keep their commitments? Because they *choose* to. Fulfilling their commitments says something about them, and it says something about the ones they love. Mature, adult relationships are based on something more than one's whim and fancy, and what one may happen to feel like doing at any given moment. Real love always includes an act of one's free will, where people mutually commit themselves to each other in a way that transcends their feelings. A friend who is only around when it is convenient is not really my friend.

If this is true for friendship, it is certainly true for marriage. The ebb and flow of one's emotional life is far too unstable and unreliable to provide the foundation for the lifetime commitment of marriage. Committed love is the love that is worthy of persons. There are some who—for one reason or another—are incapable of giving themselves in this way. They are willing to "love," only so long as the relationship brings them emotional contentment. In the final analysis, they love no one but themselves.

Real Love Is More Than a Feeling

The point I am making is that genuine love is something more than the *experience*, the *feeling*, of love. Long before Karol Wojtyla was elected pope, his pastoral work brought him into contact with many men and women in their twenties. Recall that he was a university chaplain and later a professor. His broad experience—especially with the graduate students—gave him many insights and helped him form his *theology of the body*. In *Love and Responsibility*, his book on human love written during this time, he wrote:

> It is impossible to judge the value of a relationship between persons merely from the intensity of their emotions. The very exuberance of the emotions born of sensuality may conceal an absence of true love, or indeed outright egoism. Love is one thing, and erotic sensations are another. Love develops on the basis of the totally committed and fully responsible attitude of a person to a person, erotic experiences are born spontaneously from sensual and emotional reactions. A very rich and rapid growth of such sensations may conceal a love that has failed to develop.[62]

In saying, "It is impossible to judge the value of a relationship between persons merely from the intensity of their emotions," he is making a distinction between "loving someone," and the state of being "in love." One who is "in love" is overwhelmed in a euphoria of positive emotions, where everything about the beloved is perceived as sweetness and light. Not by accident do we use the term "madly in love" to describe such lovers, as there is something of a madness or craziness about them. They may describe themselves as being out of control, "head over heels" in their love. Or they may say they simply want to sit and contemplate their beloved, spending their days gazing into each other's eyes.

Eventually the intensity wanes, and lovers begin to see each other as they really are. Some of the excitement wears off, but this is when the real loving begins. Why? Because genuine human love always requires a choice. It is volitional love—intentional love. When I no longer feel as though a freight train of emotions is running through me, when I feel I am in possession of myself, it is then that my love for you is *deliberate*. A man who is *in love* will ignore virtually anything unpleasant in his beloved; a man who genuinely loves finds *many* things unpleasant, but loves anyway. We could think of a husband who does not particularly enjoy gardening, but who waters the flowers and pulls the weeds because he knows it makes his wife happy. Or the wife who makes a dish for dinner that is difficult to prepare, knowing how much her husband likes it. We would like to think that we will always find a delight and a charm in our relationships, but our love is measured more accurately by what we willingly do for each other than by the intensity of our emotions at any given moment.

The Developing Relationship—From Dating to Marriage

The male-female relationship begins in earnest when the couple starts to date. The man and woman may have known each other for years—or they may have only recently met each other. As they spend time together, they are evaluating their compatibility in a number of areas. In their first few dates, they will likely focus on emotional compatibility. They will ask themselves, "Do I like this person, and enjoy spending time with him/her?" That, along with a sexual appeal, makes a person *attractive*. If the feelings are mutual, the couple may decide to date each other exclusively. They describe themselves as *going out, seeing each other,* or *dating*—and they are now boyfriend and girlfriend.

Among the young, it is typical to find people dating simply for the sake of dating. At this point in life, they have not yet begun thinking of someone as a potential spouse. High school relationships are often like this. And through these relationships they gain a deeper understanding, both of themselves and of members of the opposite sex.

Alex and Bonnie: A Relationship between High School Students

Alex and Bonnie are high school seniors who have been dating since the beginning of the school year. He likes being in a relationship, and so does she. It fulfills them in a way that their other friendships cannot. If you ask Alex if he is in love with Bonnie he replies, "I know that I have very strong feelings for her—feelings of love. She means the world to me. But whether I am 'in love'—well, I am not really sure I know exactly what that is."

Bonnie sees the effect that a high school relationship has on some of her friends. Seeing how it monopolizes their time, she decided at the beginning of her relationship with Alex that she would not let this happen. She wants to enjoy high school life and her high school friends, some of whom she has had since kindergarten.

Alex, for his part, agrees with Bonnie. And they have kept their relationship, as it were, "light." As he puts it, "I am 'involved,' not 'overwhelmed' in the relationship." Alex is considering his options for college. Some of his friends have made college decisions based on boyfriend/girlfriend relationships, and he is resisting the temptation to do the same. He knows that Bonnie is going to spend two years at the local junior college. And while there is an appealing side to staying at home for two years, Alex really wants to go away to school.

The two of them see each other every day at school, and they usually call to "check in" sometime in the evening. On Friday or Saturday, they try to do something together. Bonnie goes to church and breakfast every Sunday morning with her family, and sometimes sees her grandparents later in the day. This is an important part of her life, and she does not want to give that up. So on Fridays and Saturdays, she tries to balance her time between Alex and her other friends. It does not always go smoothly, but she does the best she can. The two of them very much enjoy the time they do spend together, even if it is just doing homework.

Neither one of them knows where this relationship will go next year. Alex is not sure he wants to be in a long-distance relationship when he is in college, with all the expectations that that entails. He really is not sure *what* he wants. He knows that he wants Bonnie to be a part of his life, if not as his girlfriend, at least as his friend.

* * * * *

During the time a man and woman date, they discover much about each other and much about themselves. They see, with increasing clarity as time goes by, how a member of the opposite sex sees them. The man is attracted to the woman not simply as a person—he is attracted to her femininity, which has a way of drawing out his masculinity. The same happens in the woman. This is all part of the mysterious process of falling in love. It might all come together very quickly, or take a long time to develop.

As the relationship evolves, the ways of intimately communicating need to be further developed. Couples do this in the things they say and in the affectionate way they interact. Learning how to speak intimately is a basic relating skill. People can be hesitant in communicating their feelings if they wonder whether these feelings are mutual. And one feels particularly vulnerable when saying to a person for the first time, "I love you."

They may not be aware of it, but as the relationship develops, they are forming patterns of relating. This happens in all our relationships. Over time, the couple discovers their favorite things to do when they are together which, as we saw earlier, is one of the three essential elements of a personal relationship. In a developing relationship, people often ask themselves how they feel about the other person. But part of their thought process should also include an evaluation of how well they themselves communicate their love. Those who have refined the art of loving know how their beloved likes to be loved. My favorite way of loving may not be your favorite way of being loved. It strengthens all our personal relationships when we love as we ought, and we love people the way they want to be loved.

At some point, marriage becomes a consideration. "Is this the person with whom I wish to spend the rest of my life and with whom I wish to raise a family?" It is one of the most important decisions one makes in life, and it requires much more than an evaluation of one's feelings. What does it take to be happily married? What an enormously important question that is! It is easy to *get married*. But *being* happily married—that is another story. It is a serious mistake to think that emotional bonding and sexual attraction is all we need. That only, so to speak, gets you in the door. Two other things need to be seriously evaluated.

First, besides their emotional bond, couples need to evaluate the extent to which they have a common vision about what they consider "the important things in life" and the way they envision living family life. This is a compatibility of *values*. When couples are dating, they often talk about the things they have in common and the things they enjoy talking about. But they also need to talk about their values and about the way they hope their lives will come together.

Secondly, they need to evaluate their loved one's character strengths and weaknesses. The more they spend time with each other, the more clearly these will be seen. Successfully navigating the waters of marriage and family life requires a great deal of determination and hard work. Many virtues are required to do this well. One should ask, "Does the one that I love have the *character strength* to live the vision of life that we have and to be my faithful spouse?"

Sherry and Vince: A Serious Relationship between Two People in College

Sherry and Vince are both in their third year of college. They met in a Spanish class during their first year. They became friends and later that fall they started going out. Now, two years later, they are very much in love.

Their love for each other is evident in the affectionate way they talk to each other, and in the way they warmly and lovingly interact. They talk on the phone every day, and they see each other as often as they can, but not as often as Vince would like. Vince is happiest when he is with her, and if he had his way, he would spend several hours with her every day. Sherry would gladly oblige if she could, but she cannot. She is majoring in international finance, and it places heavy demands on her time. Perhaps she makes it harder than it needs to be, but she is *driven* to succeed. Vince is studying agribusiness. They used to study together, but Sherry finds his presence distracting when she is studying, and she prefers to study alone.

So the two of them talk on the phone daily, and they spend time with each other a couple of times a week. They think about each other very often, many times each day, and doing so gives them a very positive feeling. When they do spend time together, they feel like they really connect. Vince really likes to talk—probably more than most guys. (This is why they rarely watch movies together. Vince will want to comment on things during the movie, which drives Sherry crazy.) There is a café on the first floor of the student union, and the two of them have spent many hours there just talking. Spending time in this café is one of their favorite things they do together.

As to their experience of intimacy, Vince feels closest to her when they are physically present with each other. Just being with her, looking into her eyes, sharing the things of his heart with her and affectionately touching and kissing are various ways he feels that he connects with her, experiencing their closeness. For Sherry, simply reflecting on the role Vince has in her life makes her feel close to him. For her, it is the perpetual awareness of the relationship itself that gives her comfort and security. Vince is more predictable than he is spontaneous—predictably thoughtful and responsive. Sherry likes that, and finds it romantic. He does little things all the time, like leaving short little notes or sending text messages. They give her an awareness of his presence. It is all of these things, taken together, that give her the feeling of being united with the man she loves.

One challenge the two of them will face in their future involves religion. Vince is firm in his belief and practice of his Lutheran faith. Sherry does not practice a religion, and finds herself at odds with some basic tenets of Christianity. Because it is a neuralgic issue, they do not discuss it much. Up until now, they have simply agreed to disagree. Vince and Sherry love each other very much, and they are friends in the true sense of the word. If they are to be married one day, this issue will have to be resolved. It will not simply go away, and it will greatly affect the way they raise their children.

The other serious issue they will face has to do with what they each see as his or her life's work. Sherry is eager to pursue a career in international finance. Vince is majoring in agribusiness because he wants to return to the family farm. It is not clear how all of this will come together after college graduation.

* * * * *

As we have seen, in a continuing, developing relationship be-tween a man and a woman, the question inevitably arises in the minds of each of them, "Is this the person I am going to marry?" It is a question that brings both excitement and anxiety. The woman may think to herself, "I love him very much. He is very good to me, and he makes me so happy." At the same time, she knows that marrying him will change her life in unimaginable ways. And she wonders if he is "really the one," and if the two of them will be happy together.

The man, for his part, may think much the same. Perhaps she has areas where she needs to grow—he sees this clearly, though she may not. It might be a character defect or a personality quirk. Chloe, for example, is a loving person, but when she is angry she has a violent temper. It does not come out very often, but when it does, she says very hurtful things. Her boyfriend is very much in love with her, and because of his love, he is deeply hurt by things she says in anger.

But Chloe's anger does more than hurt his feelings; it also makes him question just how emotionally vulnerable he wants to be with her. He finds it difficult to be, so to speak, emotionally exposed to someone who hurts him. He finds himself keeping a safe emotional distance even though he knows this does not help build up the relationship. They have repeatedly talked about her angry outbursts and the effect they have on their relationship, but the conversation never really gets anywhere. Her response is always the same, "If you would not make me so angry, I would not say those things." Perhaps she will eventually learn to resist the temptation to say hurtful things when she is angry. But she might not. The point is this: not everyone approaches his or her character defects with a willingness to improve. And, depending on what they are, these character defects make communicating and experiencing love more difficult. Again we see the importance of virtue and character strength in healthy relationships.

When two people first begin to date, they may know rather little about each other. As the relationship develops, their love and affection grow—and so does their knowledge of each other's peculiarities. Some of these things we could call "personality quirks." We all have them. They include the myriad aspects of our personalities that make us the unique individuals that we are. Sometimes personality quirks, which we first found to be annoying, can later become endearing. Your friend, for example, makes a peculiar noise when she chews gum. It used to drive you crazy, but over time you began to associate that noise with her and you find it endearing.

A married man, whom I know, likes to read and eat peanuts in bed before going to sleep. Sometimes his wife would find a stray peanut in bed in the morning. After several years of marriage, she told him, "If you die before I do, and if I ever find a peanut in bed, I will weep." What was once annoying had become endearing. It does not always happen, of course. But it happens often enough.

Besides personality quirks, we also discover aspects of the person's emotional make-up. We see their insecurities and their neuroses. Your friend, for example, has a neurotic fear about driving in the rain—even drizzle—for fear some disaster will ensue.

We see people's character faults too. Perhaps someone, as in the example of Chloe and her boyfriend, only rarely gets angry—but when she does, she says very hurtful things. Or someone may have the habit of lying to avoid embarrassment.

In ordinary friendships we take all these things into account—knowingly or not—as we choose to pursue a friendship. It factors into how close the friends will become. But in romantic relationships, another dynamic is at work. I may find myself in love with someone who not only has personality quirks, but also has serious emotional struggles or character faults. Some of them may improve over time, but they might not—or they could get worse. The love between the two people is real—real in the sense that they are attracted to each other and committed to each other at some level. But we must recognize that erotic love can unite two people who, in every other way, are completely unsuited for each other. *Eros* is blind and has the power to draw people together who would never have become friends, were it not for erotic love. As Lewis stated in *The Four Loves*, "For *Eros* may unite the most unsuitable yokefellows; many unhappy, and predictably unhappy, marriages were love-matches." This is why we must, so to speak, supervise our erotic love, asking ourselves, "Is the one I am falling in love with capable of becoming my genuine friend?" This is complicated by the fact that we may already be strongly, emotionally committed by the time we see the person's true self.

Looking at a developing relationship, we are legitimately concerned about the character flaws we see in the one we love. Unlike personality quirks, character flaws do not become endearing over time. Though we have the patience of Job, and we overlook and forgive many things, character faults nevertheless are stumbling blocks on the road to marital happiness. By their very nature, they impede healthy relating. As we evaluate a relationship with a view toward marriage, we must be realistic, bearing in mind that we all have things about us that make us difficult to love. No one is perfect. It is not a bad idea to ask our close friends what they think about a developing, romantic relationship. From their vantage point, they see things we cannot see—or do not want to see.

At some point, after all the thinking, evaluating, and praying, we may come to the decision—this is the person with whom I wish to spend the rest of my life. "I want us to make a life with each other, and raise a family together." Engagement has its own way of changing the way they relate to each other. Among other things, it increases one's security in the relationship. And as they think about their future, the issue is no longer *whether* they will marry, but about *how* they will live married life.

Engagement is a time when the man and woman hone many of the intimacy skills they will rely upon for the rest of their lives together. Some of the skills are difficult to acquire—such as being completely emotionally vulnerable and talking about things one is not accustomed to discussing. If these things do not fall into place during this period, when the environment is ripest, they likely never will. Tremendous growth can take place during the period of engagement. When the couple begins to prepare for marriage, they are already very much in love and have established a pattern of relating. But their relationship grows and deepens while they are engaged. And they often attest to the change they see in their relationship after six or eight months of engagement.

Some new patterns are established during this time. The man and woman in the school of intimacy discover new ways to communicate to their beloved, "I love you," and, "How happy I am that you are a part of my life." They continue to discover special things they like to do together, and they will rely on these things throughout their married life.

Brooklyn and Cooper: An Engaged Couple

Brooklyn and Cooper are both twenty-four-years-old. They met through a mutual friend five years ago. Last year Cooper proposed, and they are now consumed with the details of the wedding. If you ask Brooklyn about her fiancé, she says, "I love him and everything about him. Besides being incredibly good-looking, he is strong, yet gentle, and I want him to be the father of my children." It is that strong and gentle way about him that really attracts her.

Both Brooklyn and Cooper are athletic and played sports in school. Their favorite things to do together involve exercising. They run, bike, and swim. Asked when she feels closest to him, she responds, "I feel deeply connected to him when he holds me. He is just as strong on the inside as he is physically strong. Though we are competitive athletically, and though we enjoy kidding and teasing each other, he is nevertheless very protective of me—emotionally protective."

Brooklyn is particularly good at communicating her feelings and her appreciation for what Cooper is, and for what he does. About a year ago she got into the habit of saying, "You are my man—and I love you." Cooper seems to light up when she says it.

Cooper looks forward to the times they workout together, and the time they spend with each other afterwards. But what really connects him to her is the security that comes from knowing they have a future together. And his security regarding their future is rooted in two things: the strength of her character and their five-year history together. He knows what kind of person she is. She is a woman—and a lady—of deeply held convictions. She tells him he is strong, but, in truth, he sees her as equally strong—in a feminine way.

All of this, taken together, gives him great confidence for their future together. The two of them have forged a relationship over the past five years, and the positive way in which things have come together gives both Brooklyn and Cooper great hope. As time passes, their security continues to rise.

Cooper considers himself a traditionalist, and "family values" are important to him. He is probably more traditional than she is, though not by much. But when it comes to spending money, she is more conservative than he is. Brooklyn and Cooper rarely argue, but when they do it involves finances. It is an area they need to work on, and as a married couple they will both have to "yield" a little as they balance their spending and saving in a way that both of them can live with. All things considered, Cooper and Brooklyn have a promising future ahead of them.

Communicating Our Love

In the relationships we have seen thus far, we have observed different ways that people both communicate and experience their love for each other. This is at the heart of intimacy; it is a union of persons. The nature of the human person—made in the image of God—is such that we are fully persons only in relationship with another.[63] And we find ourselves only by giving ourselves away. Thus, the human person—who is both body and spirit—desires to unite with another person. We want to come to know the inner lives of the ones we love, knowing them "on the inside." We wish to know what our beloved thinks, feels, and hopes for the future—especially *our* future. These are all spiritual realities. But spiritual realities are communicated through the body—through our words and gestures. The key to intimate relating lies in perfecting the process whereby one effectively communicates the inner things of the mind and heart. We do this in a variety of ways.

Through Things That Are Said and the Way They Are Received

In the various ways we speak with each other we communicate love. We reveal the things of our hearts, and we communicate our acceptance and our approval. Perfecting the art of loving includes broadening one's vocabulary of loving and encouraging phrases. Well-chosen words, at the right time and with the right tone can deeply touch someone's heart.

By the Way People Look at Each Other

With our eyes and facial expressions we communicate a great deal. We can think, for example, of the "look of approval" that we desire to receive from those we love—and the "look of disapproval" that we try to avoid. It is said that the eyes are the windows of the soul. The "look of love" can be remarkably communicative. One has the sense of being, as it were, *exposed* when one permits another to look into his or her eyes. It is mysterious, and much is communicated.

Through Touching

The first ones to communicate intimacy through touching are one's mother and father. All through life, and in various ways, one communicates love through touch. These varied types of loving, physical contact include hugs, kisses, caresses, the pat on the back, playful interacting, and sexual touching.

Through Sharing Meals Together

When we eat we satisfy a basic, bodily need. Sharing a meal with someone creates an environment for one's soul to be fed as well. Whether it is a dinner with friends, a romantic dinner, or a family meal, interpersonal interaction is taking place that is greatly facilitated by the fact that they are eating together. Even when there is relatively little conversation, as may be the case with older married couples, the meal is an occasion to spend time with someone we love. Family meals are an important part of family life. And families that only rarely eat together are missing a lot.

Through the Making and Keeping of Promises and Commitments

In friendship, and certainly in marriage, we have aspirations for both the near and distant future. They may be large or small.

By our mutual cooperation with each other, these "hopes" become "realities." And over time, we discover how well any given person keeps his or her commitments. We reveal the importance of a relationship by the way we make and keep our promises. It is a way of saying, "You are important to me, and I am not going to let you down." This has a two-fold effect. It gives people confidence about the future, and it generates an experience of intimacy here and now.

Through Giving Gifts and Loving Deeds

Giving gifts to those we love is a token of the gift of ourselves. What we give, the occasion, and the way in which we give the gift, all communicate something. Whether it is a little "thinking of you" gift, or a substantial gift given for a special occasion, we communicate our love by giving gifts, and the gift itself symbolizes our love. The giving and receiving of an engagement ring, or a wedding ring, are examples of gifts that are powerfully symbolic. Other gifts include gifts of service or loving deeds. Some find it difficult to communicate love verbally, preferring instead to "do things" for those they love. It is a way of giving a gift, and it could be anything from washing a spouse's car, to making his or her favorite dessert.

Through Spending Quality Time with Each Other

One of the most precious gifts one can give is the gift of one's time. It may also be the gift that is most greatly desired. By giving our time and attention—especially undivided and uninterrupted attention—we communicate to people their importance in our lives.

Through Doing Things Together

Doing things together can be a powerful way people bond and experience each other's presence. It can be things they particularly enjoy doing together, and things they do with their children. But it might also be things they do not particularly enjoy doing, but which bind the two of them together in a spirit of solidarity. Spouses can experience this when, as a couple, they deal with a family tragedy.

In all of these things, the spiritual is communicated through the physical. The activity is the *context* for the spiritual to occur, but it might not occur. Intimacy is about making a connection with another. And while it takes place in the midst of the things we do, intimacy itself is not the same as the actions that occasion them. Take, for example, two people eating together. It might be an occasion where they both experience a connection and a sense of unity with the other—or it could simply be two people eating at the same time. Similarly, if a companion gently grasps my upper arm to communicate sympathy, it does not have the same effect as the identical gesture done by a dear friend. When a friend does it, the opportunity is there for a real connection. Intimacy is communicated *through* these activities, but it is not equated with them.

The Uniqueness of Sexual Intimacy and Its Connection with Marriage

As we continue our conversation about male-female intimacy, we turn to the topic of sexual love. Sexual expression—a term that I use to connote explicitly erotically motivated interaction—is connected with deep human emotions and passions. The deepest connection one can *experience* is a sexual connection, and it is a complicated dynamic.

Views on the proper context for sexual expression have varied widely through the ages. I suspect that no one reading this book subscribes to the "Puritanical" position, which sees human passion in general—and sexual activity in particular—as something dirty, an evil to be tolerated for the sake of begetting progeny. Further, I suspect that my readers equally rebuff the "friends with benefits" phenomenon, where people with casual connections to each other "hook up" for recreational sex, or treat sex as a commodity.

So having thus narrowed the field, what more can we say about human sexuality? If it is the case that sex *means* something, if it is a type of bodily language, then one should only *say* with one's body what one genuinely means. Otherwise one is being dishonest with one's bodily language. All of our communications, both bodily and verbal, should be honest and genuine.

Even if we agree that sex is bodily language, and that one should be honest in one's bodily communications, how is the "meaning of sex" determined? Do *we*, individually or as a society, determine it? Or does sex have a meaning, so to speak, built into it because of the multifaceted and somewhat mysterious nature of human personhood? If we could discern a meaning in sexual intercourse—a meaning which we *discover*, but do not give to it—then certain things would naturally follow from that.

Pope John Paul II understood this very well, and his *theology of the body* is his attempt to reveal the goodness, the truth, and the beauty, of human sexuality. I use the term "human sexuality" to emphasize an important point. Animals have sex; people make love. And when we talk about love, we are talking about something mysterious, be- cause God—who is love—has made us in his image, and has put into us the desire and the ability to love as he loves. Jesus even com- mands his disciples to love each other as he loves us. So when we talk about love, we are talking about something that is deeper than what is readily observable and richer than what we experience. The human body, male and female, somehow reveals this mystery—the mystery of the God who is love. This is a fundamental point in John Paul II's *theology of the body*. As far as our bodiliness and our sexuality are concerned, there is more here than meets the eye.

The Language of the Body

When considering the mysterious reality of human sexuality, we seek to draw insights by pondering human nature and reflecting on the things God has revealed to us. John Paul II's approach in his *the- ology of the body* was not to lay out a logical argument: "If premises A and B are true, then conclusion C must logically follow." He does not think that is the way to approach a mystery. It is, as it were, a different kind of logic. It is an attempt to discern a vision of the hu- man person—body, soul, and spirit—that takes all of the reality into account, including the following facts.

- We were made in the image of God
- We were made for interpersonal union
- We were made male and female
- We desire fulfillment and completeness through union with the opposite sex
- Man leaves father and mother and cleaves to his wife
- Our human nature is both fallen and redeemed
- Evidence and effects of our fallen nature (our "woundedness") remains

The *theology of the body* gives one a "vision" of the human person. It is a vision that seeks to integrate these various aspects of our per- sonhood and gives an account of sexuality, marriage, and celibacy.

Sexual intercourse is more than an expression of love and the experience of a profound interpersonal connection. It is a covenantal act that renews the marriage covenant. The husband and wife "say" with their bodies the words they said when they exchanged their marriage vows. If that is the meaning, so to speak, built into sexual intercourse, then in the case of sex outside of the marriage covenant there is "a disconnect" between what one is saying with one's body, and what one really means to communicate. And if that is what is going on—if I am saying with my body what I do not, in fact, really mean—then I am being dishonest.

Within the context of renewing the marriage covenant, I think we can further specify its meaning without contradicting it. Beneath the umbrella of their marriage covenant, a husband and wife may make love to further communicate a variety of things. It can be a celebration of joy, a comfort in sorrow, an expression of support, or simply a thanksgiving for their mutual love for each other. But it is always within the larger context of the total gift of themselves, which is the marriage covenant. This is the natural meaning of sex, and as such it is profoundly beautiful. It is beautiful because of what it communicates—committed, faithful, spousal love in a bond that lasts until death.

Before going further, we must consider whether we ourselves can give sex its meaning. That is, after all, the view that many hold—that the meaning of sex is a human convention that we ourselves determine.

I do not think that we can absolutely *prove* that sex has a built-in meaning. However, I do think we can offer a response to those who deny it, and who maintain instead that it has whatever meaning the participants choose to give it. Rather than trying to argue against it directly, I think one can show that those who claim to hold such a view do not hold it consistently. Imagine a couple, Damon and Stef, who are in a "committed relationship." They both believe that sexual intercourse has the meaning that they choose to give it. The two of them are in love with each other, and they communicate that love sexually. Suppose further that Stef occasionally has sex with another man. When Damon discovers this and confronts Stef, she responds, "It does not really mean anything, not to me anyway. He is a friend, and I know he is lonely. And sex is a way of showing him that I care. But when I am with you, sex means deep love. It is not like that when I am with him." Would Damon be satisfied with that response? I suspect not. But he *should* be satisfied if he truly believes that one can give to sex whatever meaning he or she wishes to give to it.

Sexual intercourse has a meaning because *marriage* has a meaning. But this truth has been obscured in our time, for in the minds of many people, marriage is simply "a relationship" that might endure for life—but it is not something that, by its very nature, is irrevocable and indissoluble. Even people who generally believe that marriage is for life can consciously or subconsciously accept the idea that a marriage can end if they are unhappy, or if "things do not work out." Marriage is seen more in terms of a couple being together for as long as they want to be together. And in their hierarchy or ranking of values, "permanence of marriage" ranks lower than "the right to choose different or more fulfilling options as that need arises." Interestingly, that is not the approach people have toward their children—they grasp the permanence of parenthood. No one ever says, "We had two children, but it did not work out." Again, sexual intercourse has a meaning because marriage has a meaning—and the meaning of marriage is clearly stated in the marriage vows. But if sexual intercourse has a meaning built into it, and if it is a bodily way of renewing the covenant the man and woman made on their wedding day, then one can expect that as the meaning of marriage is clouded or obscured in people's minds, the meaning of sex will be clouded as well.

When considered from the specifically religious point of view, we see throughout history that God has established covenants and has given us a means to celebrate and renew them. On Mount Sinai God established a covenant with the people of Israel. And through Moses, he established the yearly observance of Passover as a way to both celebrate and renew the covenant. God established the new and eternal covenant through Jesus' sacrificial offering of himself. This is the Paschal Mystery. And each time the Eucharist is celebrated, the covenant is renewed. In a similar way, and in similar fashion, God established the covenant of marriage as a tremendous good for the couple and for their children. Marriage itself, and marital love, are an icon of God's faithful love for us. Each time the husband and wife make love, they celebrate and renew their marriage covenant.

What Is Meant by Lust?

It is perhaps worth noting that the three Western religions, some-times known as the "Religions of the Book"—Judaism, Christianity, and Islam—all view sexual activity apart from marriage as something sinful, i.e., as something prohibited by God himself. It is mentioned in the Scriptures of each of these three religions. Jesus takes the is-sue further, stating in the Sermon on the Mount that even looking lustfully at a woman is equivalent to committing adultery in one's heart.

Not everything that presents itself as love is authentic. But when it is authentic, it involves the giving of oneself to another, resulting in the two, as it were, abiding in each other. Love elicits a response from the beloved, so that in the context of self-giving we receive the gift of the other. We enjoy receiving this self-gift from the ones we love. We take delight in it, find it fulfilling—and perhaps charming. In all of the ways we love, mutual giving and receiving is, so to speak, built into the system—it is a part of the inner logic of love. And those who love each other, easily identify with the idea that they live *for* each other.

But suppose one were to try, so to speak, to circumvent the system. As such, I want to receive from you, but not as a part of our mutual self-giving. This entails an altogether different way of saying, "You are *for* me." And the look with which I look upon you is not a look that sees you as a *person* with whom I live in a relation-ship of mutual self-giving. Rather, with this look I see you as some-*thing*—as one sees an object—from whom I seek the satisfaction of some need or desire. That, when it is in a sexual context, is the "look of lust." It is the antithesis of love, and a violation of the true good of the person. Hence, it is always a moral evil. It is, as Jesus put it, adultery of the heart.

By admitting that the look of lust is evil, and is a possibility for all of us, we come face to face with the reality of our fallen human nature. Examples in the extreme are easy enough to identify. But in our fallen condition, we are susceptible to yielding to the look of lust in subtle ways too. And their subtlety makes them all the more difficult to recognize. But by acknowledging that we are subject to it adds something to the conversation that was not there before. It changes the landscape. And this framework enables us to discern an ethic that is applicable in all male-female relating.

Let us look further at the topic of lust itself. What is it? Definitions are not consistent. Some use the term to describe any kind of sexual desire. But more commonly, it refers to sexual things that are somehow tainted or defective in one way or another. We have the paradoxical expression, "sinful love." But how can love contain within it the seeds of moral evil? Clearly, lust cannot simply be identified with sexual desire, but with sexual desire of the "disordered" variety. But what makes it disordered? That is the issue.

To begin with, our *spontaneous* emotional and physical responses to sexual stimuli are neither morally good nor bad in themselves. They provide "the raw material for love," but they are not yet love. They become expressions of love when they are integrated into the larger reality of the couple's relationship. They do not stand alone, but are part of something larger.

At this point I want to introduce the term, "the larger context of committed love." Later on, I will further specify it. And in the end, the "larger context of committed love" will turn out to be marriage. But that conclusion is a ways off yet. For now, assume I am simply referring to a committed relationship of love.

Being made male and female, we desire sexual fulfillment through the opposite sex. Those desires, in response to internal or external stimuli, begin to make their presence felt. The *inclination* to seek the *sexual value* of another is what appears first—and it is not something over which we have direct control. It is there because of our sexual nature. When the spontaneous sensual responses make their presence felt, and one becomes aware of their presence, he or she must then choose, so to speak, what to do with them. Should they be pursued? Should they be resisted? The individual is faced with this choice. It is precisely at this point that one enters the "moral arena." Morality involves the way one *chooses*. When one is presented with a variety of options—which may simply be the option to do, or not to do something—the person determines himself or herself *existentially* as the particular kind of person he or she chooses to be by the choice made. This is why choices are important—I am what I choose.

The choice to seek or pursue the sexual value of another (either interiorly or exteriorly) outside the larger context of committed love is what is meant by lust. Note that it is not just sexual intercourse we are talking about. When the sexual value of another is sought as part of the larger orientation or commitment toward the other, and flows from it, then our sexual response itself is part of a larger context, which changes its meaning and its significance. It is not simply sought for its own sake. But when it *is* sought for its own sake, apart from the larger context of committed love, then it is lust. One is, in a certain sense, using the other. Pope John Paul II wrote,

> The truth of original sin explains a very basic and very widespread evil—that a human being encountering a person of the other sex does not simply and spontaneously experience 'love,' but a feeling muddied by the longing to enjoy, which often overshadows 'loving kindness' and robs love of its true nature, leaving only the outward appearance intact.[64]

Therefore we cannot, as it were, simply follow our instincts. Rather, our desires must be "filtered." We spontaneously desire the sexual value of the opposite sex, and when it is part of the larger context of love, it is good. Pursuing it apart from the larger context of love is disordered. Here lies the temptation that opens the way to "sinful love." It is not simply "wrong thinking." It is intentionally and willfully pursuing the sexual value of another, apart from the larger context of love.

Chaste love, on the other hand, involves a certain *interior transparency.* The notion that one's love is in need of being purified causes some to bristle. Commenting on the resentment some have to the concept of chastity, Pope John Paul II wrote:

> Resentment arises from an erroneous and distorted sense of values. It is a lack of objectivity in judgment and evaluation, and it has its origin in weakness of will. The fact is that attaining or realizing a higher value demands a greater effort of will. So in order to spare ourselves the effort, to excuse our failure to obtain this value, we minimize its significance, deny it the respect which it deserves, even see it as in some way evil, although objectivity requires us to recognize that it is good.[65]

Hence, the desire that one has to "enjoy" is naturally part of—but must be subordinated to—the larger context of love. It is a love that is marked, says John Paul II, by a "readiness to show loving kindness in every situation."[66] Even when we clearly recognize that chaste loving is good and is beautiful, we will not pretend that it is easy. The road to self-mastery is uphill for most of the way.

But even granting that sexual love, when properly ordered, must be part of a larger context of love, why must that larger context of love necessarily be marriage? Clearly, that is the real issue here.

Why cannot the love between the man and woman, which they are expressing sexually, be a genuine and committed love, but not the lifelong commitment of marriage? Is there an ethic, which we humans do not create, but which we discover and discern by examining human nature and the demands of interpersonal relatedness? If there is such an ethic, then it is not the genuineness of emotions that make expressions of love authentic, but whether they are in accord with this ethic. Further, if we discern such an ethic governing sexual interaction, then if one were willing to pursue the sexual value of another outside the parameters of such an ethic, it would be hard to deny that the person is in some sense "using" the other. And while it would not perhaps be *experienced* as using the other, nevertheless, "enjoying" replaces "loving" when this occurs. When one willingly violates a discernible ethic, then the virtue of love is replaced by an unhealthy preoccupation with sensual and sexual enjoyment.

The discernment of an ethic of sexual relating will turn on the meaning of the word "matrimony." It is derived from the Latin, *matris* and *munia*: maternal duties. Children are conceived by the sexual union of the man and the woman. Both the woman and the child have the need for the man to be a permanent part of the picture. The woman needs a spouse, and the child needs a mother and father who love each other and stay together until death. What clouds people's vision is that artificial contraception has broken the link between sex and conception—at least in people's minds, if not always in fact. And once one has the "power" to remove the conception of children from sex, then the value of marriage itself is called into question. "Why do I need to be married at all?" If sexual love is, as it were, disconnected from children—it is a short step also to disconnect it from the permanent relationship of marriage. This is precisely the situation today, and it was the motivational force driving the so-called sexual revolution: disconnect sex from marriage and from child bearing, and we would all be freer—freer in our communicating and experiencing love. But is that, in fact, what has happened? Now that we are several decades into the sexual revolution, are we really happier, freer, and relationally better off? It seems, rather, that we are lonelier and more disconnected inasmuch as "permanent, lifelong commitment" has been replaced in our hierarchy of values with the freedom to do as one pleases. Certainly, not every marriage is a happy one. But the

and the love between them runs deep. Every day when Kevin comes home from work, she smiles as soon as she sees him. He said, "I look forward to that smile all day."

* * * * *

There are several moments in the life of a married couple that strongly impact the way they experience life. The time when the last child leaves home is one such moment, and the time and energy they spent raising their children now needs to be refocused. If the first and last child are ten years apart, then mom and dad have had kids at home for nearly *thirty years*. And in their mind and heart "family life" means being at home with the kids. Once the last child has moved out of the house, the parents' whole life seems different. Some describe the first few months as a time of mourning. It is the "empty nest" experience. It requires a real adjustment in the way they live, and it does not always go smoothly. But going "smoothly" and going "well" are not the same thing. Anything that is experienced as a sort of dying will be unpleasant—but it can also bring new opportunities for growth.

If a husband and wife neglected their marital relationship, that fact will become painfully obvious when the last child leaves home. Some couples, whose mutual love had long-since died, stayed together for the sake of the children—and they separate once the last child is gone. Or they continue living under the same roof but live almost completely separate lives. But many couples, after they get over the initial distress of the empty nest, experience something like a new springtime in their marriage.

Keith and Sylvia: Marriage in the Later Years

Keith and Sylvia were both twenty-four when they got married. They had known each other since high school and started seriously dating soon after graduation. Once they were married, they bought a home in a rural area just outside the town where they grew up, and both of them were eager to start a family. The first of their four children was born in the second year of their marriage.

After the birth of their fourth child, Sylvia's father was diagnosed with inoperable cancer and died within the year. It was a difficult time all around. She spent a lot of time with her mother during the last two months of her father's life, while Keith looked after the kids. A couple of times a week Sylvia spent the night with her mom. That helped her mother immensely but added to the stress of her own home. Nonetheless, they got through it. Sylvia was grateful to be able to assist her mother and spend that time with her dying father. She could see the toll it took on her husband, and she will forever be grateful to him for his generosity through it all.

Looking back on it years later, Sylvia and Keith believed the ordeal of her father's death brought the two of them closer inasmuch as it gave them the security and confidence that comes from effectively facing a serious challenge. Having successfully negotiated that difficulty, they had the confidence that if they could get through that, they could get through anything. It gave them a sense of reposing in each other and looking for—and receiving—support from each other. They did not always agree on things, but somehow they always managed to work things out. And their religious faith played a role in that, too. Both of them are devout, but Keith has always had a firm trust in Divine Providence, believing that God allows things happen as they do for a reason. His wife and his children heard him say many times through the years, "In God's Providence, there are no accidents." It was an idea he had gleaned from Pope John Paul II.

Their four kids are all out of the house now, and their eldest is married. When the kids were living at home, it was always a struggle to find the time, or the money, for Keith and Sylvia to do things together—things like getting away for a weekend. But now it has become a regular part of their lives. They both continue to work, and they plan to continue doing so for a while—at least until their grandkids come along. Their marriage is a multi-layered relationship, which gives it its richness. It is plainly obvious that Keith and Sylvia love each other. The interpersonal union they experience is the fruit of various elements of marital love. To begin with, Keith and Sylvia continue to be very dear friends, with all that that entails. Their generosity and willingness to serve each other is evident in their day-to-day relating, and after all these years they genuinely enjoy doing things for one another. They acknowledge this trait in each other, which in turn seems to bring it out even more. Among the married people they know, Sylvia and Keith are aware that some of their married friends are not particularly generous—a fact that is evident in the way they relate. Somehow, seeing this lack of generosity in some of their married friends makes Keith and Sylvia more appreciative of each other.

Besides their character strengths, the two of them continue to be deeply interested in one another. They have never taken each other for granted. Over the years, they have discovered their beloved's favorite ways of being loved, and they have grown accustomed to loving each other in those ways. Once a week, Keith stops at the grocery store on his way home from work. Along with the groceries he picks up a small, inexpensive bouquet of flowers that the grocer always has on hand. If Sylvia is out when Keith gets home, he puts the flowers in a vase with a note next to it: "For the love of my life."

Besides Keith and Sylvia loving each other in the way they want to be loved, they have also learned to accept *being* loved in the way their beloved wants to communicate it. Sylvia does a lot of things—little things—that Keith does not particularly want or need to have done. She still irons his handkerchiefs, even though they are permanent press, because she thinks a gentleman should have a neatly ironed handkerchief. It means more to her than it does to him, but he gladly allows her do it because it is one more little way that she shows her love. It is sort of like when Keith washes Sylvia's car—it means more to him than it does to her. But by acknowledging and thanking each other for these little acts of kindness, they show that they continue to be grateful for each other's expressions of love.

Keith and Sylvia are also bound together by their sense of accomplishment. They look at the lives of their children, and they are rightly filled with a noble pride. Looking back, they know they were not perfect. Still, they know they were good parents, and the fruit of their labors is seen in the lives of their kids. They have a sense of satisfaction and accomplishment from their marriage and the home life they have created.

Finally, the two of them have a healthy confidence in the future, and this unites them as well. In the immediate future, they look forward to the trips they continue to take together. More than that, they look forward to having grandchildren and the joy that they will bring to their lives.

Keith and Sylvia are not what one would call elderly, but they are getting on in years. Their faith and hope in God enables them to talk about what awaits them in the years ahead. They do indeed look to the day when they will be together in the Kingdom with all the blessed. Both of them know that it will be a sad time for the surviving spouse when the first one goes to God. But they try to keep the big picture in mind, remembering why God has made us, and remembering that the separation between those in heaven and those on earth is more of an illusion than a reality. Many times, at the funeral visitation for a departed friend, they have heard the priest pray, "But for those who believe in your love, death is not the end, nor does it destroy the bonds that you forge in our lives." And though they know that the bond of marriage ends with death, they know that their relationship in the Kingdom will be real, it will be meaningful, and it will be intimate. Keith says he wants to live one day longer than Sylvia—so that he can be there *for* her as she dies, and then be there *with* her in the Kingdom.

A Multifaceted Diamond

The love between a husband and wife is like a multifaceted diamond. They are attracted to each other, they desire each other, they want to give themselves to each other and be received by the other in a reciprocal and fruitful relationship of intimate love. All of these things—and more—seem to come together as they make love. And the love they celebrate and experience in their lovemaking is a love that is capable of bearing fruit.

In *By Love Refined: Letters to a Young Bride,* Alice von Hildebrand (the wife of the eminent Catholic philosopher, Dietrich von Hildebrand) carries on a correspondence with Julie who is recently married to Michael. In one letter she speaks of marital intercourse and the need for inner preparation. She writes:

> With regard to sexual relations in particular, I think it's a great psychological mistake for spouses to enter the mysterious garden of sexual self-giving without any interior preparation. Quite apart from its link with the great event of conceiving a child, your bodily union with Michael in the secret of your intimacy is so great and so mysterious that it calls for an inner preparation. It should be the climax of attention revealed through loving words and loving deeds: a symphony of tenderness manifested in many different ways in the course of the day. (Your heart will teach you what to do.) Then—and only then—will your sexual union acquire its full value as a canticle of love.[69]

As Mrs. von Hildebrand makes clear, the lovemaking between spouses should be the climax of all their other ways of communicating love. It is as though all their acts of love and sacrifice are, so to speak, gathered together and re-presented to each other as they make love. It is, as she points out, something that requires "inner preparation."

As beautiful and powerful as sexual intercourse is, it is not the highest and greatest act of love—though it is perhaps the greatest *experience* of love and unity. The greatest *act of love, the greatest expression of love,* is found in the laying down of one's life. This is the love of a martyr. "Greater love has no man than this, that a man lay down his life for his friends."[70] Most will never have the opportunity to die for their spouse in the sense of a martyr's death, but there is an insight here that we do not want to lose. We find ourselves, and we are ennobled, by the *sincere gift of ourselves.* One sees this lived most beautifully where a husband or wife cares for a spouse who is dying from a terminal illness such as cancer. It is difficult physically, mentally, emotionally, and spiritually. In a sense, they are both dying, though in different ways. Jesus, who loved his own in the world, *loved them to the end.*[71] These husbands and wives have loved their spouses *to the end.* The *idea* of living that kind of life may seem romantic, though actually living it out may not be experienced as such. But, romantic or not, it is a beautiful gift of oneself. They stood before God and swore that they would love their spouses *for better or worse, in sickness and health, until death*—and this indeed they have done. Pope Benedict XVI beautifully describes this love between a man and a woman as a mutual self-giving that is simultaneously life giving:

> Love is indeed "ecstasy," not in the sense of a moment of intoxication, but rather as a journey, an ongoing exodus out of the closed inward-looking self towards its liberation through self-giving, and thus towards authentic self-discovery and indeed the discovery of God: "Whoever seeks to gain his life will lose it, but whoever loses his life will preserve it.[72]

Questions for Philosophical Consideration and Personal Growth

1. How are expectations in a relationship typically communicated?

2. What is the relationship between genuine love and emotional contentment?

3. What did Karol Wojtyla mean in *Love and Responsibility* when he wrote, "A very rich and rapid growth of [erotic] sensations may conceal a love that has failed to develop"?

4. What is the difference between loving someone and being in love?

5. What, as you see it, is masculinity? What is femininity? What does it mean to say that in the masculine-feminine dynamic, the man *encounters* the femininity of the woman, and the woman *encounters* the masculinity of the man? What does it mean to say that a spiritual reality is communicated through the body?

6. Imagine the following scene—it is a common one. Jim and Susan have been dating for a long time. Jim's friend, Charles, asks him if he really loves her. Jim says he does not know. What is Jim really asking? What is the real issue here?

7. There are a variety of ways of measuring love. What are they?

8. What would a healthy dating relationship between high school students look like? What would be warning signs or symptoms of an unhealthy relationship?

   What about a couple in college?

   What about a couple preparing for marriage?

9. What role does character strength play in marriage?

10. What would you say to a married man with children who regularly wants to spend his evenings in recreation away from the family?

11. It seems as though the marriage relationship changes when the husband and wife no longer spend time doing things they enjoy doing together. Comment.

12. Look at the various people in your life. What are your favorite ways of communicating your love? Do you know their favorite ways of being loved? What are your favorite ways of receiving their love?

And further, "Many are called, but few are chosen,"[76] and, "The gate is narrow and the way is hard, that leads to life, and those who find it are few."[77] But a different image of Jesus comes to mind when we read that Jesus, seeing the crowds, "had compassion on them, because they were like sheep without a shepherd."[78] And when none remained to condemn the woman caught in adultery, Jesus says to her, "Neither do I condemn you."[79] And who can fail to see the compassion revealed in the familiar story of the prodigal son?

Putting all of this together can be a challenge. God hates sin with a perfect hate. But he loves sinners—and that is all of us. And though we make progress in our lives of discipleship, leaving some of our sins behind, we continually discover new ones. We cannot completely eliminate it from our lives. Archbishop Fulton Sheen was famous for saying, "Sin is in the blood."

On the one hand, we want to avoid "living in the shadow of a Puritan god." Accordingly, God is a severe God—always demanding and never understanding, and we seemingly never do anything but displease him. Those who think this way see themselves as never measuring up and always in trouble with God. I am characterizing this in the extreme—but many clearly have tendencies in this direction.

But on the other hand, neither should we see God as some sort of celestial Pillsbury Doughboy. "I can do what I want, and God will understand, or I can rebel against God without consequence—because he loves me." Pope John Paul II addressed this issue in a document entitled *On Reconciliation and Penance*. In it he stated:

> But when we ponder the problem of a rebellious will meeting the infinitely just God, we cannot but experience feelings of salutary "fear and trembling," as St. Paul suggests. Moreover, Jesus' warning about the sin "that will not be forgiven," confirms the existence of sins which can bring down on the sinner the punishment of "eternal death."[80]

So what is one to make of all of this? Keep in mind, this is not a book about salvation. I am not describing what is necessary to go to Heaven. Rather, my focus is the issue of what it means to have a real friendship with God. But the way that we see God has a discernible impact on the way we relate to him. We want to have a concept of God that encompasses everything that he has revealed about himself.

We have seen all along that there are three key elements to every personal relationship. They are present as well in our friendships with God.

Mutual Interest in One Another

God desires an intimate relationship with each of us which, if it is going to be real, requires that we be sincere participants. This reminds me of a line from St. Augustine who somewhere said, "God, who made us without our help, will not save us without our help." I am writing specifically about friendship, not salvation, but the point here is the same. As we have seen throughout this book, every friendship requires that there be a *mutual* interest. The first stage in one's relationship with God is often the recognition that Our Lord loves me personally and individually.

For the Christian, our love for God means having a relationship with each of the three members of the Blessed Trinity, and the relationship with each of them is different. We speak to the Father with the confidence of a child talking to dad. It is an intimate relationship—but the intimacy like that of a parent and child.

The relationship with Jesus is different. The Son is just as divine as the Father, but he became one of us, being born of the Blessed Virgin Mary. So we do not relate to him as a father, but as a brother—a brother who is like us in all things but sin. The devotion to the Sacred Heart of Jesus stresses this very point. Jesus loves us with a human heart—a heart that loves, a heart that rejoices, a heart that can break.

And we relate to the Holy Spirit as the divine person who dwells in our heart. Spiritual writers have referred to the Holy Spirit as "The Great Unknown." He is the love of the Father and the Son, proceeding from both. He enlightens our minds and inflames our hearts that we may know and love the things of God.

Loving God is more than respecting God, and respecting God is more than fearing God. He is interested in a relationship of love, but if it is to take shape, then we must desire it as well.

Virtue and Character Strength

What is the role of virtue, goodness, and character strength in our friendship with God? God does not love us *because* we are good. God's love *enables* us to be good. Recall that one of our principle assumptions here is that God always acts first. He is the source of every good thing and the giver of every good gift. We become good, and we grow in holiness, by cooperating with God's saving work in us.

Living out our friendship with God, we can be frustrated by our own failings. We can genuinely desire to live noble and upright lives, yet we are aware that we often fall short. St. Paul had the same experience, and he wrote of it in his Letter to the Romans:

> I do not understand my own actions. For I do not do what I want, but I do the very thing I hate. Now if I do what I do not want, I agree that the law is good. So then it is no longer I that do it, but sin which dwells within me. For I know that nothing good dwells within me, that is, in my flesh. I can will what is right, but I cannot do it. For I do not do the good I want, but the evil I do not want is what I do.[81]

He clearly does not sound like a man who, as is said, "has everything together." And we, like St. Paul, daily face the struggle to live the life that God wants us to live. And each day we ask for his mercy, knowing we fall short.

This side of the grave, our work is never complete. People can change, and people can grow. I have seen this happen in the lives of some people whom I have known for many years. There is a transformation that takes place, and they become more and more like Christ. The older St. Augustine bore rather little resemblance to the man he was in his youth. This gives us an insight that helps us to be patient with our spouses, our friends, and ourselves. Growth and change *can* occur, but it does not typically happen overnight. But as the growth does happen, we indeed become better—better friends and spouses, and better friends of God. We become like our friends. And if Jesus is our friend, we will become more like him. We grow in goodness and virtue, and that enables us to keep our commitments to God. It is a *process*, and God is with us through our personal journey. He does not wait until one is living a noble and holy life to be our friend. We all, to one degree or another, struggle to live a good life. Each of us is the prodigal son, making his way back to the Father's house.

Favorite Things Done Together

Finally, if the friendship is to be real we have to have things we do together. At first glance, we might ask, "What could I possibly do with God?" In reality, everything we do can be done with him and for him. In the three types of intimate relating we have looked at in this book—with friends, with one's spouse, and with God—we gain insights about each relationship by looking at the other two. Human friendship and marriage give us insights about how to relate to God. So, for example, we can imagine a married man who, after many years of marriage says to his wife, "You are a part of me and a part of everything I do. Everything I do, I do for you and the kids. And I do not know where I would be without you." He means it sincerely. He does not *think* like a bachelor. Everything passes through a filter in his mind, and he habitually asks himself, "What would my wife think about this? What effect will this have on the family?" Their lives have become so intertwined—their roots have so grown together—that you cannot separate them without doing damage to both of them. We see something very similar in a deep and richly lived relationship with God.

Intimate conversation is more than talking. It entails two people encountering each other—consciously coming together. Prayer can provide the same experience. In a soul inflamed with the love of God, there arises the desire to spend quality time in prayer. We naturally desire to spend time in conversation with the ones we love. Many have the praiseworthy custom of talking to God spontaneously throughout the day. Spiritual writers speak of this as "living always in the presence of God." But we still have need for focused attention during the time we reserve exclusively for prayer—the time when we give him our undivided attention. Whether we are talking about friendship, marriage, or the relationship with God, we need quality time spent together. Time constraints often make this difficult. But if we see it as something truly worthwhile, we are more likely to make time for it. And we should expect that being attentive and responsive to God in prayer will sometimes come easily, and other times it will require sustained effort on our part—just as it does in every other relationship we have.

For Catholics, receiving the sacraments worthily is the most intimate thing we can do *with* God. This is most especially true of the Eucharist. But in each of the seven sacraments, Jesus and the individual (through the mediation of the priest, who at that moment is acting for Christ) do something together which results in the individual's growth in holiness. We may not feel any different—but we are. (We do not feel any older on our birthday, but we are. We are a day older than we were the day before.) But we do not have to feel different for the effect to be real.

Finally, all of the things we do in the fulfillment of our vocations are things done for God. And for the recollected soul living in the presence of God, they can also be done *with* God. This is especially true of the corporal and spiritual works of mercy. They are things we do for others and things we can do with God.

Communicating Our Intimate Love for God

Jesus told us that we love him by keeping his commandments. And there is no greater act of love for God than the laying down of one's life for the faith. But I wish to focus here on the seemingly smaller, more intimate ways of showing one's love for God.

Throughout the book I have tried to help the reader see that we can gain valuable insights about intimate relating by looking at other intimate relationships we have. Spouses, for example, can learn about marriage by reflecting on lifelong, loyal friendships—and *vice versa*. And a healthy marriage can give us clues about how we might relate to God.

In the last chapter, we looked at several ways people communicate their love in the context of marriage. *Mutatis mutandis*—making the necessary changes—we can apply this to our relationship with God. We do not love our loved ones *in theory*, but in the concrete ways we interact with them. So, too, growing in our love for God is more than an increased sense of religiosity. Like all of our relationships, it entails concrete ways of interacting with the one we love.

Through Things That Are Said

We do not want to sound like bureaucrats when we pray—saying everything very properly. We open our hearts and let words of love spill out. When people love each other, words of love spontaneously spring forth. It is a venerable custom to have short prayers (commonly called "aspirations") that one frequently says to God. One of my favorites is a line from St. Peter, "Lord, you know everything; you know that I love you."

By the Way We Look at Each Other

Can we look at God when we pray? St. John Vianney, the patron saint of parish priests, seemed to think so. He spent a good deal of time in prayer before the Blessed Sacrament each day, and someone once asked him, "What do you do when you pray?" He responded by saying, "I look at the Good God. And the Good God looks at me."

Through Touching

St. John began his first letter, "That which was from the beginning, which we have heard, which we have seen with our eyes, which we have looked upon and touched with our hands, concerning the word of life."[82] In his case, as one who lived with Jesus, he had the experience of seeing, hearing, and touching Our Lord.

In the Gospels one finds a surprising number of instances where Jesus touches people. He touched the eyes of the blind so they could see,[83] and the tongue of the mute so they could speak.[84] When Peter's mother-in-law was ill, "he touched her hand, and the fever left her, and she rose and served him."[85] A leper approached Jesus and said to him, "'Lord, if you will, you can make me clean.' And he stretched out his hand and touched him, saying, 'I will. Be clean.' And immediately his leprosy was cleansed."[86] And Sts. Peter, James, and John, after the Transfiguration, fell to the ground in awe. "But Jesus came and touched them, saying, 'Rise, and have no fear.'"[87]

In our prayer, we can imagine Jesus' loving hand on us—tenderly touching us—confident that he loves us. And, of course, when we receive the Eucharist we encounter Jesus bodily.

Through Sharing Meals Together

We do not sit down to dinner with God, though I know people who mentally converse with Jesus when they are eating alone. But let us not forget that Jesus instituted the Eucharist at a meal. And it was not just any meal—it was the Passover. The Mass is more than a meal—but it *is* a meal. It is a meal hosted by Jesus that is an integral part of the Paschal Mystery.

Through the Making and Keeping of Promises and Commitments

Promises and commitments can be large or small. Besides vows and solemn promises, we can make little promises—like the ones we make for Lent. We can promise, for instance, to make the Stations of the Cross on the Fridays of Lent. Anytime of the year we could promise Jesus in the morning that we will spend thirty minutes in prayer that afternoon. By keeping our commitments we show our love.

Through Giving Gifts and Loving Deeds

Our giving a gift to God resembles little children giving gifts to their parents. Everything we have comes to us by the grace and favor of God. Nevertheless, we can give back in love and in gratitude. Some people, moved to generosity, give a gift that is sacrificial. But very small gifts can be beautiful and done with great love. I know a man who cuts the roses from his garden and places them in front of his statue of Our Lady. He says it is a little way of showing his love and affection.

In his first letter, St. Peter wrote about "spiritual sacrifices." These are spiritual gifts presented to God. Many people have the custom of making a morning offering each day, offering to God all their "prayers, works, joys, and sufferings" of the day. When we do them for Our Lord, out of love for him, they become, as St. Peter said, "Spiritual sacrifices acceptable to God through Jesus Christ."[88] Like with any gift-giving, the spirit in which it is given is what really matters.

Through Spending Quality Time with Each Other

We looked at this when we talked about prayer. Good husbands and wives live their lives for their family. They could say, "Everything I do, I do for them." Still, it is important for their spousal relationship that they spend quality time just with each other. A woman trying to live a devout life could say that everything she does, she does for God. Nevertheless, we communicate his relative importance in our life by spending time in prayer and worship. How beautiful it is when someone says to another, "I do not have much time right now, but some of the time I do have—I want to spend with you."

Through Doing Things Together

This is an enormously broad category. It is our task to build up the Kingdom of God here on earth, and we cooperate with Jesus in doing so. It does not have to be specifically "religious activity." God gives to everyone a specific vocation which is the work he wants the person to do at that moment in his or her life. Whether it is teaching math, caring for the sick, stocking shelves, playing with the kids, or waxing floors, we can do it with the awareness that we are doing it with and for Jesus. All of the *Works of Mercy* can be something we do with Our Lord and done out of love.

Modeling Our Life on the Paschal Mystery

On the day of his ordination, every man who is ordained a priest hears his bishop say, "Model your life on the mystery of the Lord's Cross." But these words are equally fitting for a couple on their wedding day or for two people who are becoming friends. I sometimes tell the people at a wedding Mass that if Jesus were to speak to this couple right now, I think he would say to them, "Love one another as I have loved you."[89] This is the "new commandment" that Jesus gave to us at the Last Supper, and it reveals one of the great mysteries of human life and human love. At the heart of it is the Paschal Mystery—the mystery of the suffering, death, and rising of the Lamb of God. Embracing it is not a "task to be accomplished," but rather a transformation of one's thinking and choosing—modeling one's life on the mystery of the Lord's Cross. And it is precisely what St. Paul had in mind when he said that we are to "put on Christ."[90]

The Paschal Mystery is the predominant theme in the New Testament. In the third year of Jesus' public life he faced a choice. He knew that his enemies—the official leaders of the Jewish people—sought his death. Aware of this, three options would have naturally occurred to him:

- He could have escaped to a far-away land, never to be seen or heard from again;
- He could have used his divine power to keep his enemies at bay;
- He could have permitted himself to fall into the hands of his enemies.

But both of first two options would, in effect, nullify the very reason of the Incarnation. By escaping to a far-off place Jesus would be leaving us the following example: when things in life really become difficult—flee. And had Jesus used divine power to keep his enemies from harming him, he would no longer be an example to us of how to live—since we do not have such divine power at our disposal.

The only real option Jesus had was to permit himself to fall into the hand of his enemies. He did so, confident of his Father's power—including power over death. Further, Jesus understood that as the Messiah, he would save his people by being the Lamb of God—the Lamb of Sacrifice.

The concept of the sacrificial lamb is of particular importance in understanding the Christian mystery. If we are to model our lives on the life of Jesus, we need to see the significance of Jesus as the Lamb of God.

Every pious Jew living in Palestine in the time of Jesus was familiar with the story of the deliverance of the Israelites from their enslavement in Egypt. Those unfamiliar with the story can read it for themselves in the Book of Exodus. What saved them was the blood of a sacrificed lamb which they applied to their doors. God had revealed to Moses that when the Angel of Death descended upon Egypt, he would *pass over* their homes. Every year thereafter Jews recall this event as they celebrate Passover.

Christians believe that the events of Passover were a prelude to the deliverance made possible by Jesus, the Lamb of God, whose blood was shed for us. We would be saved by Lamb's blood—not some little farm animal—but the blood of Jesus, the Lamb of God.

At a certain point it seems logical to ask, "Why is the Father pleased with Jesus' Death?" It is a reasonable question. I think the best answer is that the Father was pleased—not precisely with Jesus' Death—but with Jesus' willingness to live his vocation to the full, even if it killed him. So on the evening of his Last Supper, he made the definitive choice to proceed, knowing what that would entail. Jesus had prayed, sweating blood, that this cup of suffering could pass him by—but he concluded his prayer with, "Thy will be done." Jesus abandons himself into his Father's hands with complete trust and confidence.

At the Last Supper, Jesus participated in the annual celebration of Passover, where they ate the sacrificed lamb, recalling how their ancestors had been saved by its blood. To drive home the point that he himself was the new Passover Lamb, he gave them his own Flesh, commanded them to eat it, and mandated that they repeat this in his memory. "Take this and eat it. This is my body, which will be given up for you. . . . Do this in memory of me."

The following day, events unfolded as Jesus knew they would. His enemies had sought his death, and now they would get their wish. They killed him, "nailing him to a tree," and all the while he prayed for those who brought about his Death. "Father, forgive them; for they know not what they do."[91]

But Jesus knew that his Father would respond. And that is precisely what we celebrate on Easter. The Father was pleased with Jesus' willingness to fulfill his vocation—his mission and life's work—even if its fulfillment would bring about his Death. And it *did* bring about his death. But the Father responded by raising Jesus from the dead.

All of this, taken together, is the prototypical Christian life and a model for our own life. Each of us has a life to live—a mission and vocation. John Henry Cardinal Newman said, "God has created me to do him some definite service; he has committed some work to me which he has not committed to another. I have my mission—I may never know it in this life, but I shall be told it in the next." When we live that life well, our life is pleasing to God. Faithfully fulfilling the demands of that vocation may give us a tremendous sense of satisfaction and joy. Or, it might result in our persecution. More likely, there will be aspects of our vocation that we enjoy and aspects that cause us suffering. But the goal of life is not the maximization of the pleasant aspects and the elimination of the difficult ones. The goal of life is to fulfill all the demands of our vocation, regardless of the outcome. "Seek first his Kingdom and his righteousness, and all these things shall be yours as well."[92] As the Father responded to Jesus' generosity and fidelity—so too will he respond to us. This is a unique and distinctly Christian way of looking at life. And it takes faith and hope to achieve it: faith that God is who he says he is, and the hope—or confident expectation—that he will keep his promises. The difficulty in accepting God's offer lies in the fact that while Jesus promises us a hundredfold in this life to those who sacrifice for his sake, or for the Gospel, we will not receive our full recompense until the next life.

A man who had recently returned to the United States from England commented on his experience watching a game of cricket. He understood baseball and tried to use the same basic framework to understand cricket. After several hours, he could still make no sense of what the players were doing. I cannot help but think that something similar happens when trying to understand the Christian Faith using secular values.

The life of a believer entails more than the embracing of the civic virtues (like honesty, dedication, and commitment). And it is more than living a life of piety—saying one's prayers and attending

Church on Sunday. It is something far richer. Rather, it is a vision of life that enables one to discern the "tiny whispering sound" of the Spirit, prompting one to live heroically for the sake of the Kingdom. It is, as St. Paul calls it, "A fresh, spiritual way of thinking."[93] It is a life where one seeks at every moment the will of the Lord.

It regularly happens in our lives that we face choices—big and small. It is not always a choice between good and evil. Often the options before us are all good ones—but which one should I choose?

- Should we take the kids camping or take them to Disney World?
- Should I ask her to marry me, knowing that we differ in significant ways?
- Should I accept this promotion?
- Should we buy a car now, or wait? And when we do, should we buy it new or used?
- Should we try to have another child now?
- What should I do with my aging father?
- Should I join this fraternal organization?
- How will I spend my time this weekend?

At every turn God is present and wants to be "part of the conversation." And in the exercise of one's freedom, God is there—trying to lead us one way or another. The life of grace and intimacy with God entails placing oneself, as it were, at God's disposal—becoming an instrument in his hand.

Living life this way gives one a sense of adventure—we cannot always predict where God will lead us. We want to be able to let God take us by the hand without first asking him where he will take us. Adopting this way of thinking, certain notions from the New Testament are seen in a new light. "Take up your cross and follow me" and "Try to enter through the narrow gate," encourage us to live generously, reminding us that a life of greatness entails real, personal sacrifice. "The last shall be first, and the first shall be last," helps us see that the hierarchy of values in this world does not correspond with those of the Kingdom. And "as you did it to one of the least of these my brethren, you did it to me," asserts that Jesus identifies with each of us personally in the family of God.

The Effect God's Friendship Has on Our Life

Growth in a relationship is not a task to be accomplished, but the result of a transformation. We become like our friends, and as our friendship with God increases we become more like him. This happens as we increasingly place our *faith* in him, as we live in the *hope* that he will fulfill his promises, and allow his divine *love* to take possession of our souls. We become more like God, and grow in holiness. Holiness, like goodness, is not *a* virtue but a general quality or orientation of one's life.

As the transformation occurs, several things happen. Among other things, egoism—or pride—begins to be replaced with humility. The word "pride" has several connotations, some of which are very good—such as when a father says he is "proud" of his daughter, or when a woman says she is "proud" to be Catholic. The sin of pride has nothing to do with that. The sin of pride places one, so to speak, in competition with God—and with everyone else. Accordingly, my way is always the best way, and I will not yield to anyone. Humility, on the other hand, entails a realistic evaluation of who I am and what my role is *vis-à-vis* God and everyone else. Humility is a beautiful virtue, enabling us to be, so to speak, *genuine*.

By understanding who we are, and what we have received, we are thus enabled to bestow mercy. Because the humble woman knows that she has been forgiven, it is easier for her to forgive. The humble man is aware that he has received mercy, thus prompting him to be merciful.

This inner transformation, brought about by a loving friendship with God, manifests itself by the handing over of one's life to God—in a spirit of abandonment. It is harder than it sounds. We all have an idea of what we want to do with our lives, and the way we want them to unfold. We have an idea, for example, of whether we wish to marry, where we want to live, the kind of work we want to do, and how many kids we will have. And to get these things to fall into place, we use our wit and wisdom, our hard work and determination, and our social, familial, and political connections. And we often believe that if we are bright, hard working, well-connected, and lucky, we will get what we want. We make plans for our lives, present them to God, and ask him to bless them.

But what if our beautiful and well-thought-out plans differ from the plan that God has in mind for our lives? It is not God's job, after all, to help us get what we want. We are *his* servants, not the other way around. And suppose further that God's plan for us entails things we will never be able to accomplish with our own strength? It is precisely at this point that one stands at the threshold of abandonment to the Will of God.

Father Walter J. Ciszek: Abandonment to the Will of God—in the Gulag

Father Walter J. Ciszek was a Jesuit priest who came to understand what it means to abandon oneself to the Will of God. He was born in 1904, a Polish-American from the coal region of Shenandoah, Pennsylvania. As a youth he was a tough, scrappy kid—known for his grit and for being something of a bully. In eighth grade, his father asked the police to send his son to a reform school.

Walter shocked his family when he announced his intention of going to the seminary. In 1929, Pope Pius XI was acutely aware that the Communists had decimated the Church in Russia, and he asked the Jesuits to send missionaries there to meet the spiritual needs of the people. Walter volunteered for this undertaking and was sent to study at the Russia Center (*Russicum*) in Rome. On June 24, 1937 he was ordained and said his first Mass in the Russian rite.

Since no priests were allowed to enter Russia openly, Father Ciszek was sent to Albertyn, Poland, where he taught ethics to seminarians. But on September 1, 1939 Hitler invaded Poland; and shortly thereafter Russia invaded from the east. For Father Ciszek, it was as though Russia had come to him. Since the Jesuit mission at Albertyn was no longer operational, he and a priest-friend decided to make their way deep into the heart of Russia where they could tend to the spiritual needs of the Russian people. Father Ciszek envisioned it as being a great adventure. He had no idea.

Though he was using an assumed-name, the secret police knew exactly who he was, and in very little time he was arrested. He was charged with being a Vatican spy. He spent some twenty-three years in Soviet prisons and in the labor camps of Siberia. Later he wrote of his experiences in the Gulag in two books, *With God in Russia* and *He Leadeth Me*. In the later book he describes a moment of conversion that is worth examining in detail. It is the moment when he discovers—for the first time in his life—what it really means to abandon himself completely to the Will of God.

Shortly after his arrest, Father Ciszek was sent to Lubianka. Here, in the Gulag—the dreaded Soviet prison—the NKVD (Soviet secret police agency, and forerunner of the KGB) did its best (or worst) work. He spent months in solitary confinement in a six-by-ten-foot cell which was completely empty except for a bed (which one was forbidden to use except at night), a toilet-bucket, and a naked light hanging from the ceiling. During this time he was regularly interrogated, the purpose of which was to determine the exact nature of his espionage and to get him to admit to his crimes. The NKVD had many means at their disposal. Father Ciszek put it, "They were relentless, and they were thorough, and they were good at their trade."[94]

From the very beginning, he believed that they would eventually realize that they had made a mistake. He was not a spy—not for the Vatican, or for the Americans, or for anybody else. He was simply a priest who was carrying out his priestly work.

The interrogations could be brief, or they could go on for twenty-four or even forty-eight hours—with no rest or food for the prisoner. They might occur daily for months, and then not at all for several months. At times the interrogators were brutal, demanding, and harsh; at other times they seemed understanding, almost sympathetic. It was not as though Father Ciszek had secret information that he was withholding—he was simply a priest doing priestly work. After each session, he would return to his cell where he would be tortured by his own self-examination: Did I say the right things? What if I had said it this way? How will this be conveyed to the "higher-ups"? Will they finally understand? What can I do to make them understand?

After twelve months, his interrogators presented him a very lengthy document that was a "summary of his testimony." While the words were largely his, the one who prepared the summary had twisted the meaning of his statements. He was overwhelmed by confusion, by his desperation, and by his desire to have the whole matter done with. And in the end, he signed it.

Back in his cell, he was overwhelmed with shame and grief—with the feeling of being a coward, a traitor, and a failure. Why, he wondered, did it come to this? Why did God not give him the strength to stand up to his enemy at this critical moment? He not only felt broken and embarrassed, he felt that God was very, very far away. Little did he know that he was on the verge of the greatest conversion of his life.

For his entire life, Walter Ciszek had relied on his vigor, his intelligence, and his strength of endurance. From the time, years ago, when he entered the novitiate, he had seen his strong will as one of his great strengths. It never occurred to him that it could also be a serious flaw and an obstacle to spiritual growth. Now God had placed him in a situation that, on human strength alone, he could not handle.

While we will likely not face the horrors of the Gulag, we may face a tragedy that seems to shake the foundations of our very existence. In this sense, we can identify with Father Ciszek. When pushed to his limit, he came up with two possible solutions: God was either to give him the strength to withstand the pressures brought by his interrogators, or God was to enable them to see that he was not a Vatican spy and release him. God did neither. It had not occurred to Father Ciszek that he had "boxed-in" God. God was expected to select from one of the more-or-less acceptable options. And when God chose neither of the "acceptable" options, Father Ciszek was overwhelmed. I believe that many people have this very same experience. What if God's "solution" to our problem is not one that we find acceptable? It is at this point that we discover the depth of our faith in God, our hope in God, and our love for God. We see whether we trust enough to abandon ourselves to God's plan.

How do we respond when God does not select one of the options we have pre-determined to be acceptable? Perhaps you know people, as I do, who have responded with resentment and bitterness. Others feel as though they have been hurt by him and they maintain a "safe distance" so as not to be hurt again. They distance themselves from God, no longer counting on him to "do the things God is supposed to do." But some are blessed with a belief in Divine Providence that touches the depth of their soul. It is the "stuff" of which the saints are made.

This moment in the Gulag was a turning point in Father Ciszek's life. Having come to the point of virtual collapse, he was now beginning to see things anew. What did it matter if they killed him? What did it matter if he had to spend the rest of his long life—or short life—in that prison? He could not let himself predetermine the outcome. That was up to God. His role was to embrace each day as it came, and to deal straightforwardly—as Christ did—with each person he met. That included his interrogators. In a passage I find very moving, he wrote:

> Somehow, that day, I imagined I must know how St. Peter felt when he had survived his denials and been restored to Christ's friendship. Even though our Lord had promised that he, being once converted, would confirm his brethren, I doubt very much that Peter ever again boasted that he would never desert the Lord even if all others deserted him. I find it perfectly understandable that Peter, in his letters to the early churches, should have reminded his Christians to work out their salvation in fear and trembling. For just as surely as man begins to trust in his own abilities, so surely has he taken the first step on the road to ultimate failure. And the greatest grace God can give a man is to send him a trial he cannot bear with his own powers—and then sustain him with his grace so that he may endure to the end and be saved.[95]

His book is fittingly named, *He Leadeth Me*. Living one's life in abandonment to Divine Providence entails believing just that: that all along the path of one's life, in what seems like good times, or extremely difficult ones—God is there, leading us. It requires both love and trust. And it is one of the greatest effects of God's friendship in our lives.

Experiencing Intimacy with God

In all of our relationships, we enjoy the experience of being loved, and it is no different in our relationship with God. When writers refer to "spiritual consolations," this is what they mean. It is the experience—subtle or powerful—of being loved by God, and being united with him. In this relationship, as in any personal relationship, one can intellectually *know* that he or she is united with God—but not be feeling much of anything at the moment. As we have seen repeatedly, love is something that often includes feelings and experiences—but at the core of genuine love is an act of the free will. It is intentional. And it can be present with positive emotions, negative emotions, or no emotions at all.

I have found that many people, when they first begin the habit of spending time in prayer, have the very positive experience of feeling close to God. For some, it is the first time they have experienced God's presence. But after a time—maybe a month or two—they no longer have that feeling. Sadly, some abandon the habit of prayer at that point, thinking they are no longer "getting anything out of it." Others persevere.

Why do the feelings of closeness ever fade? It is hard to say. Perhaps the novelty of it has worn off. Or perhaps God is trying to purify the soul, to see whether they are praying for the sake of the warm feelings, or out of love for him. But we need to look more deeply at these experiences that come to us during prayer because they give us insights into our topic of love, and we will see parallels for friendship and marriage.

Mount Tabor and the Transfiguration

The "religious experiences" that people describe vary broadly. They encompass everything from a mild awareness of God's presence to interior visions, locutions, and visible signs of God's presence such as the stigmata. Spiritual writers—especially the mystics—have written about this through the centuries, describing ecstatic mystical experiences. St. John of the Cross is one example. Ordinary folk, such as me, often wonder what to make of it all. But I think it must be something like the experience that Sts. Peter, James, and John had atop Mount Tabor when Jesus was transfigured before them:

> After six days Jesus took with him Peter and James and John, and led them up a high mountain apart by themselves; and he was transfigured before them, and his garments became glistening, intensely white, as no fuller on earth could bleach them. And there appeared to them Elijah with Moses; and they were talking to Jesus. And Peter said to Jesus, "Master, it is well that we are here; let us make three booths, one for you and one for Moses and one for Elijah." For he did not know what to say, for they were exceedingly afraid. And a cloud overshadowed them, and a voice came out of the cloud, "This is my beloved Son; listen to him." And suddenly looking around they no longer saw any one with them but Jesus only.[96]

The Transfiguration was truly an extraordinary event. Even for Sts. Peter, James, and John—who were used to witnessing miraculous healings and the like—this was not an ordinary day. They would remember this event for the rest of their lives.

There are various plausible explanations as to why God did this. I happen to think he wanted to give them something that would sustain them for what they would endure later. Why was it only Sts. Peter, James, and John that witnessed Jesus transfigured in glory? Why were they not permitted to tell anyone of the vision until the

Resurrection? I do not know. But in all of this, two things continually come to my mind: mystery and gift.

Bl. Teresa of Calcutta (Mother Teresa):
Her Experience of the "Dark Night of the Soul"

There is another side to all of this. The side where one feels nothing; where one feels abandoned; where one is certain of nothing—not even the existence of God. Spiritual writers describe this as the "dark night." While nearly the whole world may be familiar with Bl. Teresa of Calcutta (Mother Teresa), many are surprised to hear of the darkness she experienced for several decades.

Father Brian Kolodiejchuk, M.C., who was the Postulator for the cause for her beatification, gathered information about Bl. Teresa. Beatification is the step before canonization, or the declaration by the Church that one is officially enrolled on the list—or "canon"—of saints. Father Kolodiejchuk described Bl. Teresa's spiritual life as four unfolding phases.[97]

Agnes Gonxha Bojaxhiu—the future Mother Teresa—was born August 26, 1910. From her earliest years she was pious, and from the day she received her First Holy Communion, at the age of five and a half, she had a great love for souls within her. At the age of eighteen, moved by a desire to become a missionary, she left home to join the religious community known as the Sisters of Loreto. It was there that she received the name Sister Mary Teresa, after St. Therese of Lisieux. Later, she departed for India, arriving in Calcutta in January 1929. Because the Sisters of Loreto was a teaching community, she worked as a teacher and principal. From that time on she would be called "Mother Teresa."

The second phase of Bl. Teresa's spiritual life began in 1942. At this point she was thirty-two-years-old and had been a religious sister for fourteen years. But Bl. Teresa felt strongly moved, while on retreat, to make a further vow to give herself completely to Christ: "To give God anything that he may ask . . . not to refuse him anything." She did this with the permission of her spiritual director.

Bl. Teresa spoke of having received a "Call within a Call." This is the third phase of her spiritual life, and it began in 1946. She was traveling by train from Calcutta to Darjeelling for her annual retreat. She had the experience that Jesus was asking her to give more of herself and to serve him radically—not just in the poor—but in the poorest of the poor. What became known later was that these were more than simple interior promptings. Jesus, in fact, appeared to her and spoke to her. "Will you not help me?" "Will you refuse?" Jesus was asking her to leave her familiar and happy life as a Sister of Loreto, exchange her religious habit for an Indian sari, and abandon herself to an uncertain life. But it would be a life where she would "radiate his love on souls." "Come be My light," Jesus begged of her. He revealed his great sadness over the neglect of the poor, and their ignorance of him. Repeatedly Jesus asked her, "Will you refuse? You have become my spouse for my love. You have come to India for me. The thirst you had for souls brought you so far. Are you afraid now to take one more step for your spouse, for me, for souls?" After nearly two years of testing and discernment, Bl. Teresa had permission to leave the convent and enter the world of the poor.

The fourth stage of Bl. Teresa's life was the Dark Night, and it would last four decades of her life. During the period when Jesus manifested himself to Bl. Teresa in such extraordinary ways—appearing to her and speaking to her—she experienced profound union with Christ. But soon after, not only did the visions cease, but all "spiritual consolations" were gone. And in its place—inner darkness, loneliness, abandonment, and doubt. God seemed absent, and her sufferings and sacrifice seemed to count for nothing. She revealed to Archbishop Perier, and to successive spiritual directors, "just that terrible pain of loss, of God not wanting me, of God not being God, of God not really existing."

By all accounts, Bl. Teresa's life was truly extraordinary. She received numerous awards for her work, notably the Nobel Peace Prize in 1979. But what I find even more amazing than the work itself is the fact that she did it all without interior experience of God's love and gratitude. Carol Zaleski, in her article on Bl. Teresa's dark night, commented, "It gave her access to the deepest poverty of the modern world: the poverty of meaninglessness and loneliness."[98] Intellectually she knew God was pleased. But for forty years she never felt it. Imagine loving someone for forty years without experiencing love in return! Zaleski continues:

> To endure this trial of faith would be to bear witness to the fidelity for which the world is starving. "Keep smiling," Mother Teresa used to tell her community and guests, and somehow, coming from her, it doesn't seem trite. For when she kept smiling during her night of faith,

it was not a cover-up but a manifestation of her loving resolve to be "an apostle of joy."

Pressing the Issue and Drawing Some Conclusions

Bl. Teresa's life was not one of stoic resignation, but a life of love—though she did not *experience* or feel God's love. She felt the opposite. We can learn a great deal about love—loving God and loving one another—by reflecting on the life of this great woman. Throughout this book we have looked at many of the questions of love:

- What does it mean to really love someone?
- Can I still genuinely love in a context where I am not experiencing love?
- What does it *mean* to love in that context?
- Must I feel our unity in order to be truly united to you?
- Is it possible that the love I feel for another is merely an illusion?

Love is the gift of oneself. By the giving of this gift we are fulfilled. When one is willing to give a gift of oneself, that very fact unites the persons. The more one is willing to give, the greater is the gift—and so is the unity between them. Bl. Teresa's love was greater than most because her sacrifice was greater than most. Her lack of emotional feedback in fact increased her love since it required her, so to speak, to reach deep within herself as she continued to give.

How did she have the strength to do all that she did? Surely, it was more than a firm act of the will, grinding away for forty years. Had it been a sheer act of her will, she likely would have either abandoned the effort, or become bitter. She did neither. She was motivated by love, but not a love of the emotional variety. Pope John Paul II said in his homily for Bl. Teresa's Beatification Mass:

> Her life is a testimony to the dignity and the privilege of humble service. She had chosen to be not just *the least* but to be *the servant of the least*. As a real mother to the poor, she bent down to those suffering various forms of poverty. Her greatness lies in her ability to give without counting the cost, to give "until it hurts." Her life was a radical living and a bold proclamation of the Gospel.

Though deprived of the emotional experience of God's love, she knew that God's love for her was real, and that in spite of this *experiential depravation*, she could nevertheless love those whom she was called to serve—seeing in them the suffering Jesus on the Cross. Again, in his homily for her beatification, Pope John Paul said:

> The cry of Jesus on the Cross, *"I thirst"* (Jn 19: 28), expressing the depth of God's longing for man, penetrated Mother Teresa's soul and found fertile soil in her heart. *Satiating Jesus' thirst for love and for souls* in union with Mary, the Mother of Jesus, had become the sole aim of Mother Teresa's existence and the inner force that drew her out of herself and made her "run in haste" across the globe to labor for the salvation and the sanctification of the poorest of the poor.

Regarding her experience of darkness, the Pontiff had this to say:

> In the darkest hours she clung even more tenaciously to prayer before the Blessed Sacrament. This harsh spiritual trial led her to *identify herself more and more closely* with those whom she served each day, feeling their pain and, at times, even their rejection. She was fond of repeating that *the greatest poverty is to be unwanted*, to have no one to take care of you.

Looking at all that Bl. Teresa did for the poor out of love for God, we could ask why God permitted her to experience such darkness. She had dedicated her entire life to him and to the service of his poor ones. Why would God deprive her of the experience of his love? It is a mystery, and it is a gift. But did it not draw out of her an even greater gift of herself? Did it not draw out of her an even greater love than would have been the case if she had the experience of God's love to carry her through and lift her up in difficult moments?

We often like to think of the saints as "God-intoxicated" men and women who sort of floated through life by their continual experience of God's love. It somehow gets the rest of us "off the hook." We see from the life of Bl. Teresa that we are not off the hook. Not only did she do truly extraordinary things, but she did them while she herself was deprived of the feeling of love and gratitude that we all naturally desire. God permitted all of this. In a sense, he *extracted* from her a profound gift of self. And *that*, in itself, was one of God's gifts to her. Bl. Teresa *became* what she would not have become had her experience been different. And what she became, she will remain—for all eternity. She is certainly experiencing the love of God in Heaven, and her experience in Heaven is what it is, because of the life she lived on earth. Her experience of the Kingdom would have been different had her life on earth been different. That is the point.

To steal a line from the movie *Shadowlands*, "The pain *now* is part of the happiness *then*. That is the deal."

God plays for the long haul—the eternally long haul. He knows that we are not all the same in heaven any more than we are all the same here on earth. And what differentiates us is the way and the degree to which we have given of ourselves. By making a deeper gift of ourselves, our capacity to receive God's eternal love increases. When Jesus said, "So the last will be first, and the first last,"[99] he is saying that there will be a differentiation among the Blessed in the Kingdom. But it will not be based on the criteria often used to differentiate here and now—money, status, intelligence, appearance, etc. Instead, it will be based on how much we gave of ourselves, given what we had to work with.

This gives an entirely new perspective to the way we view suffering and hardship. It is like finding the Rosetta Stone, enabling us to make sense of what was previously unintelligible. Suffering no longer seems meaningless, and God no longer appears heartless. We have not eliminated the mystery—there will always remain unanswered questions in God's providential plan for his creation. But at least we have some clues that point us in the right direction. They point us in the direction of Love.

If the way we give of ourselves here and now makes a difference in the way we will experience eternity, then simply living a comfortable life now loses much of its attraction. God did not put us on earth to live a comfortable life, but to give generously of ourselves. This is the key to understanding our existence, and the meaning of life.

We are told over and over in the New Testament that we are to love another. If we, so to speak, squeeze as much as we can out of our lives and really love the people that God has placed in our lives, it will benefit *them* here and now—and it will benefit *us* eternally. Sometimes this seems easy and at other times excruciatingly difficult. And in the midst of it all, God has his hand firmly on the throttle. With some, like Bl. Teresa, the engine is running full speed ahead. Most are traveling at a much more moderate pace. But he knows what he is doing, and he will not push us beyond our limits, though at times, it seems as though our toes are right on the line. His purpose is to enable us to give—to love—to the fullest extent of our individual capacities. He knows that there is a love that can only be found on the far side of suffering and abandonment.

Questions for Philosophical Consideration and Personal Growth

1. Why do you suppose some people have a difficult time believing that God is interested in a friendship with them?

2. When you pray, do you pray like a Trinitarian (i.e., to each Person of the Blessed Trinity in a slightly different way)?

3. What are your favorite ways of communicating your love for God? God communicates his love in a variety of ways and everything God does manifests, in one way or another, his love. His love is creative, and he loves by giving gifts. Do you think we can speak of God having, as it were, favorite ways of loving us? What would they be?

4. Both the Passover sacrifice and the Eucharist were instituted in the context of a meal. He also told the Apostles that they would eat and drink at his table in his kingdom (cf. Lk 22: 30). Do you see parallels between humanly important meals—such as the family dinner—and sacred meals where God is explicitly present? Are there insights that we can gain about each of them by observing the other?

5. What does it mean to say, "In God's providence, there are no accidents"?

6. If you were giving a class on *He Leadeth Me* by Fr. Walter Ciszek, what ideas would you want to leave with your audience? How would you describe the transformation process whereby we allow ourselves to be led by God?

7. If you had asked Bl. Teresa what her plans were for the future of her community, she would have told you that they do not make plans. Rather, they allow themselves to be led. There is a middle ground we are searching for here. We are not supposed to sit and do nothing—waiting for God to tap us on the shoulder. But neither are we to have everything planned out and then expect God to make everything fall into place. How are we to sort this out? What is the role of prayer? Of the voice of the Church? Of the "voice" of the circumstances and events going on around us?

8. What is the difference between *being* close to God and *feeling* close to God? How does one measure—if one *can* measure—closeness to God? Can one use insights from other relationships—such as friendship or marriage—to answer this question?

9. Imagine someone saying, "I read the account of Bl. Teresa's dark night. I just cannot imagine God doing that to such a good person." How would you respond? What does Bl. Teresa's dark night teach us about genuine love? What insights does it lend regarding the following:

    What does it mean to really love someone?

    Can one still genuinely love in a context where one is not experiencing love?

    What does it *mean* to love in that context?

    Must one have the experience of unity to be truly united with another?

    Is it possible that the love one feels for another is not genuine?

10. Describe a mature and balanced view of the emotional life *vis-à-vis* genuine love?

11. What does it mean to say that there is a kind of love that can only be found on the far side of suffering and abandonment?

Chapter Eight

Putting It All Together

"Let us not love in word or speech
but in deed and in truth."

1 John 3: 18

The Loves "Learn" from Each Other

St. Paul wrote in his Letter to the Ephesians that the union of husband and wife in marriage is "a great mystery." God created marriage to tell us something about himself and about his faithful and fruitful love. In other words, we get insights into the meaning of marriage by reflecting on God's love for us. And it works the other way around. When we see a marriage that is lived well, lived faithfully in spite of difficulties—we see an image of God's love. Each, in a way, reflects the other.

We see something similar in other relationships. We can discern insights about marriage by observing vibrant friendships. Some people would have a happier marriage if they treated their spouses like they treat their good friends. Friends who are especially close are continually feeding—"putting energy into"—their relationship. If they lose personal contact with each other—because they no longer do things together and no longer talk much to each other—their friendship slowly begins to unravel. When that happens in a marriage, it spells disaster.

I think that we intuitively grasp that in order for our friendships to endure through the years, we must continually put energy into them. And if I am not willing to "put anything into it," we will not be friends for very long. Certainly, we have friends whom we only see infrequently—and these friends can be very dear to us. But occasionally opportunities present themselves for us to talk or spend time together. If I consistently let these opportunities slip by, our relationship will suffer because of it. Married couples need to do the same. The energy generated by their mutual erotic attraction is not a substitute for the feeding of their marital friendship. The marriage itself needs to be fed by finding and doing things that they both enjoy.

Another way we put effort into a marital friendship is by changing and adjusting to please our spouses. There has to be a healthy give-and-take and a willingness to change and improve. If everything has to be done my way, with you simply acquiescing and going along—that is not much of a marital friendship. If our friends would not tolerate that, we should not expect our spouses to tolerate it either. Marriage is, after all, a kind of friendship. And the happiest of marriages are the ones where the spouses relate to each other like the best of friends.

Friends, for their part, can learn a few things by observing good marriages. Friendships are intensified when people are willing to share their lives deeply—analogously to the way spouses share their lives. It is not the same, of course, but intimate friendship has more in common with marriage than it does with companionship.

Looking at our relationship with God, we see that it can be enriched by imitating the love we see in marriage and in friendship. We speak and otherwise interact in a familiar way when we are with our families and friends. That familiarity can be appropriately imitated when speaking with God. We should avoid being too formal, always speaking as though we were in a courtroom or some other formal gathering. There are times for that, but we must learn to speak from the heart in the way we speak with those who are closest to us, like our intimate friends and our spouses.

All of our intimate relationships can benefit from reflecting on the dark night that is experienced in the relationship with God. There will be times in every relationship—especially in long-term relationships—when the emotions seem "flat." How long can one continue as a dear friend, as a devoted spouse, or as a faithful son or daughter of God, when the emotional well has run dry? Bl. Teresa of Calcutta (Mother Teresa) continued loving for forty years.

What Hinders Us from Loving Heroically?

Why do not we love like we might? What keeps people from loving heroically? Perhaps what hinders us more than anything else is the desire to experience being loved. We may be edified by Bl. Teresa's heroic loving and, at the same time, feel completely incapable of that kind of love. It is not so much the *giving* that is so difficult, as much as it is the *not receiving* the experience of being loved. When we have the experience of being loved we can do extraordinary things. But when our "love-tank" is empty, then everything seems difficult.

Our desire to experience love is a legitimate one. C.S. Lewis described our very existence as humans as "one vast need."[100] We enter the world that way, and as we get older our needs change, but the reality of our neediness does not. Our *restless heart*, spoken of by St.Augustine, is an aspect of our neediness. We cannot fulfill ourselves, and whether we realize it or not, we reach out to others—including God—to complete our being. Scripture testifies to this, and this need to achieve fulfillment through other people is something that precedes Original Sin. "*It is not good that the man should be alone.*"[101] In loving selflessly, one is fulfilled—though it does not always give the *experience* of being fulfilled.

So we have these two things going on at once. We want to give of ourselves—to love. At the same time, we want to experience others loving us in return. We in fact need both. We need to give and we need to receive. And we want our giving and receiving to be *experienced* as love. How do we balance these two? Am I expected to continue loving—to keep giving—when my "love-tank" is empty? This is the great question. Must I continue loving when I am not loved (or not feeling loved) in return?

I will let you answer that last question for yourself. But before you answer it, let us first look at three things.

First, as for the one who "is not being loved," is it really the case that he or she is not loved—or, rather, is it the case of not being loved the way he or she *wants* to be loved? Your spouse, for instance, may genuinely believe that he or she is effectively communicating love, but love is not what you are hearing. Perhaps your spouse likes to communicate love by his or her deeds—but you prefer romantic conversation. It is not that you are not being loved; you just are not being loved the way you prefer being loved.

Secondly, does your friend or spouse *know* how you prefer to be loved? It may seem obvious to you—but what is obvious to one, is not obvious to others.

Thirdly, are your expectations for experiencing love realistic? I think this is a source of disappointment for many people—they did not get what they expected. But some have expectations that are unrealistic, expecting everyday to experience an outpouring of love, of gratitude, of sympathy, of appreciation and affection. Relationships are not like that, even among particularly generous people. "The highest does not stand without the lowest." And there is a rhythm to our relationships and a rhythm to our love—with ebbs and flows, high points and low ones.

Even when we take all of this into account, we cannot deny that some folks have people in their lives that are very difficult. They might scratch their heads and ask, "How did it get this way?" Maybe it is a wife who is controlling or narcissistic. Or a husband who, like a proud devil, will never admit he is wrong. Perhaps it is a friend who is chronically unhappy, or a girlfriend who is dishonest. What is one to do? Certainly, bad behavior should be pointed out. Sometimes that helps, sometimes not. We will search in vain for a "one size fits all" solution.

The "Divorce Mentality"

Let us look at the case of a marriage that is not experienced as emotionally rewarding and fulfilling. Nobody should have to tolerate physical or mental abuse, but there is a tendency in our age to give up on a marriage "because I am not happy right now." It reveals an unwillingness to work through difficulties, or a lack of maturity, or the "hardness of heart" which Jesus said was the reason Moses permitted divorce. No one can deny that loving someone for the long haul presents many difficulties—and that it is not without some degree of heartache. Yet we see people "giving up" on their spouses in a way that they would not "give up" on their children. As I said earlier, we never hear someone say, "I had two kids, but it did not work out." We continue to love our children, even when it is emotionally difficult to do so, and when they do not love us back. Is not that, indeed, what couples vow to do when they marry? They vow marriage for better or *worse*, richer or *poorer*, in *sickness* and in health, until death. If marriage were only for the good times, for the times when we are rich, healthy, and everything is great—we would not need a vow. It is precisely because of the difficult times that we *vow* to do it until death.

When I prepare couples for marriage, I sometimes tell them about the famous Eng and Chang Bunker, the original "Siamese twins." Born in Siam (now Thailand) in 1811, they were connected at the chest by a band of flesh five inches wide. In spite of being conjoined twins, they lived a relatively normal childhood and adult life. They played, ran, did chores, and helped support their family by selling duck eggs in their small village. When they were older, they earned money giving lectures in North and South America and in Europe. They eventually married two North Carolinian sisters, Adelaide and Sarah Yates. They were married over thirty years and had twenty-one children between the two families. They died at the age of sixty-three, two and a half hours apart.

Conjoined twins are no more likely than other siblings to see things the same way, but they learn from a very early age that they simply have to get along because they cannot get away from each other. In what they say, and in what they do—no matter how angry or frustrated they may get—they can never "drop the nuclear bomb." If the idea floats around in the back of people's minds that they could get out of a relationship if they really wanted to, that would change the dynamic of how they relate. It is admittedly very difficult to escape the "emergency exit" mentality when so many people around us are running through those doors. The *divorce mentality*—the idea that one can back out of a difficult or otherwise unfulfilling marriage—can hinder one from loving generously. It lowers one's motivation to give generously, to practice forgiveness, and to tend to the day-to-day business of strengthening a marital friendship.

Tools for Generous (and Even Heroic) Loving

Virtuous Living in General

All through the book we have seen that virtuous living is an essential element to our relating well. "Quality individuals" make good friends and good spouses. Mature reflection enables us to see the importance of the "cardinal" virtues: prudence, justice, fortitude, and temperance. Author James Stenson describes them as sound judgment, responsibility, personal courage, and self-mastery. They are part of one's interior development, and they are essential to the living of a noble life. It is not a matter of either having them or not, but the degree to which they are developed.

I think most people want to be decent folk. And with a select group, and up to a certain point, they make it a point to be particularly honest, respectable, generous, and loving. So, what is the problem? The problem is that we also can be lazy, soft, temperamental, and stubborn. It is not that we are wicked—we are just weak on the inside, and we have a disordered desire for a "comfortable life." In these days when so many people are going to great lengths to be physically fit, even going so far as to have a "personal trainer," we do well to keep in mind that we need training on the inside, too. Whether we "go it alone" or have the assistance of spiritual director—a coach for one's interior life—our interior development should not be ignored. Communities, including our families, are blessed by the presence of those who attend to their interior development as much as serious athletes attend to their physical fitness.

It requires humility. The proud man or woman will say, "Leave me alone. This is just the way I am—it is my character." But it is *not* their character, it is—as St. Josemaria Escriva put it—their *lack* of character. But it requires humility to accept that.

Growth in virtue involves more than behavior modification. It nearly always includes an adjustment to one's way of *thinking*. Take, for example, a married man with small children. All of his decision-making needs to take his wife and children into account—especially as he makes decisions regarding the way he allocates his time, and the way he spends money. He must not, as a married man, continue to think and act like a bachelor. And this process may well be experienced as a sort of dying. Growth in virtue nearly always involves a death of sorts, a death that can be painful. But it is also freeing—freeing in the sense that it enables us to become the men and women we were made to be.

When St. Augustine was in his early thirties, he experienced a period of tremendous inner turmoil—the greatest of his life. He was well-aware that many parts of his life were simply a mess. He wanted to change his life, and yet he felt incapable of it. He both wanted—and did not want—to change. Within himself he kept hearing the words "Presently, presently." But he responded with "Leave me alone a little while." The tension within him was building like two driving forces—the habit of his former way of living and the certain knowledge that he was made for something incomparably more. He was intellectually convinced that he needed to change his life, but he found himself utterly incapable of surrendering his "old life."

Angry with himself and frustrated with himself, he was soul-sick and tormented as two wills struggled within him. (How many people have identified with St.Augustine's inner turmoil, experiencing the same interior struggle in their own lives!) It came to a head when he was in the town of Ostia. In his autobiography he wrote:

> Now when deep reflection had drawn up out of the secret depths of my soul all my misery, and had heaped it up before the sight of my heart, there arose a mighty storm, accompanied by a mighty rain of tears. That I might give way fully to my tears and lamentations, I stole away from [my friend] Alypius, for it seemed to me that solitude was more appropriate for the business of weeping. . . . I flung myself down under a fig tree—how I know not—and gave free course to my tears.[102]

He heard what seemed like the voice of a child singing, "*Tolle, lege; tolle, lege*"—"take and read; take and read." He had next to him a copy of St.Paul's letters. And, opening it at random, he came upon the words from the Letter to the Romans, "Let us conduct ourselves becomingly as in the day, not in reveling and drunkenness, not in debauchery and licentiousness, not in quarreling and jealousy. But put on the Lord Jesus Christ, and make no provision for the flesh, to gratify its desires."[103]

This was not the end of the process, but a critical step along the way. There would still be many more "deaths" he would have to die. But he had finally "given in" and was willing to grow.

In a sense, all growth in virtue is this way. First we see virtue for what it is, and we understand what it means specifically for our lives. Then, perhaps after a long interior struggle, we give in—as we just read St.Augustine doing—and choose to pursue it. Finally, we begin the (perhaps lifelong) process of integrating that virtue into our lives. In the case of St.Augustine, he was struggling with the virtue of chastity. But we must go through this process for *all* the virtues and the other aspects of living a noble life. This is how we grow in virtue—grow in holiness—and it is the work of a lifetime. And it is what enables us to be a good friend and a good spouse.

Forgiveness

On one occasion St.Peter approached Jesus and asked him, "Lord, how often shall my brother sin against me, and I forgive him? As many as seven times?" Jesus said to him, "I do not say to you seven

times, but seventy times seven."[104] Forgiveness is part of every relationship that endures through the years. Though we do not mean to,
we hurt the people we love. We hurt them by what we say, and what
we do—by what we do not say, and what we do not do. A husband
can hurt his wife by forgetting something that is important to her.
He himself can be hurt by his wife belittling something important
to him. Friends can hurt each other, too.

I am not so much referring to the annoying little (or not so little)
things people do such as ignoring the "check engine soon" light.
These are more bothersome than hurtful. I am talking about those
hurtful things that directly bear upon the relationship itself—the
kind of hurt that only those close to us can inflict, because only *they*
have access to our hearts.

We hurt each other in different ways, but at the root of the hurt is
the belief, "If you loved me as I love you, then you would have done
things differently." It is a kind of rejection that leaves one feeling
embarrassed or even humiliated. This embarrassment leads to sadness, which if unresolved, becomes anger and bitterness.

Unwillingness to forgive is a serious—perhaps insurmountable—
obstacle in a friendship or marriage and it is perhaps the greatest
cause of divorce. If one is unwilling to forgive, then no real reconciliation is possible. And the forgiveness I am talking about is much
more than *saying*, "I forgive you." It is a deep, genuine forgiveness
that touches the forgiver's heart, and perhaps the heart of the one
forgiven.

Before we look at deep forgiveness, I want to first look at what
forgiveness is not. Some people do not *want* to forgive because they
have a mistaken notion of forgiveness. They think, perhaps, that forgiveness is a denial of the wrongdoer's offense, or a denial of the
harm it caused. Or they think forgiveness is simply forgetting, con-
doning, or excusing, or that forgiveness means they must continue
to permit someone to do harm. But forgiveness, properly understood,
is none of these things.

First of all, let us make it clear that forgiveness is for real offenses—not imaginary ones, or things that I am angry about though
they are not anyone's fault. For example, suppose we agreed that I
will come over to your place, and we will spend the afternoon together, but on the way there my car breaks down. By the time I make
arrangements to get my car fixed, the afternoon is shot. Of course, I

called you as soon as I realized I would not be able to make it. Now, you may be frustrated, sad, or angry—but this is not something for which I need to be forgiven. I did not do anything wrong. So, forgiveness is not in order here. (I might add that "forgiving God" is never in order. We do not understand many of the things God does and things God permits. But he always knows what he is doing, and it is always for our good.)

Forgiveness is for real offenses, though they need not have been done maliciously or with the specific intention to do harm. It could be for an offense that is devastating—such as marital infidelity. Or perhaps one uttered deeply hurtful words such as, "I wish we had never gotten married." Or it can be, by comparison, something seemingly insignificant but which nevertheless causes hurt.

Forgiveness is the conscious decision to willfully abandon resentment, including all that goes along with it, and attempt to respond to the offender with beneficence.[105] Forgiveness is a *moral gift*. People who harm us may not deserve to be forgiven. In some cases, they clearly *do not* deserve to be forgiven. But I can choose to forgive them anyway. And I forgive them for my sake, not for theirs. It is the nature of a gift that it be given freely. Something I *owe* to another cannot be given as a gift.

Forgiveness is also a process. While the decision to forgive takes place at the actual moment when one chooses to forgive, that only begins the process. And depending on the harm that was done, the process can take a very long time. Letting go of resentment can be exacting work; until one chooses to forgive, the process will not begin.

The attempt to come to a deeper understanding of the one who caused the harm often helps the process to move along. This is especially true in cases where the offense was not done with the specific intention to cause harm. It also helps us to forgive when we realize that we, ourselves, have been forgiven by the ones we have harmed—including God.

If we are going to love people through the years, we will have to resist temptations to define them in terms of their shortcomings. We all need to be forgiven—and we all need to forgive. It brings us freedom, and it brings us peace.

Loving Well Requires Effort on Our Part

Most of what follows is directed to married people since it is easy to demonstrate the need to put forth effort in marriage. But clearly, one can draw parallels for friendship and for one's relationship with God.

Even the best of lovers and the best of friends, who never seem to think of themselves and are cheerfully and generously attentive, will have their moments when they are not 100%. Dating couples who expect, as they spend more and more time with each other, that *all* their moments together will be deep experiences of closeness may be disappointed by the ordinariness of day-to-day relating. Married couples, too, can be disheartened when their emotional life seems to flatten out. Some people, I believe, are unhappy because somehow they did not get what they expected. It is not *hard times* as much as it is *unmet expectations* that cause unhappiness. Our expectations of the experience of intimacy and interpersonal closeness must be realistic. Marriage is not like a very long date. Sometimes two people (friends or spouses) happen to have the same favorite way of communicating and experiencing love. If the husband's favorite way of loving is also his wife's favorite way of being loved—that makes loving easier for both of them. Those who are temperamentally similar to their spouses may wonder why many people struggle with married life. But spouses are not always temperamentally similar. People are different, and men and women are different—which means that our favorite ways of giving and experiencing love often differ.

Some people's work, and some people's temperament, keeps their lives new and exciting all the time. But this clearly is not everyone's experience. Few would describe their life as magical. Much of it is ordinary and humdrum. We face, as Pope Benedict XVI once put it, "The tiring pilgrimage of everyday existence." But we can do great things with "ordinary life." We can overcome boredom and monotony by keeping a supernatural vision, seeing the richness of daily life that comes from the innumerable opportunities to give and to serve. We must work at loving. We rarely have the opportunity to do "big things." But we can do little things with tremendous love, seeing persons that are behind ordinary tasks. A husband, for example, might know that his wife particularly appreciates having the garbage taken out each night. It makes the house seem clean and neat in the morning. Though he finds it bothersome, the devoted husband takes out the trash every night, *knowing how much it means to her*. It is a little thing done out of love. This is real love at work. Those relationships that have endured over the decades, those friendships—especially the friendship between spouses—teach us a lot about love and intimacy.

We may put persistent effort in our relationships, and things still may not come together in the way we had hoped. St.Paul reminds us, "We know that in everything God works for good with those who love him."[106] This is not simply Pollyanna optimism, nor wishful thinking. It is an expression of our hope in God. God keeps his promises, and he does make all things work together unto good, though our experience is that it is not always *when* we would like, nor the *way* we would like. God sees all that we do, and he promises us that all our efforts will be rewarded in the Kingdom.

Even in the best of marriages, when husband and wife have been joyfully married for many decades, the human heart still longs for more. It cannot *not* long for more. That is because the human heart cannot be completely satisfied with human love. St.Augustine, in the very first paragraph of his autobiography, wrote, "You have made us for yourself, O Lord, and our hearts are restless until they rest in you." Our hearts will not be completely at rest until we are in the Kingdom.

One Last Look

Here is a summary of the things we have seen throughout this book. It is the "here it is in a nutshell" description of the three basic relationships we have seen in this book. I will very briefly cover "Making and keeping friends," "Happy marriages," and "Developing a friendship with God." They are each different ways of communicating and experiencing interpersonal union or intimacy. True unity comes about by the mutual *gift of self*. People are united more by their mutual self-giving than in their mutual desiring. And at times our self-giving can be experienced as a sort of dying. We see here a paradox of love. In all of our relationships of love, there is paradoxically a dying that is mysteriously life-giving.

Making and Keeping Friends

Some people seem to make friends with great ease and naturalness. Others have a more difficult time of it, causing them stress and anxiety. Often they do not really know where to begin. Well, the natural place to begin is with our companions. They are already a part of our lives in one way or another. Someone only very rarely goes directly from being a stranger to being a friend; our friends begin as our companions. So the first place to look for potential friends is among our peers, co-workers, schoolmates, teammates, neighbors, etc.

We pursue friendships by seeking to engage some of our companions more deeply, looking for areas of common interest. If one is afraid to engage people in conversation, thinking that he or she has nothing worthwhile to offer, that in itself is a serious obstacle to friendship development. This type of person will always struggle with friendship and will resist engaging people in anything other than shallow ways. Naturally, this will have an effect on spousal and parental relating as well.

When seeking to develop deeper relationships with companions, we do well to focus our attention on those who seem to have good qualities—character strengths and virtues. Those qualities are far more important than superficially attractive ones, and people with character strength are more likely to have the relational wherewithal to be a good friend.

Getting a friendship "off the ground" takes effort. But we move the process along by taking a sincere interest in people. When someone takes a personal interest in us, we can tell. We like it when someone notices, say, the work we have done, or at least the effort we have put forth—or when they remember details of a conversation from several days earlier. By taking such an interest in people, we make it more likely that companionships will evolve into friendships. When a *mutual* interest is discernible, the friendship is beginning to come together.

As the friendship develops, look for things the two of you really enjoy doing together. Having favorite things to do together is important in every friendship and it provides the matrix for the relationship to be lived out. Over time, these favorite activities can be broadened so that the friends have *several* favorite things to do together. This is particularly important in a marital friendship. Through the years, we can permit our former favorite activities to pass away as we find new ones, more suitable to our ages, maturity, and circumstances of life.

Our friendships will be experienced as intimate ones to the extent that we share ourselves and open our hearts. Those who are not accustomed to letting someone see them "on the inside" can be intimidated at the thought of this, but it is a natural part of every close relationship. Because of the dangers inherently involved with self-revelation, it is important that we choose our friends carefully.

If we continue to put effort into our friendships, practicing the virtues of honesty, generosity, forgiveness, and especially loyalty, we will experience our friendships as one of our greatest treasures.

Happy Marriage

What can people do so that their marriage will last a lifetime? As couples prepare for marriage, they are immensely optimistic and hopeful for the future. Yet many experience anxiety as they approach marriage, noticing so many people around them whose marriages have failed. Naturally, they do not want to end up that way. Is there some kind of relational vaccine against it? Marriages do not come with a guarantee, but there are three qualities seen in happy, life-long marriages. Their presence in a marriage increases the likelihood that a couple will stay together for life.

First, husbands and wives, if they want to have a happy marriage, need a strong marital friendship. And all the qualities of friendship that we have seen throughout this book need to be present in the couple's marital friendship.

Second, to be happily married and raise a family together, the man and woman need a common vision of life. If they do not see life the same way, with common hopes, expectations, and values—they are sure to struggle. This is something that needs to be seriously evaluated *before* they get married. When the common vision of life unites the couple in a richly lived common faith, the unifying effect is a powerful one.

Thirdly, we see in happy marriages that the spouses try to love each other in the way their spouse wants to be loved. Earlier in the book I listed several ways we communicate our love. And we all have our favorite way, or ways, of being loved. Perhaps your favorite way of being loved is to have people spend quality time with you. Or perhaps physical touching is your favorite way of loving and being loved. The point is that people often make the mistake of thinking that their own favorite way of receiving and giving love is also their beloved's favorite way of receiving love.

Lovers can go to great lengths, and with real, personal sacrifice, to show their love—but if it is not the way the beloved wants to be loved, the lover's efforts may go unnoticed. A man, whose wife had recently moved out, said that he worked three jobs to buy her "everything she could have wanted." What his wife really wanted was quality time spent with him. He thought his love was overflowing, like a bountiful harvest. From her perspective, she was being starved.

In the chapter on love I addressed the issue of sympathy. It is the experience people have of being, as the saying goes, "on the same page." When people are loved the way they want to be loved, their mutual sympathy remains high. It gives one the sense of being appreciated and valued—of being loved.

I think the image of a cistern is illustrative. In areas where water is not readily available, people sometimes have a cistern to collect rainwater. As long as it rains, the cistern supplies their needs. During a draught the cistern runs dry, making life difficult. We each, so to speak, have a cistern that is filled by experiencing love. When we feel loved and appreciated, it can motivate us to do great things. But when the cistern runs dry, life in a relationship is difficult. Things we used to do effortlessly are now seen as burdensome. And people may ask themselves, "Why am I bothering with all of this?"

If we love people in the ways they want to be loved, so that they experience the love we are trying to communicate, our cisterns remain full and our love remains fresh. The richness and the beauty of married life is most evident when the love between the man and the woman is a marvelous interweaving of both *love as desire* and *love as goodwill*, with each person putting the other first. People who love well seem to be constantly on the lookout for ways to respond to the ones they love. This makes them less likely to miss the *cues of love*. We see this in marriages where spouses place themselves at each other's service—where both the husband and wife habitually seek to discover what makes their spouse happy, loving each other as they want to be loved.

Finally, as we all know from experience, there are times when we let each other down. Good spouses—like good friends—know how to ask for, and receive, *forgiveness*.

Developing a Friendship with God

A friendship with God is, at the same time, the easiest and the most difficult friendship to establish and maintain. It is the easiest because God greatly desires our friendship; he is infinitely loving and infinitely lovable; he is always available and attentive to our needs. Friendship with God is difficult because his presence is not experienced in the way one typically thinks of "being present" to another; and because "God's ways are not our ways."

But once one gets past the initial difficulties, it is clearly experienced by many as something that is very much "real," and the anchor of one's life. Those who profess the Christian Faith speak of having a separate relationship with God the Father, God the Son, and God the Holy Spirit. We relate to the Father as his sons and daughters; Jesus is our brother, and the Holy Spirit dwells within the soul that is in the state of grace.

Like all our personal relationships, the relationship with God grows and matures over time. Two friends must learn how to be each other's friend, and husbands and wives discover how to be a spouse to one another. We do the same in our friendships with God. Through the years we discover what it means to be God's friend, and what it means to have him for our friend.

As in every personal relationship, communication is very important. Communication with God, of course, is prayer. There are many varieties and styles of prayer: mental prayer, vocal prayer, liturgical prayer. One can pray in one's bedroom, before a tabernacle, in the woods, or on a streetcar. Regardless of the form it takes, everyone who is a sincere friend of God has some kind of life of prayer.

To say that one has a life of prayer is not to say that prayer comes easily. Spiritual writers through the ages have written of the "battle of prayer." Friends struggle—if they are otherwise busy people—to make time for each other. Spouses work at finding or making time for the two of them to have each other's undivided attention. The friends of God have the same experience as they search for ways to spend time with him. In spite of the many distractions that come up, perhaps at times struggling even to stay awake, the friends of God reveal to him their lives and their hearts, their sorrows and their joys. Sometimes God makes his loving presence felt which naturally makes it easier to pray. But typically, these "spiritual consolations" ebb and flow in the rhythm of the relationship.

We become like our friends, and becoming friends with God entails our becoming more like him. He leads us, but does not push us—at least not in a way that takes away our freedom. God respects our freedom even more than we do, because he understands the significance of our freedom better than we do. As St. Augustine said, "The God who made us without our consent, will not save us without our consent." And when we do consent, he transforms us—making us more like himself. This is what is meant by "growing in holiness."

Our deepest personal relationships have a way of affecting every other relationship in our lives. A relationship with God does the same. Because he personally identifies with every man and woman he has created, he bids us to treat everyone as members of the family, reminding us that—as we treat the least of our brothers and sisters—we treat him."

C.S. Lewis says an old author once asked, "Is it easy to love God?" And he says the old author responds, "It is easy to those who do it." Whether they find it easy or not, the ones who have loved God heroically are the ones we call "saints."

Intimacy in the Kingdom of Heaven

We began our considerations of friendship by saying that everything begins with the Blessed Trinity. The Father, Son, and Holy Spirit are three distinct persons who live in complete interpersonal communion and intimacy with each other. Because of their unity, they are one—one God, not three. Being made in the image and likeness of God, we too were created for intimacy. But like many of the gifts given to us by God, our full participation in them will not be experienced until we reach the Kingdom of Heaven—when God will make all things new.[107]

What will the Kingdom be like? We know that God is preparing a "new heaven and new earth."[108] And while much of it is veiled in mystery, we do have bits and pieces that have been revealed in the Scriptures. St. Paul tells us that "what no eye has seen, nor ear heard, nor the heart of man conceived, what God has prepared for those who love him."[109] And many times in the Gospels Jesus speaks to us about the Kingdom of God.

Life in this present world is like the womb; what we anticipate is the "real world" of heaven. If, in our conception of things, this present world seems more *real* than heaven—there is something wrong with our theology. All of us must struggle to expand the horizons of our thinking. C.S. Lewis in his book *Miracles* drew an enlightened comparison when he said explaining Heaven to us on earth is like explaining the raptures of sexual love to a child. The child has not the capacity to understand sexual intimacy, and wonders if, in the throes of carnal rapture, one can eat chocolate at the same time. In vain does one attempt to explain that lovers have far more interesting and appealing things on their mind than the eating of candy.[110] We are like that child. We really have no way of grasping the fullness of supernatural happiness.

With that in mind, remembering that what awaits us is *fullness*, though our present experience is one of *privation*, we press on in our search for a fuller understanding of that life for which we were made. Our Lord, in his priestly prayer before the Last Supper, prayed for the unity of his Apostles, asking "that they may all be one; even as thou, Father, art in me, and I in thee, that they also may be in us."[111] St. Paul speaks of life in the Kingdom in terms of there being one body, with Christ himself as the head.[112] Imagine if you could get *inside* someone. Imagine being able to perceive as the other perceives, think as the other thinks, feel as the other feels. If people could achieve this sort of complete interpersonal union, it would be enriching beyond our imagining. In such a state, I would see more because I also see what you see; I would think in a fuller and deeper way because I think as you think. And being able to feel as you feel would exponentially expand my own experience. This would be *true unity of persons—true intimacy*. This gives us a hint of the intimacy of the Kingdom.

Such union, of course, is not possible in this life. However, it is not only possible in the Kingdom, but it is indeed the life for which all of us were made. I cannot help but think that upon entering Heaven the soul is overwhelmed with a sense of awe. In the Kingdom (please God we get there), we will experience intimacy with *all* the Blessed in Heaven. This is why marriage (and therefore sex) is, so to speak, obsolete in the Kingdom. The experience of intimacy of the Kingdom will be more profound than sexual intimacy because it will entail a complete union of persons that is not possible in this life. As for the procreation of children—that is part of life in this world and will not be part of the next.

To say we will experience profound unity with all the Saints in Heaven (and everyone in Heaven is a Saint) is not to say that our most dearly beloved (like our spouse) will simply be just one more face in the crowd. As our unity with everyone increases, our unity with them will increase as well. Nobody will, as it were, bump St. Joseph from his favored place in Mary's heart.

As we become increasingly more in tune with God in prayer, we see with ever-greater clarity that he has an individualized plan for our lives—our vocations. And by fulfilling it, we become God's partners in the building up of the Kingdom. "No longer do I call you servants, for the servant does not know what his master is doing."[113] In this infinitely wise and loving master-plan, God arranges for us to meet and interact with people, and he brings about many things by our participation in each other's lives. And much of it happens without our being aware that it is taking place. God our Father is always at work building up the Kingdom, though this fact is not always clearly visible—or not visible at all. It begins very small, like a mustard seed.[114] And there are many difficulties along the way as "the weeds and the wheat grow up together"[115] until harvest time. And though there is much that tests our faith, there is plenty of evidence of God's activity in our life. We need the eyes to see it and the ears to hear it.[116]

Because God is busy building up the Kingdom and preparing us for eternity, he places people in our lives—and us in theirs. What may have appeared as a chance meeting of two people, in fact had been planned from all eternity. Think of the really important people in your life. You never would have met if, say, your parents purchased a different house, if you attended a different school, if you decided not to go out for the team, had you accepted a different position, etc. Christ is the organizer of our relationships. He is, as C.S. Lewis put it, the "secret master of ceremonies" who is always at work.[117] The important people in our lives are not the reward of our discriminating taste, but a gift from God. And we should strive to relate to others as such and think, "God has placed me in your life for a reason—and he has placed you in mine." With that in mind, it is appropriate to ask God to place people in our lives whom we can serve, and whose loving interaction will bring us joy, satisfaction, and fulfillment. And while we earnestly pray, we also wait patiently, remembering that many worthwhile things in life require lengthy preparation.

In the end, for those who love God and have served him faithfully, it will all come together in the Kingdom of Heaven. And just as two children who are playing on the living room floor are aware that their father is sitting on the sofa watching them play, so too in the Kingdom we will have the awareness and experience that God our Father is near to us, watching us, and loving us. We have a *sense* of it now—we will experience it fully. We will experience ourselves and others as members of the Divine Family as we live a new life in the Kingdom of Heaven—the life for which we were made.

God did not give us a timetable for when all these things will come to pass. Though we do not know when it will happen, we do know that the world as we know it will come to an end. This world, disfigured by sin, will be transformed into a new heaven and a new earth, "and whose blessedness will answer and surpass all the longings for peace which spring up in the human heart."[118] All will be refashioned. All will be remade. What was sown in weakness and corruptibility will be clothed with incorruptibility. The old order will have passed away, and all things will be made new. This is the world for which we all were made, and all who have not rejected it shall rejoice in it.

The Fathers of the Second Vatican Council stated it beautifully, and I can think of no more fitting way to conclude these reflections on friendship and love:

> For after we have obeyed the Lord, and in His Spirit nurtured on earth the values of human dignity, brotherhood and freedom, and indeed all the good fruits of our nature and enterprise, we will find them again, but freed of stain, burnished and transfigured. This will be so when Christ hands over to the Father: "a kingdom eternal and universal, a kingdom of truth and life, of holiness and grace, of justice, love and peace." On this earth that Kingdom is already present in mystery. When the Lord returns, it will be brought into full flower.[119]

Questions for Philosophical Consideration and Personal Growth

1. Why did St. Paul say of marriage that it is a "great mystery"?

2. What does friendship teach us about marriage and about our relationships with God?

   What does marriage teach us about friendship and about our relationships with God?

   What does the relationship with God teach us about friendship and about marriage?

3. What is "appropriate familiarity" with God? How would that be lived out?

4. What are the things in your life that keep you from giving more than you do?

5. People are frustrated when they do not get what they expected. What do you expect from God? What do you expect from your friends and from your spouse? Might it be the case that your expectations are not realistic or reasonable? Do you think the expectations that God, that your spouse, and that your friends place on you are realistic and reasonable?

6. Is there a difference between "being fulfilled" and the "experience of fulfillment"? If they are different, what is the difference between them or the relationship between them?

7. Why do our emotions ebb and flow in all of our relationships? If someone sought your advice in this matter, how would you describe "realistic emotional expectations" in friendship? In marriage? In our relationships with God?

8. Jesus said that Moses permitted divorce because of the "hardness of their hearts." What does that mean?

9. What is "interior development," and how is it related to relational life?

10. What area in your life needs further development?

11. What does it mean to say that forgiveness is a process? In what sense is it a moral gift?

12. What does it mean to have a supernatural outlook on life? How does one foster it?

Endnotes

Chapter One

1. Sirach 6: 14-15.
2. C. S. Lewis, *The Four Loves* (Orlando: Harcourt, Brace, Jovanovich, 1960), 88.
3. The Second Vatican Council, *Gaudium et spes*, 24.
4. 1 John 4: 8.
5. Cf. John 15: 13.
6. Genesis 1: 27.
7. *Gaudium et spes*, 24.
8. Genesis 2: 20.
9. Josef Pieper, *Faith, Hope, Love* (San Francisco: Ignatius Press, 1986), a commonly used phrase throughout the section "On Love."
10. Michael Collopy, *Works of Love are Works of Peace: Mother Teresa of Calcutta and the Missionaries of Charity* (San Francisco: Ignatius Press, 1996), 35.
11. Cf. Mark 14: 42.
12. *Faith, Hope, Love*, ibid.
13. Luke 17: 10.
14. Matthew 13: 31-32.
15. John 12: 24.

Chapter Two

16. *De Amicitia*, 20.
17. *De Amicitia*, 18.
18. *De Amicitia*, 20: *"Est enim amicitia nihil aliud nisi omnium divinarum humanarumque rerum cum benevolentia et caritate consensio."*
19. *De Amicitia*, 37.
20. *De Amicitia*, 33.
21. St. Augustine, *Confessions* (Nashville, Tennessee: Thomas Nelson, 1999), Bk. IV. Citations by section, not pages.
22. Epistle 258 to Martianus (Cited in Sr. Marie Aquinas McNamara, O.P., *Friends and Friendship for Saint Augustine* (New York: Alba House, 1964), 219).
23. Epistle 258 to Martianus, Ibid.
24. *Confessions*, Book IV.
25. Aelred of Rievaulx, *Spiritual Friendship* (Kalamazoo, Michigan: Cistercian Publications, 1977), I. 46. Citations by section, not pages.
26. *Spiritual Friendship*, I. 32.
27. *Spiritual Friendship*, III, 134.
28. Michel de Montaigne, "Of Friendship" in *Michel de Montaigne: The Complete Works* (New York: Knofp, 2003).
29. *The Four Loves*, 88.

Chapter Three

30. Exodus 33: 11.
31. John 15: 15.
32. *The Four Loves*, 98.

Chapter Four

33. *Confessions*, Book IV.
34. John 21: 7.
35. John 11: 11.
36. John 15: 15.
37. Mark 5: 37; cf. Luke 8: 51.
38. Matthew 17: 1-13; cf. Mark 9: 2-13; cf. Luke 9: 28-36.
39. Matthew 26: 37; cf. Mark 14: 33.
40. Matthew 16: 13-20.
41. John 21: 15f.
42. John 13: 23; 19: 26; 20: 2; 21: 7; 21: 20.
43. John 15: 15.
44. Judas is identified numerous times in the Gospels as Jesus' betrayer.
45. Cf. 1 Samuel 18: 1 and 1 Samuel 20: 17.
46. Pope Benedict XVI, *Deus caritas est*, 7.
47. 'Caritas amicitia quaedam est hominis cum Deo,' *Summa theologiæ*, II-II, q. 23, a. I: 'Utrum caritas sit amicitia.'
48. *Deus caritas est*, 18.
49. *Deus caritas est*, 4.
50. Genesis 1: 31.
51. St. Josemaria Escriva, *Furrow* (New York: Scepter Press, 1988), no. 733.

Chapter Five

52. *Spiritual Friendship*, III: 83.
53. Pope John Paul II, *Letter to Youth*, 3.
54. Cf. Luke 5: 4.
55. Josef Pieper, *A Brief Reader on the Virtues of the Human Heart* (San Francisco: Ignatius Press, 1991), 9.
56. Galatians 6: 2.
57. 1 Corinthians 13: 4-8.
58. Luke 2: 19.
59. *De Officiis* III, 133 (PL 16, 191-192), (Cited in Sr. Marie Aquinas McNamara, O.P., *Friends and Friendship for Saint Augustine*, p. 96).
60. *Faith, Hope, Love*, 187.
61. *De Officiis* III, 133 (PL 16, 182), (Cited in Sr. Marie Aquinas McNamara, O.P., *Friends and Friendship for Saint Augustine*, p. 96).

Chapter Six

62. *Love and Responsibility*, 145 (emphasis in original).

63. There are various ways of being united with another: friendship, marriage, a relationship with God, etc. But one who is absolutely and existentially alone cannot be fulfilled. Some authors, such as C. S. Lewis, see such absolute aloneness as the defining experience of Hell.

64. *Love and Responsibility*, 161.

65. *Love and Responsibility*, 143.

66. *Love and Responsibility*, 170.

67. *Deus caritas est*, 6.

68. *The Four Loves*, 152.

69. Alice von Hildebrand, *By Love Refined* (Manchester, NH: Sophia Institute Press, 1989), 81.

70. John 15: 13.

71. John 13: 1.

72. *Deus caritas est*, 6.

Chapter Seven

73. Matthew 11: 28-30.

74. Francis Cardinal George, taken from "Be Prepared to Give an Account," given at Georgetown University, 1997.

75. Luke 17: 10.

76. Matthew 22: 14.

77. Matthew 7: 14.

78. Mark 6: 34.

79. John 8: 11.

80. Pope John Paul II, *On Reconciliation and Penance*, 17.

81. Romans 7: 15-19.

82. 1 John 1: 1.

83. Matthew 9: 29.

84. Mark 7: 32-34.

85. Matthew 8: 15.

86. Matthew 8: 1-3.

87. Matthew 17: 6-8.

88. 1 Peter 2: 5.

89. John 15: 12.

90. Cf. Romans 13: 14.

91. Luke 23: 34.

92. Matthew 6: 33.

93. Ephesians, 4: 23.

94. Walter J. Ciszek, *He Leadeth Me* (San Francisco: Ignatius Press, 1995), 61.

95. *He Leadeth Me*, 71.

96. Mark 9: 2-8.

97. Cf. "The Dark Night of Mother Teresa" by Carol Zaleski, © 2003 *First Things* 133 (May 2003): 24-27.

98. Ibid.

99. Matthew 20: 16.

Chapter Eight

100. *The Four Loves*, 13.

101. Genesis 2: 18.

102. Confessions, Bk. VIII.

103. Romans 13: 13.

104. Matthew 18: 21-22.

105. Cf. Enright and Fitzgibbons, *Helping Clients Forgive* (Washington, D.C.: American Psychological Association, 2000).

106. Romans 8: 28.

107. Cf. Revelation 21: 5.

108. Cf. Revelation 21: 1.

109. 1 Corinthians 2: 9.

110. C. S. Lewis, *Miracles* (New York: Macmillan, 1960), 159-60.

111. John 17: 21.

112. Cf. Ephesians 1: 22-23, cf. Colossians 1: 18-19, cf. 1 Corinthians 12: 12-27, cf. Romans 12: 4-8.

113. John 15: 15.

114. Matthew 13: 31-32.

115. Cf. Matthew 13: 24-30.

116. Mark 4: 11-12.

117. *The Four Loves*, 126.

118. *Gaudium et spes*, 39.

119. *Gaudium et spes*, 39 (the quotation used by the Council Fathers is taken from the Preface for Christ the King).

Index

Acceptance (also see: Love/Loving as acceptance): Environment of: 90-93

Acquaintances: 36, 45, 47, 128

Adam: 7-8

Adultery in the heart: 170

Aelred, St.: 43-45, 125

Affection (also see Philia): 5, 13, 99; And the other loves: 102-109

Affirmation: 92-93

American Sociological Review: 4

Appreciative love: 15-16

Aquinas, St.Thomas: 101

Aristotle: 38-40, 47-50, 59, 65-66

Attraction: 11, 24, 69-70, 157, 215

Attraction: Mysteriousness regarding: 14-15, 69

Augustine, St.: 41-43, 89, 191-192, 225, 230; Conversion: 220-221; On intimacy: 46, 148; Restless heart: 42, 144, 217, 225

Benedict XVI, Pope: 97, 224; *Deus caritas est*: 102; On *eros*: 108, 174, 184

Bodily language: 128, 166-170

Celibacy: 112, 116, 168

Character flaws: 159-162

Character strengths: 57-64, 158, 178, 226, 191-192, 220

Charity (also see St.Aelred): 5, 38, 42-43, 101-102, 115; St.Thomas: 101; And the other loves: 105-109

Children, childhood: 32, 109-110, 130-132, 135

Choices: 59, 130-133, 145, 171-172

Cicero: 40-41, 49, 56, 62

Ciszek, Fr.Walter: 202-205

Comfortable life: 211, 220

Commitment/Duty (also see Intimacy): 23, 75-77, 153-154; Every relationship has them: 19, 24-26,

Common vision of life: 158, 174-178, 227

Communicating our love: 92-93, 163-166, 178-184, 194-196; At the heart of intimacy: 163-166; For God: 194-196; Spiritual realities communicated through the body: 164, 166; Things said in passing: 98; Tone of voice: 98-99, 137, 142, 164

Companions/Companionship: 34-37; May become our friends: 37, 67

Compatibility of values: 158

Confidence: 3, 6, 27, 91-92, 101, 181; For the future: 128, 163, 165, 182

Contraception: 173

Conversation: 128

Credibility: 135

Culture: 89-92; As environment: 109-111; In a family: 90; Of friendship: 90

Custody of the heart: 117

Dark night of the soul: 207-209, 216

Defensiveness: 131

Dependability: 60-61; Illustrated: 61

Different ways of being close: 94-95

Discernment: 134

Disconnected: 2, 4, 110, 147-148, 174

Discretion: 81, 136

Divine indwelling: 102

Divine providence: 43, 181, 204-205

Divorce: 175, 177, 222; Divorce mentality: 218-219

Early twenties: 133

Egoism: 154, 174, 201

Emotions/Emotional love: 12-17; Compatibility: 155; Do not make expressions of love authentic: 173; Ebb and flow: 154; Emotionally constipated: 99; Emotionally needy: 112; Emotionally present:

179; Response to internal stimuli: 115; Why we have them: 14

Engagement: 118, 162; Illustration: 162-163

Eros: 5, 100; Begins as an interest in the other: 151-152; Needs to be disciplined and purified: 108, 172, 174; And the other loves: 106-109

Escriva, St.Josemaria: 119-120, 220

Esprit de corps: 8, 35

Eucharist: 169-170, 193, 195, 198

Evangelization: 118-120

Faith: 26-27

Femininity: 152, 157

Forgiveness: 63, 221-223; What it is not: 222

Four Loves (also see Lewis): 98-102

Four orders of reality: 71

Friend/Friendship: As a habitual way of relating: 57; Adequate theory must include: 49-50; Aelred, St.: 43-45; Affection between: 70-71; Agreement between: 41, 63; And charity: 43, 105-109; And common interests: 48; And duties/commitments: 24-26, 83; And evangelization: 118-120; And intimacy: 58-59, 125-138; And moral quality: 59-66, 100; Aristotle: 38-40, 65-66; As means to Christian perfection: 44; Augustine, St.: 41-43, 148; Best friend: 95; Between men and women: 114-118; Briefly described: 100-101; Capacity for 57, 60-61; Casual friendship: 36; Cicero: 40-41; Click with one another: 66, 69; Connotation in this book: 8; Creates a culture: 89-92; Different levels: 93-95; Distinguished from *eros*: 115-116; Distinguished from marriage: 76; Equality of: 56; Essential elements: 57-58; Experience of union: 45; Favorite common activities: 57, 72-75, 226; Favorite friend: 95; Form concentric circles:

94; Freedom regarding: 53; Friend from the past: 75, 85; God's role in : 41, 43, 45, 46, 232; Good vs. close: 79-80; Hear each other: 71; Humanly fulfilling: 54; Incarnated in favorite activities: 57, 72-75; Lewis: 46-48; Losing interest in : 85; Making and keeping: 225-227; Midway between companionship and marriage: 75; Montaigne: 45-46; Mutual interest in each other: 67-72, 226; Often begin as companions: 67-69; Phases of development: 82-85; Prepares one for marriage: 54, 75-77; Primordial interpersonal relationship: 54, 148; Rare: 40-41, 46, 49; Recurring themes: 48-50; Requires good qualities: 59-60; School of: 76; Some things that resemble: 31-33; Spiritual: 44; Supporting and elevating other loves: 102-109; Sympathy of: 95-98; We become like our friends: 187, 201; What makes people friends: 56-59; What one pursues when pursuing: 54-56; With God: 187-196, 216, 229-230

Fulfillment: 209, 217

Generosity/Heroism: 21, 109-114; More of a process than a goal: 138

George, Francis Cardinal: 189

Gift love: 16-17

God (also see Divine providence): Abandonment to his will: 201-205; As Pillsbury Doughboy: 190; Draws love out of us: 210; Effect of his friendship in our life: 201-202; Friendship with: 187-196; Image of: 5-6, 167; Increases our capacity to love: 211; Puritan: 189-190; Responds to fidelity: 199; Therapeutic: 189; Wants to be "part of the conversation": 200

Goodness (also see Character strength) (also see Virtue): 10-11, 15-16, 39-41, 59, 62-63, 66, 98-99; Makes one naturally attractive: 63, 66; Measuring it: 62

Hardness of heart: 218

Hell: Endnote 63

Holiness: 188, 192-193, 201, 221, 230, 233

Honesty: 26, 135-136

Hope : 26-28; As theological virtue: 28

Human nature: 167, 170

Humility: 201, 220

Inferiority: 131

Inner life: 6, 143-146, 164; And intimacy: 145

Insecurities and neuroses: 161

Intentional love: 12-13, 155, 175; Arising from duties/commitments: 18; Why we have it: 17

Interior preparation: 183

Interior transparency: 172

Interpersonal union (also see Intimacy): 2, 6-8, 58, 76, 126, 133-134, 167, 225, 231; Masculine-Feminine: 151

Intimacy: 7, 58, 125-128; And commitment: 128, 152; And conversation: 128; As interpersonal union: 126, 163; Between men and women: 151-152; Capacity for: 132, 144-148; College seniors illustration: 138-144; Development: 128-134; Ethic regarding: 116-118, 171; Fear of: 144; Illusion of: 147, 176-177; In the Kingdom of God: 183, 230-233; Modern errors regarding: 4-5; Realistic expectations: 144; Sexual: 166-170; Skills: 162; With God: 205-207

Jesus: Calls us friends: 56, 232; Faced three options: 197; Had friends: 93-94; Last Supper: 197-198, 231; New Commandment: 197; Not alone when he died: 91, 137; Sacred Heart: 191; Secret master of ceremonies: 232; Transfiguration: 195, 206

John Paul II: Illusion of intimacy: 147; *Love and Responsibility*: 1, 154, 172-173; Love as gift: 109; Lust: 172-173; Mother Teresa: 209-210; On youth: 132; Personalist Philosophy: 6; Providence: 181; *Reconciliation and Penance*: 190; School of self-mastery: 62; Theology of the body: 167

Kingdom of God: 28

Language of the body: 167-170

Lewis: 1, 14, 31, 46-48, 78, 230, 231; Mrs. Fidget: 72, 79; On common interests: 74

Living in the dimension of gift: 109

Loneliness: 5, 19, 32, 58, 82, 141, 148, 208

Love/Loving (also see Romance):"I love you": 10, 157, 162;"Love-tank": 217;"Sinful love": 171-172; And expectations: 152-154; And liking: 11; As a response to a perceived good: 11; As acceptance: 22-23; As desire: 11, 98; As discovery of God: 184; As ecstasy: 184; As giving/gift of self: 7, 109-110, 184; Being "in love": 154, 174-175; Between men and women: 151-152; Chaste: 172-173; Cistern analogy: 228; Communicating: 92-93, 163-166; Communicating it as the other desires it: 180-183, 217, 227-228; Cues of love: 228; Disinterested: 62-63; Form blocks of a pyramid: 102-109; Genuine love is more than a feeling: 154-155; In little things: 224-225; Is there an essence?: 5; Loves "learn" from each other: 215-216; Loves restraining one another: 118; Loving "in" God: 89; Questions regarding: 209, 217-218; Requires effort: 23, 62, 85, 138, 172, 175, 216, 224-225; Responding to love with love: 98; Tools for generous loving: 219-225; Twofold dimension of giving and receiving: 11, 97

Loyalty: 40-41, 63-64, 136-137; Illustrated: 64-65

Lust: 170-174; As "using" another: 173; Defined: 172; Look of: 170

Marriage: A "great mystery": 215; A multifaceted diamond: 183-184; And duties/commitments: 25-26, 165; As a covenant: 169-170; As intimate and domestic friendship: 175; Communicating marital love: 178-184; Empty nest experience: 180; Happy marriage: 178, 227-228, Love-matches: 161, 177; Marital compatibility: 175-178; Matrimony: Meaning of: 173; More than a "relationship": 169; Spouses need a common vision: 174-178, 227; Spouses should be friends: 174, 215, 227; Vows: 25, 73, 168-169, 178, 218

Martyr: 184

Masculinity: 152

Maturity/Maturation: 19, 60, 82, 110, 127, 132, 218, 226

Mental and emotional associations: 90-91

Mercy: 192, 201

Monotony/Boredom: 24, 44, 224

Montaigne: 45-46

Moods: 96

Moses: 169, 198, 206, 218; Intimate friend of God: 56

Mother Teresa (see Teresa of Calcutta, Bl.)

Natural grouping: 68

Need love: 14-15

Newman, John Henry Cardinal: 199

One vast need: 217

Ordinary life: 224

Overlapping interests: 24

Paschal Mystery: 169, 195, 197-200

Passover: 169, 195, 198

Paul, St.: 137-138, 190, 192, 197, 200, 215, 221, 225, 230-231

Personal information: Revealing and receiving: 7, 81-82, 132-133, 140, 144, 147, 188

Philia: 38-39, 47

Pieper, Joseph: 10, 134, 147

Plato: 34, 70

Positive role models: 81

Prayer: 20, 194-196, 199, 205-206, 229, 232; As intimate conversation: 193, 195; Battle of: 20, 205, 229

Pride: 201

Raw material: 171

Reciprocation/Reciprocity: 39, 97, 133, 148, 183; Illustrated: 3, 68

Rejection: 64, 131, 136, 222

Relating/Relational/Relationship: And hope: 26-28; Both an art and a science: 1, 5, 132, 144-145, 157, 164; Breadth and depth: 23; Categories of: 78; Continuum: 2, 36, 129-130; Cowboy story: 3; Development in : 76, 147; Have a rhythm: 218; Patterns of: 92; Relational laziness: 85; Take time to develop: 81-85; Trigonometry: 54

Religious experiences: 206

Romance/Romantic: 24, 91, 115, 117-118, 151, 159, 161, 178, 184

Sacraments: 193

Sadness: 80, 95, 131, 152, 222

Secrets (see Personal information)

Security: 83, 92; And Confidence: 101; And Engagement: 162; Emotional: 14; From facing challenges: 181; From knowing we are loved: 85; From shared history: 163

Self-mastery: 62, 173, 219

Self-understanding: 132; And intimacy: 144-146

Sense of accomplishment: 182

Sex/Sexual/Sexuality (also see *Eros*) (also see Intimacy) (also see

Romance): And the Kingdom: 231; Appeal and Attraction: 155, 157; As bodily language: 166; As covenantal act: 168; Bodily expresses marriage vows: 178; Communicates several things simultaneously: 168; Friends with benefits: 107, 166; Hooking up: 107, 166; Intimacy: 166-170; Meaning of: 168; Need for purification: 108, 172, 174; One flesh union: 152; Puritanical view: 166; Sexual revolution: 173-174; Sexual value—inclination to seek: 171; Spontaneous emotional and physical responses: 171

Shadowlands: 211

Sheen, Fulton: 190

Siamese twins (Eng and Chang Bunker): 219

Solidarity: 49, 67, 75, 91, 93, 95, 165

Spiritual consolations: 201, 205, 208, 229

Spiritual director: 220

Spiritual sacrifices: 196

Stenson, James: 219

Suffering and hardship: 211

Supernatural vision: 224

Sympathy: 95-96, 228; And friendship: 95-98

Temperament: 2, 5, 69, 73, 103, 127, 189, 224

Temperamental: 220

Teresa of Calcutta, Bl. (Mother Teresa): 21, 112, 207-211

Therese of Lisieux, St.: 207

Tolerance: 63, 216

Trust (also see Character strength): and intimacy: 129

Union of persons: 6, 163, 231

Union/Unity (also see Intimacy): Can be real without being felt: 8; Different types: 8-10; Rooted in the goodness one perceives: 10

Unkind kindnesses: 79

Unmet expectations: 224

Vianney, St. John: 194-195

Virtue (also see Character strength) (also see specific virtues): Admirable qualities: 37; And holiness: 201; And sustained intimacy: 134-135; And the relationship with God: 191-192; Aristotle on: 38-40; As something habitual: 77; St. Augustine on: 148, 221; Cardinal: 219; Cicero on: 40-41; Civic: 199; Determines capacity for friendship: 60-65; Enables very different people to be friends: 70-72; Essential element of friendship: 3, 49, 57, 69, 120; For those considering marriage: 158; Growth in: 220-221; Has natural appeal: 66; Is not itself friendship: 65-66; More important than superficial qualities: 226; Not the first thing one notices: 68; Pieper on : 134;"school of": 31; Why it is important: 59-60

Vocation/Vocational: 116, 199; Commitments: 19

Volitional love (see Intentional love)

Voluntary association: 69

von Hildebrand, Alice: 183-184

Vulnerability: 148

Works of mercy: 194